THE HEROIC TRIAD

By Paul Horgan

NOVELS

The Fault of Angels
No Quarter Given
Main Line West
A Lamp on the Plains
A Distant Trumpet
Far From Cibola
The Habit of Empire

The Common Heart
Give Me Possession
Memories of the Future
Mountain Standard Time (*containing*
MAIN LINE WEST, FAR FROM CIBOLA,
and THE COMMON HEART)
Everything to Live For

OTHER FICTION

The Return of the Weed
Figures in a Landscape
The Devil in the Desert
One Red Rose For Christmas
The Saintmaker's Christmas
   Eve

Humble Powers
Toby and the Nighttime
   (*juvenile*)
Things As They Are
The Peach Stone:
   Stories from Four Decades

HISTORY AND OTHER NON-FICTION

Men of Arms (*juvenile*)
From the Royal City
New Mexico's Own Chronicle
   (*with Maurice Garland Fulton*)
Great River: The Rio Grande
   in North American History
The Centuries of Santa Fe

Rome Eternal
Citizen of New Salem
Conquistadors in
   North American History
Peter Hurd: *A*
   Portrait Sketch from Life
Songs After Lincoln

The Heroic Triad: *Essays in the Social Energies*
of Three Southwestern Cultures

*Essays in the
Social Energies
of Three
Southwestern
Cultures*

THE
HEROIC
TRIAD

By PAUL HORGAN

Holt, Rinehart and Winston

NEW YORK
CHICAGO
SAN FRANCISCO

Copyright © 1954, 1955, 1970 by Paul Horgan

All rights reserved, including the right to reproduce
this book or portions thereof in any form.

Published simultaneously in Canada by Holt, Rinehart
and Winston of Canada, Limited.

Library of Congress Catalog Card Number: 70-102145

FIRST EDITION

Designer: Winston Potter
SBN: 03-084520-3
Printed in the United States of America

Contents

Preface

In an earlier year, I published a large work which attempted to bring to the reader a survey of the historical life—pre-Spanish, post-Columbian, pre technological, and proto-modern—of the American Southwest. This was *Great River: The Rio Grande in North American History*. The information I presented there—some half million words of it—was all related to the immense course of the river, for it always seemed to me that the Rio Grande was the most importantly unifying feature of the vast lands through which it carried many confluent streams of action and spirit, as well as a generally meagre, though sometimes flooded, flow of water. The river's geography, its qualifying landscape, was everywhere in my narrative, against which the events of history were placed.

Three dominant cultures were projected in turn against that land —the Indian, the Latin, and the Anglo-American; and their known historical movements would, it seemed to me, be barren of intimate interest if they were merely chronicled. Instead, at significant changes of racial or national dominance, they had to be seen through expressions of social backgrounds which gave to the three cultures their violently distinct characters.

Accordingly, I undertook to weave into the more formal, or perhaps more active, aspects of Southwestern history, various re-creations of those elements of belief, custom, group behavior, and social energy which gave to each of the three cultures its own style.

Now, in the belief that those passages of social study do not wholly depend for their usefulness and interest upon their emplacement in the larger narrative of historical events for which they first served as backgrounds, I have gathered out of my longer text the following group of essays about our three Southwestern cultures. These cultures seem to me without undue romanticism to justify the term "heroic triad"; for the Southwestern experiences of the Indian, the Latin, and the Anglo-American peoples carry out of our earliest continental history into our own time the quality and dimension of the epic.

History may strictly be taken to describe *what happened*—the known events of period and place. Less strictly, but in great relevance, social or cultural studies may try to tell us *how they were,* the people to whom history happened, in whatever context.

With certain revisions, I have set the following studies in the simple sequence of chronology, in an attempt to suggest, for their own value, those cultural styles which lay behind the active events of ten centuries and more of the great Southwest: the peoples there, and *how they were,* of which today we may still see countless evidences in historical laminations, almost as metaphors of the geological eras recorded in the land itself.

To give the reader a sense of place, I offer here as prologue, for the first time in full, a sequence of little geographical and landscape notes made during the years of my study of the area.

P.H.

Center for Advanced Studies, 1969.
Wesleyan University.

BOOK ONE

Prologue

Place

Pages From a Rio Grande Notebook READING FROM SOURCE TO MOUTH

i

It is born of winter, this river, in one of the longest seasons of cold in the United States. The source mountains in the Colorado Rockies are hard and wild. The air is thin and at such altitude subject to swift crystalline changes of condition which may bring blue darkness at mid-day, and yield snow during nine months of the year.

Past monstrous peaks of ragged lifeless rock, clouds tear and roll from wall to wall up in the sky. Wind cries there much of the time, and when the atmosphere is overcharged with electricity, the cut and flare of lightning, the trundle and bounce of thunder after its first valley-sharpened crash seem to require new senses, capacities, to be wholly heard.

ii

There seems no end to the mountains when you are in them. Every turn, every small advance along a hidden public way, reveal new angles of vast imprisonment in the always changing magnificence of mountain color, light, and air. A new canyon, another gorge, a farther union of facing mountainsides in a deep V; cupped cloud, a range side in shadow with snow reflecting the blue of the glistening sky; the dark slices of evergreen stabbing over and over at the dark rock background or blackly arrowing out through ten feet of snow; in the sky far away an apocalypse of light, and cloud, and ray and shadow—gold shimmering with gray, white bounteously underlighted with gold. Amidst all visions, every kind of rock and tumble imaginable shows in the tortured forms of earth, as though an analogue of cloud turbulence once came to earth, and rock and root, crust and forest and upland, slope and valley, all such heavy matter, were tossed by winds more unimagined and powerful than those bearing endlessly against the calm rocky peaks which seem so eternal in their sterile peace and massive hostility to any form of living growth.

Exiled from them by his perishability without plants and creatures, man can only see them as alien, formidable, alarming, even while he admires their abstract magnificence. But in the end an accident cannot be loved. We must come lower on the slopes to find what will, if we use it well and wisely, reward us, as it has rewarded men throughout ages.

iii   The river's course—here as in its whole career—widens and narrows by turns. Where it is narrow, the slopes are dark, the stream is shadowed all day but for a little while at noon, when straight fingers of sunlight reach down through the forest. The stream is clear and icy, going rapidly over polished brown speckled stone. They remind us of something. At a glance the diamond water going over its stony bed makes the image of the fish it carries—the same speckled colors, the same watery flicker, the same half-lights of reflection and golden flecks. In and out of leaf shadow, protected by the dazzle of moving water, the trout in plain sight is safe because he and his river are so close in likeness.

iv   In a wild park, the grassy expanse often looks like a dry lake, with its defined edge, its trees rising away up the banks, its little bays and capes and points of trees and rocks. And at one time, many such parks were in fact lakes, and are now glacial meadows, old terraced lake basins, which have been drained long since, and filled through time with sediment, and gone to grass.

v   A true mountain lake, in the depth of winter, often freezes over with glassy purity. The ice is unruffled and polished. Images plunge still and upside down as though in a mirror. The high sky is deep steel blue in the ice, and mountain pyramids taper downward below the dark line of lake's edge. Such a lake is like a great secret, proper to the scale of mountains, where nothing is mysterious except to mankind.

vi   In the source valleys there are no towns, hardly an organized group of cabins anywhere, mostly a few places, these, where in the short summertime the austerity of the high mountain character is made a little gentler by the sun in the north, and those who love to be deafened to ordinary life by the resounding silences of the peaks and the forests can come to worship the outdoors. Such men and women revisit something real and remote in their own natures, an atavism of animal society, for which comfort and release are waiting in the echoing high wilderness where the first waters run.

vii

If the mountains are a great rocky hand laid upon a table top, with streams coming from between the fingers and finally converging on a plain, then where they meet and go free there is a sense of greater ease; more use of the land itself; more sky and more vision and less mystery.

viii

The Colorado Rio Grande towns—Monte Vista, Del Norte, Alamosa—are pleasant young communities whose life in each place parallels the railroad tracks for a mile or two. They are much alike, as all towns less than a century old are apt to be. Water tower hovering above the plain; a drive-in movie on the outskirts; nerves of neon exhibiting a diagram of the corporate economic anatomy of the settlement; one-story houses, and trees along the streets, and (our faith and love projected) brick and moulded-concrete high schools, colleges, churches; and invisible in the plain air, but audible, the spoken personality of the town reaching out by radio with aching commercial desires to the incoming motorist and the resident alike. In the age of universal communication no settlement, even on plains east of the Rocky Mountains, is remote.

ix

About twenty miles southeast of Alamosa the first sign of Spanish adobe culture appeared in a little village—Los Sauses, with houses built of earth, under grand cottonwoods, on a gentle slope above the river, encircled by fine hills. This scene, made of slow water, bounteous tree, earthen brick and irrigated field, is like a symbolic image of much that is to follow as the river goes south. It is the kind of cell of family, primal want and basic sustenance made visible, from which, downriver, grew clusters of kinsmen, and then of neighbors, and then of material dependents, and then of parishioners, and then of descendants, in turn, until a village became a town which became a city, all originally and even now dependent upon the Rio Grande for life. In many places along its course you can see preserved illustrations of different ways and times of its human society, as though the river cut through the laminations of history as it does through those of the earth's crust.

x It is still winter in the canyon above Taos. The water is dark and clear and ruffled with rocky white. A little snow hides in the shadows of the biggest black rocks. From day to day the level of the river comes up a little. The winds are still cold when they come down the gorge before dawn or sunset. The occasional trees by the water side are still mostly bare.

But here and there is a breath of change to be felt. Overhead in the first rifts of day, cranes flying north; up on the sage plain, a new weedy fragrance in the warming wind of midday; down in the canyon, a feather or two of pale yellow-green among the tender willow stalks. Winter is unlocking its hold far back in the founding peaks. More water comes. More birds return. The plain shows a straggle of wild flowers. Snow stands high above the mesa, but spring is coming up the valley, and with it, a new character of the river.

xi It is an immense mesa in northern New Mexico through which the river cuts that black tumbled gorge, and it steps down first at Questa, where the early lace of cottonwoods is appearing. Aspens are turning faint smoky green in the hills. The mesa runs on until it turns into Taos plain, which reaches southward for forty miles before it steps down again and the river claims its wide valley.

xii Over the three communities of Taos—the pueblo, the middle commercial town, and the old Ranchos—there is a piercing, sweet, illimitable clarity of light and sky. Sounds carry. Meadow larks, mockingbirds, blackbirds have returned. Over the long plain breathes the wind, sharply sweet and already warmed, disturbing nothing but the senses. Space is so great, vision is so plain, air is so clear that human activities can be seen from afar. Small figures like humanity in Breughel go about their tasks. Earthen buildings go up. Carts travel. Winter rubble is cleared off the fields and out of the acequias. Furrows are seeded. Out in the sagebrush of Taos plain, where the old road winds toward the canyon, tiny newborn lambs take fright and scamper before the gusty sand devils whipped up by the darting wind. Flocks move more slowly than cloud shadows. Shepherds sit on a modern culvert and watch what the road brings. Their dogs, showing wide smiles on their intelligent faces, with long clean jaws open and tongues curled out, work the straggling edges of the flock. The valor and pity of men and women in their renewed use of a corner of the earth is as much a part of spring as everything else.

Canyon silence is made of many sounds, and their echo is loud in the memory—deep rush of water, silky play of breeze, the talk of aspen leaves clattering in their new green, the metallic strike of a dislodged rock bounding down to the water, the piercing astonishment of the call of the male canyon wren, with its seven loud notes descending the scale, and ringing again off the face of solid stone.

xiii

Somehow in spring the unimaginable age of the river seems even greater, and makes spring seem even younger than it is. The sandy bottoms are almost a pale flesh pink. The sky is both golden and blue, the air clear as a diamond (a Spaniard said as much four hundred years ago) and poignant when you breathe it deeply. It seems charged with the joy of all past sweetnesses, and with the faint melancholy of all promises, even those made by spring itself.

xiv

Here—above Albuquerque—begins the lyric grace of the river in its richest passage of the pastoral life. Where life is fed by water, the landscape here recalls the opulence and grandeur and occasional vistas of order in the image of classical country painted by Nicolas Poussin, who left so many celebrations of grove and meadow, shady leaf and column of light, reflecting stream and stepped mountain and composed bodies. There is more than a reminder here, there is a real likeness. It is a likeness of grace and plenty in the midst of dramatic nature; nourishment in the desert; bounty summoned by the most ancient of agricultural rites out of the most inscrutable of antiquities; cool for the heated, slaking for the parched, food for the

xv

hungry, rest for the weary, ease for the eye blinded in the un-impeded sun. This middle-valley landscape not only looks like this today, it looked like that to all who ever came upon it, and was used in just those ways by them, from the first pueblo builders to the earliest Spanish soldiers; from the American adventurers of the last century to the farmers, poor and anonymous, or rich and chic, of this.

xvi   There is no design too fantastic to occur in a sky above moun-tains. Bastions of light, clouds cubed, rain curtains shaped like the aurora borealis, darknesses and confusions and sheets of blinding vi-sion like apparitions above the peaks. The peaks echo in endless change those fantasies of vapor and illumination and invisible cur-rent.

xvii   In spring's slow twilight, which comes filtering like falling ash out of the lucid darkening sky, there are bonfires above Bernalillo on the eastern side of the river. The ground is darkening, but the horizon is still as bright as a page in a book, and the bonfires dance, letting up their long flickers of smoke, and tongues of fire run along the ground. What are they doing there?—And then you see that the fires follow the elevated banks of the acequias, and it is plain that they are burning out what did not decay but simply dried up—the weeds and the grasses of the year before which must be removed from the acequias so the irrigating water will run readily and safely from the river to the fields, and, eventually, downstream, when it has been used enough, back again into the river.

xviii   The chaparral cock, or road runner, a crested bird which manages to give a notion of severe style and temperament, has a talent which bears out the appearance. An early observer of the Rio Grande re-marked that the paysano, or chaparral cock, "ventures to attack the rattlesnake, and, as if aware of the latter's venom, protects himself from its fangs by using his wings as a shield. Many instances have been related to me by eye-witnesses of contests between the rattle-snake and this bird, in which the latter always comes off the con-queror." With far more tail than wing, this contentious bird runs more often than it flies. Oddly enough, its cry is out of character.

You would expect an irritable exclamation, suggesting one who has been tried to the limits of nervous endurance. What you hear instead is a melancholy, dovelike coo.

xix

On a wide plateau on the west bank below San Marcial, where the river makes a generous bend to the east, are the ruins of Fort Craig, a former nineteenth-century post of the United States Army. Troops issued forth from it to fight Confederate forces coming up the Rio Grande for the first real battle of the Civil War on New Mexico soil. Some of the adobe walls are eroded to low mounds; some have been worn down to mountain, mesa, and butte forms, miniatures of grander erosions; and some fragments of wall stand almost intact but for doors and all wooden parts.

Any place once built by men and lived in and abandoned is far lonelier than an open piece of country, however big and vacant, where there is no evidence of human use. In the landscape silence there will sometimes be a sudden sound as of something dry cracking loudly; but if you turn and look into the wavering heat, and listen again, though you know there must be one, there comes no explanation. You think, instead, of the officers and ladies, the troopers, the trumpeter and the post surgeon, the clerks and the armorers and the Indian scouts of Fort Craig a hundred years ago.

xx

There are places where time seems to flow as slowly as the Rio Grande, and to leave unchanged from long ago much that took its original character from the immediate river land. Such a place is the village of Mesilla, New Mexico. It is built entirely of adobe. Roof lines of the one-story houses rise and fall gently like natural earth contours. House walls are cracked and wrinkled like arroyo walls that have been wet and dried. Deep domes of cottonwood trees rise over the roads of the town, with their deep pits of sweet-smelling white dust, and all is slow and placid. But history had its storms, floods, and furies, like the river, between intervals of even flow, here, and upstream and down.

xxi

At Mesilla are several examples of a style which can be called Rio Grande Palladian. Wooden window and door frames are topped with beautifully proportioned classic pediments in miniature, let into adobe walls. Square panelling on shutters or doors often accompanies them. Such refinements can turn a long, uneven, hand-plastered mud wall into the façade of a palace. The line of inheritance through centuries is clear, from Rome, to Spain, to Mexico, and up the Rio Grande. Mud and wood served the builders, lacking marble. Spirit moved. It survives, as it always survives materials.

It rings, too, in the bells of Mesilla. They hang in the church tower on the plaza, and are named San Albino, María Albino, and Sagrado Corazón de Jesús. They were cast in Mesilla in the 1870s. The parishioners brought their articles of bronze and silver to be melted down. When the bells ring today, what sounds is the devotion of the grandfathers.

xxii A river can have moments of almost microscopic intimacy, when all signals of life are received, and if not understood entirely, respected for their simple and unceasing activity. Sometimes the eye must be laid at the very waterline, the ear on the very earth.

On blades of salt grass growing out of the dried white crust of old high-water marks, gold-headed flies light and nod and then depart, surely along an invisible dotted line, of which they make an image in sound as they buzz away.

A frog croaks out of sight; not often, but with an effect of stated interval, as though his nature in a given time fills to capacity with accumulated riverdom, and must be expressed. It is a hard, knobby, metallic sound.

Listen to the western mourning dove, forever sorry, but not about anything.

There is a dog barking just at the far edge of hearing; a dutiful sound, reassuring.

A train whistle sounds far off. Just over a lifetime ago there were no tracks going down the riverside from Belen to Mexico. Now a whole continental valley, with all its outlying desert and mountain needs, is answered by the train whistle and the air liner. The valley towns are mostly older than the railroad. It was the river, not the railroad, which led to their making, just as it was the river which showed the way to the natural roadbed. Except along the Jornada del Muerto, the tracks follow the river today.

Trucks go by from time to time on the dirt roads of the levees.

Business or pleasure, you wonder; and then remember that to our people, these are the same thing.

Someone fires a shotgun, twice, across the river. At this distance, in this quiet air, the sound is flat, like the slamming of a door. On what living thing was it slammed, one, two, just now?

Beyond a brake of salt cedar an ancient pick-up has come to rest. Two voices climb out of it. No words are clear, only the burr of men talking as they haul their bait cans with scrinch and clank out of the rear of the car. At first they have much to talk about, in high, nasal plainsmen's voices, full of rising inflections of interest and incredulity and falling tones of general disgust and an implied capacity for unenlightened violence. One of the men wades into the stream and back. Gradually both men settle down. The talk gets widely spaced and presently is silenced entirely, as the river works its spell. Who, even though he does not picture it in his mind, is impervious to the mystery and power of a river which is born in mountains way beyond the curve of the earth, and comes to where he is, and without ever ceasing to come yet passes him by, going on out of sight through unimaginable time and place until it joins the sea?

Across the river on the west bank comes a band of sounds like the first news of a parade. Voices, man or animal; small metallic music; little jarrings of the ground by many. It is a little herd of white-faced cattle being driven up the riverside by a man on a horse. All are trotting lazily. The cows long out loud with their voices, for what who can say. The rider has an encouraging whistle he can make, and also a sweet and mournful falsetto cry. Brass cowbells make a junkling sound. It is about noontime, and hot, and still, and sounds carry. They carry from the past, too, with this procession; for there trots amid the golden riverside dust the character of a whole segment of life in the southwest; there thirsty herds have always been driven beside the slaking river.

Up to now, going south, when you looked across the river, you knew exactly how things were on the other side—just more U.S.A.

xxiii

But at El Paso with the new concept of a boundary between nations, things are no longer the same on the opposite bank. It is another country, with another people, and with other ways. Many manners and customs have remained common to both sides of the Rio Grande since the time a little over a century ago when the river was not a frontier—when in fact both its banks and all its course were Spanish or Mexican. But in the United States, subject to a more powerful energy in a more technical society, such survivals remain as exotic, quaint, or commercially glamorous; while in Mexico the same expressions are sincere and not self-conscious. From El Paso southeastward, every United States town has its Mexican counterpart across the river. Commerce, appetite, and corruption draw them together. Language, national boundary, and law keep them apart. The river itself is hardly an obstacle anywhere, for it can be waded for most of the year, whatever else its common uses may be.

xxiv   There is violence in all the energies of the Rio Grande empire. Even in parched seasons, when nothing happens day after week after month except the pour of the sun, the very abstinence from rain, in its results upon the deserts through countless small acts of climate and earth condition, is violent.

And when rain does come, it comes violently, in summer cloudbursts, often accompanied by hail, created out of furies in contrasting temperatures high in the sky. Baked by the relentless sun, the desert surface becomes hard and crusty. Water falling upon it tends rather to run away on any slope than sink into the ground, and the desert growth is too meagre and by nature indifferent to water to stay the flow as upland vegetation would.

So for brief spells the river, hundreds of miles below its sources, is often greater in volume and more violent in action than it is upstream. But that upstream flow is what makes the upper and middle river perennial.

Though cloudburst creates tremendous incident and has immediate effect upon the river, it does small lasting good, for the violence of the desert's reaction to it is too sudden and short-lived. Clash of hot and cold winds, the travels of cloud, mountain influence, act and desist in a matter of an hour or two. There is thunder in the canyons, sheeting back and forth from rock face to face and multiplying itself. Everything movable seems to scurry toward the river from all the wide heights of the uplands, and the brown hissing and tumbling waters go in sheets of silver reflection to the valley floor. The sky may be clear, the storm gone, even while its wild aftermath wears out its life, rolling rocks and trees, brush and weeds, motor cars, pieces of road and of canyon wall and of arroyo wall with the general pull of the movable upland toward the river levels.

From June through September this destructive drama can take

place. It does nothing to relieve the heat—indeed, it seems to be simply another declaration of summer's nature, when the mountains in the distance look to be made of heat itself.

XXV

The carcasses of dead coyotes shot by ranchers for bounty are strung along wire fences, and bake and glaze in the sunlight until they have a varnished shine. There is a lean and rangy style to these skinned, dead animals, which manages to suggest even as they dry up that they were clever, delicate, and perhaps elegant enemies. A row of them on a single fence looks like a frieze of a hilarious animal dance, arrested in full career.

xxvi

A noble sight to living things who do not need to fear it is the great brown and white hawk sailing low in the sky over the desert Rio Grande. The white underside of his wings reflects the sandy light off the ground, just as a cloud does on a bright day over the desert.

xxvii

Seventy miles below El Paso, mountains reach in on both sides of the Rio Grande and present to it another of its many obstacles; but the stream bed passes between them and continues upon its depleted way. The river is dying. The desert finally seems ready to triumph over it and drink out of sight the last crawling trickles of the flow that was born in the Colorado Rockies.

And so it would; but relief and replenishment are on their way from another mountain system lying deep in Mexico, where the Rio Conchos with its major tributary the Rio San Pedro courses northeastward to join the Rio Grande at an altitude of twenty-four hundred feet a few miles above the old Texas town of Presidio. With it comes new power for the river, to create dramatic, and even melodramatic, phases of its career, in the accomplishment of water over rock, as demonstrated by the vast implausibilities of the earth features of the Big Bend.

Early surveyors familiar with only the border country spoke of the Conchos as the "mother stream of the Rio Grande," and said that it brought "the first permanent water to the main river." This was an attitude often directed toward the Rio Grande throughout its history, for along its great length (nearly two thousand miles), and in different times, on different missions, travellers discovered the river in segments, named them differently, found contradictory characters in them, and for many generations did not form a comprehensive theory of the river's continuity, variety, and use.

XXVIII At Presidio the replenished river fashions another of those green and easy valleys which, as at Alamosa, Española, Algodones, Albuquerque, Belén, and Mesilla, lie on ancient fertile flats of old river bottoms between gravel terraces and outlying mountains. After the bare and voracious desert in which it nearly died, the river brings again willows and cottonwoods, lilac mountains and attendant clouds, blue sky and emerald-green fields and pink sand, with a sweetness in the air made from all these together.

Summer is a long season here, after the harsh, bitter wind storms of spring, with their abrasive white dust that flies out of rocky arroyos to the north, casting a steel-blue obscurity across the sun. In the long summer days there is relief for vision in the wide belt of bosky green in which little adobe farmhouses, some whitewashed, shine in the light. All commonplaces of human work and relationship take on in this lyric landscape a timeless, a symbolic air; for the acts of nature and of man seem to show themselves in their most simple terms, and you find in them reminders of the first deep springs of the cultural memory, through all interpretations of life, from religion to the great arts.

Here in sweet dense cottonwood shadows by the water, plausibly a pagan heaven came down to visit Leda on a perishable earth, as all peoples have wanted to unite heaven and earth. Was it here in this grove that Jacob wrestled with his angel, and did Delacroix dream of the scene just as here? The treetops bespeak Saint Francis, and in the flesh his brothers knew this river and still do, in exactly his purpose and purity. What elders today have seen a girl Susanna dreaming awake and naked in the caressing river water? For there is nothing new in the myths of every breast. They only become renewed and real when nature calls them forth. But they never cease flowing through generations of human desire, whether in worship or love, making a river of their own sort. You can let them flow on the surface of thought again when you see in the classical bounty and order of the Rio Grande in its pastoral mood the background they require.

XXIX Southeastward the river continues within low banks below Presidio through inaccessible desert country. In the hazy heat of the downriver horizon, and inland to the northeast, images of another country begin to loom, almost like premonitions. Fantasies are manifest. Mountain nature has unimaginably long ago gone capricious in stunning and tremendous terms. The land has opposed the river before this, but not on the scale of what is coming. The Rio Grande is heading for all the old conditions of its course—desert, mountain, canyon—but now raised to prodigious dimensions of power in furies of sky action and earth response.

Previously the river has always been accompanied by mountains, near or far; but they lay generally parallel to its course. Now in the Big Bend the river encounters mountains in a new and extraordinary way; for they lie, chain after chain of them, directly across its way as though to impede and divert it and deny it passage to the sea. But the pull of the sea is stronger than rock, and the river was here before the mountains, and as they rose, in slowness beyond time, it cut its way against and through them.

XXX

A bush of ocotillo looks like a hank of rattlesnakes clutched together by their tails, and made to strive upward in all directions against air and sunlight.

xxxi

Northern Mexicans in the Big Bend country are almost completely cut off from the national life of their own land. The Mexican Big Bend desert is even harder country than its continuation across the river in Texas. For years the river has been a boundary of escape for hunted men of one nation crossing to hard safety in the other. Freedom depends upon which way you are facing and what you're running from.

xxxii

A man who moved from Arkansas to the west slope of the Chisos Mountains in 1909 lost about six hundred of his horses and colts to the ravages of mountain lions.

xxxiii

In the speckled land six miles from the mouth of the Santa Elena canyon there is a dwelling, a *jacal,* made of wattled mud and straw and faggots. There, as late as 1947, lived an ancient Mexican supposed to be over a hundred years old, scratching a bare dusty living out of rock and sand. His wife was a woman in her twenties. They said she was his seventh wife, and that he had sixty children, and that he was still sure of his powers. He made you think of some an-cient shelled insect, armored by his very age against the desert sun and dryness, designed to meet the ravaging conditions of a place whose only bounty lay in means of destruction, timeless and inexor-able; an anonymous triumphant mote of human life with a genius for survival—the only genius pertinent to living there.

xxxiv　　Born in mountains, and cradled by them, and then opposed by them, the Rio Grande has always been within sight of them. But below the Big Bend they start to fall away. If you can say so, now as the river goes southeastward, mountains are getting lost, like beads of a string which has broken so that the ones at the end rest separate without apparent connection with each other until finally there are no more. The last hint of mountain lies deep in Mexico below Langtry. The horizons from there on are hardly broken, and then only by long, low swells and dips which recall the rhythmic design of the sea where all will end.

xxxv　　About Del Rio-Ciudad Acuña life moves slowly in summer. The heat is not the dry flattening assault which you feel in the desert up-stream. It is here damp and pervasive, and when rain comes, it brings yet more heat. The color of the country is monotonous—limp green, brown earth, enlivened now and then by the scarlet business of a cardinal in the trees or on a fence. A crow in the distance sounds like an old man speaking through phlegm in his throat.

xxxvi　　The last decisive change in the river's character is approaching with the end of the brush desert.

Wilderness summer seems to reach its zenith here. All senses but one have received the strike and pervasion of the heat—sight, in the almost palpable impact of the light of the glaring sky; taste and smell, in the wry, acrid, herblike scents cooked out of the harsh brush by the beating sun; touch, in any step on the ground, any feel of exposed metal, any grasp of branch or rock. And now the very voice of southern Rio Grande summer assails the hearing. It is the voice of thousands upon thousands of cicadas which clutch the brush twigs like hard-shelled plant pods, varnished and sticky, and sing and sing.

In the wilderness the rising stridulation is so shrill that it is like a pressure, until your head swims, and the senses seem transposed, so that light rings and sound blazes. The collective scream of the heat is audible above the hot wind, even above the rush of a car at high speed. In high summer, through this shriek of the baking land, between pale, hot, sandy banks which go lower and lower, the Rio Grande slowly flows out of the harsh rolling brush prairie and into the ancient flood plain that declines imperceptibly for the last hundred miles to the sea.

xxxvii

Autumn is the seasonal analogy of age; and now in autumn, and here approaching the sea, the river shows its age most plainly. In its last phase with less than two feet a mile to drop, it flows slowly, making bend after bend of wide loops. Built by the drag of silt the river banks rise above the surrounding country. Everywhere are signs of former river beds which finally became too shallow and too elevated to retain the river in storm time. The river broke over, making new courses. The old ones grew grass and softened their contours. Everywhere is the green growth of semi-tropical climate. The seasons are close to one another in temper, though autumn and winter bring cooler days and nights as the sun goes south over the nearby ocean. The air is hazy with moisture from transpiration as the profuse plant life breathes its misty discharge. The land is far enough south now to make every season a growing season. The uncultivated landscape shows this, and most of all, so does the culture of citrus fruit trees. Here in the lowest valley, the Rio Grande is a garden river.

xxxviii

If the river fell faster, and flowed more swiftly in this last porch of the land, it would cut a straighter course. But the bends, loops, and meanders grow more and more tortuous and laborious as the flow seeks out the easiest way to crawl to its end. The soil is composed of alternate layers of two kinds. One is river soil, hauled from upstream and laid down in soft muddy bands. The other is sea deposit, left over from times when the ocean covered the plain. These bear witness to ancient strife between risen sea and encroaching land. The differing hardness of such deposits explains why the Rio Grande turns and turns in its efforts to run out its course. At one point in the delta the river curves back upon itself in two great loops until only a dike separates one from the other, both going opposite ways. Reed, canebrake, palmetto, willow, water plants, line the course, where the great-tailed grackle in his shiny black silk coat with blue highlights makes a hilarious clattering fuss in and out of shadow.

xxxix   At Brownsville the river still has fifty miles to go, though where it is going is only seventeen miles away in a straight line.

The citrus, palm, garden aspect of the lower valley land begins to merge east of Brownsville into white sand and salt grass, through which the Rio Grande twists from side to side, mild and nearly exhausted. Dunes accompany it and migrate with the wind. Sometimes hurricanes formed in the West Indies slash inland over the delta. But it is too late for weather to create much downstream change in the Rio Grande in its last wandering miles.

There is evidence of marsh life. The riverbanks in places are hardly an inch or two above the flow. Water fowl attend—cranes, herons, geese, ducks, curlews, plover, sandpipers. The light of the sky continuously fades and brightens according to sea clouds that hardly form but hang low and filmy, as white as the wilderness of sand on which they make glistening shadows. Salt marshes and lagoons rest like misted mirrors among the low hollows bounded by dunes. The wasted flood plain is running out with the continent.

Isolated, depleted, heavy with suspended soil, the river widens gradually to a thousand feet, and leaves the dunes between low shelves of sandy beach littered with driftwood that is polished to silver by wind and sun, or blackened by saturation. Through a waste of sand, misty air, and silence, in the presence of no human concern, having come more than eighteen hundred miles from mountains nearly three miles high, the Rio Grande at last enters the Gulf of Mexico and the sea.

xl   In vast movements, the sky keeps its life compact over all, sea and earth alike, in grand cycle.

From its first mountains to its slow and exhausted arrival in the sea, the river has been surrounded by forces and elements constantly moving and dynamic, interacting to produce its life and character. If most of the river's action can be seen, its greatest element can only be surmised from what is visible. This is that unceasing passion in all nature which in any scale or detail affirms life itself, yields a theory or sense of the whole from any part, and brings great disparate forces to interact throughout its course to make the river.

It has taken sky and ocean; the bearing of winds and the vagary of temperature; altitude and tilt of the earth's crust; underground storage of water and the spill of valleys and the hard, dry, impermeable texture of deserts; the cover of plants and the uses of animals; the power of gravity and the perishability of rock; the thirst of all growing things and the need of the sea and the breath of evaporation to create the Rio Grande, to keep its nature and to return it to the element from which it came.

BOOK TWO

Indian

Rio Grande Pueblos:
The Ancients

Rio Grande Pueblos:
The Ancients

Most intimately they could watch creation as a child was born. So from the womb of the earth itself they said all life came forth long ago. The underworld was dark and mysterious. People and animals lived there and knew their mother, who was kind and loving, even though she remained far from the daily lives of her children. So they accounted for the impersonality of nature. As all life came from the underworld, so it returned there in death. To come in life and go in death, people and animals had to pass through a lake between the underworld and the world. The first people climbed up a great fir tree through the waters of the lake and entered this world. The place where they emerged was in the north and was called Shipapu.* Emergence into the world was a tremendous act, full of awe for what was left behind, and of fear and respect for what was found above, on the earth and in the sky. A thing ever afterward could be made sacred simply by saying, "It came up with us."

With them came spirit, which could dwell in everything upon the earth. All spirit was like that of people. Rock, trees, plants; animals, birds, fish; places, directions, the bodies and acts of the sky; the live and the dead; things found or things made—all had the same spirit and behaved in the same ways as men and women. Some spirit was good and some bad, and accordingly had to be propitiated or guarded against. Sometimes spirit would leave its visible form and be gone. If it was bad spirit, people could rejoice; if good, they must mourn at having lost favor with the powers of their lives.

Everything in the world was part of the same living force, whether thought, action, object, or creature. Of all this the earth was the center, and all things existed in order to help people to live upon it. And the center of the earth—earth's navel—was in the center of each group of people and their own city. All things reached

i

Creation & Prayer

* With many variants of spelling, like all proper names in the myths.

out in widening circles of awareness from the very point of the self, individual, and the group, collective. From the center, then, of person and place, reached the six directions, each with its animal deity: north, with the mountain lion; west, with the bear; south, with the badger; east, with the wolf; the zenith, with the eagle; and the nadir, with the shrew. North and west produced the snow; south and east the rain. So the reach of Pueblo belief went across the earth, and into the depths underground and into the heights of the sky, and all tied to the place of emergence which was imitated with a stone-lined pit in the center of each ceremonial chamber, and sometimes out in the open in the very center of the town *placita* itself. All forces interacted to make life; and of these, none was greater in effect, sacredness, and poetry than the sky, with its heroes, goddesses, and ancestors.

"Our Father Sun," they said. Some said that even the sun had ancestors—two mothers, who before the people came from the underworld saw that people must have light in order to see. The mothers fashioned the sun out of a white shell, a pink abalone shell, a turquoise, and a red stone. They carried him to the east and in the morning climbed a high mountain. They dropped the sun behind the mountain; and presently he began to rise, taking his way over trails that ran above the waters of the sky, toward the evening. He set toward the lake which lay between the world and the underworld. He went down through the lake and when it was night on the earth, he shone dimly below in the underworld. In the morning again he arose and again the people saw him with joy. What they saw was not the sun himself but a large mask that covered his whole body. By his light everyone saw that the world was large and beautiful. The sun saw and knew, like any other person. And others said that he walked through the sky dressed in white deerskin which flashed with countless beads. His face, hidden by a mask, was beautiful. They said he was the father of the twin boys, Masewi and Oyoyewi, the young gods of war, who protected the people by killing their enemies. The concept of evil, menace, hugeness of danger was defeated by the dream of small, unlettered mortals—the very cast of hope in people who first imagined their survival and triumph, then willed it, and then achieved it through the spirit which towered to victory over threatening forces. Power and strength came from the sun, as they could plainly see in the daily life all about them. "Our Father Sun" governed the overworld.

But when he went down through the sacred lake at evening, the world was dark. He needed a companion god in the sky at night. So they said that the two mothers who made the sun also made the moon—taking a dark stone, different kinds of yellow stone, turquoise, and a red stone—and placed it in the sky, where it followed by night the same trails which the sun followed by day. The moon was a mystery, and some said it was a man, others a woman.

Because the moon travelled slowly, not always giving light, the stars were needed, and were made out of crystal which sparkled and shone. At morning a great star shone into the dawn, and at evening, even before the daylight was all gone, another flashed slowly in the west at the place where the sun went below. They were clear in the heavens, along with many others, hanging near in power and beauty when the night was clear and dark, making at least some things certain and pure in a world where evil spirit could bring about change among people and things, and cause fear.

When clouds came, they brought rain, which blessed the earth and made things grow. Who loved the people and blessed them? The dead ancestors, who once were people, and who came back as clouds to do good for those whose life they already knew, with its constant hope, need, and prayer for rain. Clouds were prayed to. The prayers took many forms. Feathers were used to imitate clouds and were put on top of headdresses and sacred masks. Visible prayers were put together out of little sticks decorated with feathers. These could be set about and left as invocations from earth to sky. The dead who departed to life in the clouds were in some places prepared with white paint on the forehead, and feathers and cotton placed in the hair, so that cloud would go to cloud and come back bringing rain.

Lightning, they said, was born of mischief by Masewi and Oyoyewi. The twin war godlings once came to an empty kiva in a village of another world. While all the people were elsewhere, the boys stole bows and arrows from the kiva wall and tried to escape unnoticed; but they were seen, their theft discovered, and they were chased by outraged people. Just where they had come from their own world to the other one, and as they were about to be taken, the adventurers were picked up by a whirlwind and thrust back into their own world, where they went home. On the way, Masewi sent an arrow high up to the sky. It made a grand noise. The womenfolk saw it and fainted. The boys shot many more arrows. These were the first bolts of lightning known by the people. Some days later there came rainclouds, bringing the arrows back and delivering rain with many flashes and noises. Arrows fell. The twins were glad their arrows came back to them. Sky arrows were holy to hunters, who prayed to lightning when they got ready to hunt. Thunder was made by an old goddess. They said medicine men could send for thunder and receive it at any time. The wind had a divinity, too— sometimes man, sometimes woman. There was an aged god of the rainbow. When the war twins wanted to visit their father the sun, they walked on the rainbow, which quickly took them to him in mid-sky.

The Pueblos said, then, recognizing the exchange of influences and acts between earth and sky, that the Old Man of the Sky was the husband of the Old Woman of the Earth. All things came from their union, just as the child came from the union of man and woman. Mankind and the animals, the earth and the sky with all their elements, all had the same kind of life; and a person must be in harmony with the life in all things. The way to find it was in re- ligion. Prayer and observances were part of all daily life. Bound upon the earth with other living things, the Pueblos said that the same life belonged in everything, and that life was either male or female. Everything they believed came within the frame of those two ideas.

Prayer took many forms.

Sometimes it was only the person who prayed; and sometimes the whole family, or fraternity, or town. Prayers were always visible; a stuff was used, in an act, to make plain the desire locked in the heart. Of all prayer substances, the most common was meal, ground once, from white corn. It had life in it, it came from something that once grew, it fed life in people, its seed made more life in the ground. The Pueblo person took it in his hand and breathed upon it as he prayed. "Eat," he said to it, and then he sprinkled it into the air, or over the ground, or upon the person, place, thing, or animal he wanted to bless. At sunrise he would go out and sprinkle meal and say a prayer. When holy men, or hunters, or warriors went by his house before or after doing their work, he would come to his wall, breathe upon meal, and sprinkle it before their steps. His fin- gers were bunched at his lips holding the pinch of meal. In breath- ing upon it he gave his living essence to it. His inward prayer made an arc of spirit from him to all godliness; and his arm, when he swept it widely to sprinkle the meal, had a noble reach in it; for a gesture can always be bigger than the little member which makes it.

Sometimes pollen from flowers was used and spread in prayer in just the same way.

Another form of prayer, one which lasted longer and could be left to bear testimony and intercede by itself, was the prayer stick. It was used in every group ceremonial in some pueblos, and often a whole ritual was built around it. It was also used privately. Much care, ingenuity, and taste went into its making. The prayer stick was as long as from the wrist to the end of the middle finger. It was cut from oak, willow, spruce, or cottonwood. Its stem was richly painted with colors taken from the earth. There was turquoise color, made out of malachite or copper ore mixed with white bean meal. Yellow ochre came from canyon or gully faces, exposed in stripes by long weather. Shale made black. Pale clay made white, iron-stained sandstone made red, and from cactus flowers or purple cornhusk came violet. The colors were mixed with water from sacred springs, and with flowers from the bee-plant. Honey was sprayed on the paint after it was applied. The sky was called by feathers bound upon the prayer stick. Turkey, duck, hawk, and eagle; flicker, jay, bluebird, oriole, towhee, yellow warbler feathers were used. To speak to cloud spirits, downy or breast feathers were bound in with the feather bundles. Beads were added sometimes.

When the prayer stick was made, it was prayed over and exposed to smoke. It was breathed upon and given its intention. Then it was taken to do its work. Perhaps it was set up in the house where it would stay for life, expressing its prayer forever. It might be taken to the fields and buried; or set in the riverbank; or taken to a holy spring and established at its lip; or carried high into the mountains to make a remote shrine; or put away with stored food; or sealed up in the wall of a new house; or carried in the hand during ceremonials; or put to earth with the dead. If a prayer stick was left in an exposed place, they could tell by whether it stood or fell how the spirit of its maker was. If it fell, he must have had bad thought while making it, and his offering was in consequence rejected.

Sometimes prayer and its acts were delegated. Certain persons became priests and acted for everyone else. It was agreed that nature did what the priests told it to do. The priests spoke to the world in grander ways than anyone else. When they meant "four years," they would say "four days," for example. But everyone knew what they meant when they sounded special. It was part of their having power. People watched to see that the priests used their power when it was needed, such as those times every year when the sun had to be turned back. All summer long the sun moved farther to the south, toward the badger. The weather was colder. Every year, in the same month, there came a point beyond which the sun must not be permitted to go. They would know by watching the sun come to a natural landmark when the limit of his southern journey was reached. At that point, on that day, it was the duty of the priests to halt the sun; and with prayer, ceremony, and power, make the sun start northward in the sky once again, in its proper way. Half a year later, when the sun touched the point to the north, with the mountain lion, beyond which it must never be allowed to go, the priests brought it back toward the south again. So the natural cycles were preserved. What nature had already ordered was ordered once again by the people in their prayers. To rise above, govern, and hold the natural world they imagined their own control of it and solemnly sanctioned the inevitable.

Other ways to pray and gain favor were found in imitating what nature looked like and did. And here the great group prayer was made, when the people came together in ceremony to tell nature what it must do for their lives.

They gave great splendor to the group prayer, and prepared for it with rigor, always in the same ways which had come down to them out of memory. A certain society of men learned invocations and chants which lasted for hours, and had to be word-perfect. They learned choruses and strict drumbeats to accompany them. Sacred costumes were made, and the materials for them came from expeditions, often to the mountains and even farther—boughs of the pine tree, skins of the fox and the rabbit, the deer, the buffalo, the bobcat; feathers from eagles, the bright parrots of the south; and from nearer home, gourds to dry and fill with pebbles from the arroyos, cornhusks to weave into headdresses, paint to put on the body. Groups of men and groups of women worked at practicing over and over the steps of the dance to be used in the ceremony. They must stand—the men separate from the women—just so, and to the beat of the drum, they must lift and put down their feet so, all exactly together; they must turn, and pause, and advance, facing newly, and the women's bare feet must be lifted only a little and put down again mildly, while the men must smartly raise their feet in their soft deerskin shoes and bring them down to pound on the ground with power. The singers and the dancers and the drummers learned perfect accord. Implements were made in the ceremonial

chambers to be used on the day of the group prayer, which was
held in the plaza of the town. All persons, young and old, worked
toward the day. Men and women could not lie together for a certain
period before it. Only certain foods might be eaten. For several days
before, those who were going to take part made sure to vomit many
times a day. The dancing-ground was swept clean. If there was any
refuse about the houses, it was taken away. Thoughts were put in
order, too. Some of the figures in the dance were going to be the
clowns, the spirits who mocked and scolded humanity, whose very
thoughts they could see. And above all, there would be certain
masked figures who came there from the other world. All the
women knew that these were gods themselves—the spirits of rain
and growth—who wore on their heads wooden coverings, trimmed
with downy feathers and painted to represent the deities of the sky.
These were the most mysterious and powerful of all the dancers.
They had naked arms and breasts and legs like any other men, and
wore foxtails on their rumps, and had pine boughs banded upon
their arms, and wore the woven belts and the rabbit-fur baldrics and
deerskin shoes, and used the gourds like the real men; but the
women said they were not real men, they were actual gods, called
the kachinas, and upon them depended the rainfall, the crops, and
the yield of the hunt. All year, said the women, their masks were
kept in the ceremonial chamber, and when time came for the group
prayer, they came like gods and put them on, and appeared in the
ceremony. The men knew something else. They knew that long
ago, before anybody could remember, or think of it, the kachinas
really came and danced with the people. But for a long time they
had not really come. It was actually certain men who put on the
masks and appeared as the kachinas. But they never told the women
of the substitution. Children did not know of it, either; and only
boys, when they reached a certain age, learned of it, and kept the secret among their sex. If the gods were properly imitated, then they
would do as their imitators did, and make the motions which would
produce rain, growth, and game.

When the day came, the whole pueblo was ready. Those who did
not dance sat in silence upon the rooftops or against the walls upon
the ground. All was still in the early sunlight. The houses, made of
earth, looked like mesas, and cast strong shadows. People waited as
nature waited for whatever might come. The ground before the
houses was empty and clean, dazzling in the light. What would
break the silence, and release the bodies full of prayer?

It was a thunderclap, which came suddenly and rocked from wall to wall, in the voice of the drums. The drums told the thunder what to do; and thunder, born of storm, would bring rain.

At once the first dancers came like creatures of the air out of the door in the flat roof of the ceremonial chamber; and at the same instant song began and the drums sounded with it. The chorus appeared from between two houses and came to the plaza.

Then the dancers came, great ranks of them, the men in front, the women behind them, led by a man holding a long pole into the air, decorated with eagle feathers that spoke to the sky, as from one cloud to another. They all advanced as slowly as a shadow from a high cloud on a still day; but they never ceased their movement. The men pounded the stamped ground. The women padded softly upon it. The men commanded nature. The women waited to receive it. Slowly the long columns reached out and out into the dancing-ground until they were all seen. They crossed it. They faced and returned. The chorus and the drummers sang and beat without falter. Everyone was exactly together in rhythm and action. The evolutions of the dancing and singing groups were made so gradually and in such slowly changed relation to one another that they seemed like the slow wheeling of the stars overhead at night.

In their right hands the men held the rattles of dried gourds containing seed pods or pebbles. With these at intervals they clattered upon the ground the sound of seeds falling; and again they showered together upon the earth the sound of falling rain.

In their left hands the men and women carried bunches of eagle feathers which, like those on the banner that towered above them and went with them in their grave evolutions, invoked the clouds of the sky.

In their left hands the women carried pine boughs; and pine boughs were bound upon the arms of the men. These were a prayer for everlasting life, for the pine tree was always green.

The men proclaimed by their presence the seed, and invoked it, and wet it, pounded their power into the earth, and ordered that it live and grow.

The women impassively like the earth itself showed by their presence how the seed was received and nurtured.

With their pine boughs spaced throughout the ranks, they looked like a little forest. Advancing powerfully against the light, they were like a movement of the earth in an analogy of slow time. The voices of the singers barked together and made order out of the

sounds of the animal kingdom. The arms moved, the legs rose and
fell, the bodies travelled in such unanimity and decorum that they
all seemed like a great woven construction, something man-made,
some vast act of basketry, the parts tied and yet flexible in supple
buckskin; again, moving against the sidelines, they seemed like a
cliff advancing; or if the watchers shut their eyes and only listened
for a moment, they heard the singing voices clapping flatly back
from the facing houses, and the clatter of seeds, the swipe of rain,
the breeze of pine trees, the rattle of little shells tied to costumes,
and in all of it the spacious and secret sound of the sky into which
all other sounds disappeared and were taken to the gods.

All day long the insistent pounding of the prayer went on.

The clowns—koshare—played about the undisturbed edges of the
formal dancing groups. They were painted white, with here and
there a black stripe. They were naked, and used their nakedness in
comic outrage and in joking punishment of generative power. They
leaped and ran. They now went soberly by the dancers and jogged
like them and then broke away to enact a burlesque at a corner of
the dancing-ground. A little boy or two, painted like them, capered
along with them learning the mocking idiom of the people's self-
critics. Against so much work and preparation and proper devout-
ness in the great dance, it was necessary to send a different kind of
prayer through the antics of the koshare—all the things the people
knew about themselves but would not say separately. Fun included
hurting. About that there was nothing odd. Much of life hurt.

The masked gods moved with the men.

The singers and drummers, massed closely together, turned and
changed formation, now into a solid square, now a circle, but so
slowly that the watchers hardly saw the change take place, but only
realized it the next time they looked. The drums smote the air every
time the dancing feet charged the ground with the day's stern message, in beat, beat, beat. Every now and then, as dictated by the
words of the chant and the phases of prayer, the whole united government of bodies and voices and shaken air would suddenly break,
missing a beat, and break again, missing another, making a clap of
silence, a falter like a loss of light, a chasm in design, until, still in
absolute union, legs, arms, voices, drums would resume the steady
pounding by which the power of that town was driven, beat, beat,
beat, into the earthen and airy body of nature.

And the whole day long it pounded.

According to the season, the dance took its theme from different gods. With them all, it practiced imitation of nature to influence nature. The rainbow dance, with its arches of willows carried by women, suggested rain as the rainbow could never appear in a dry sky. The turtle dance reminded the powers of water, for water came with turtles. The corn dance showered the sound of seeds and rain on the ground. The parrot dance with its blaze of feathers woven on costumes made nature think of the warm south where the parrots lived, and the hot sun, also, which made crops grow. The eagle dance, in which men soared along the ground with eagle wings tied to their arms, reminded of how strong an eagle was, and how such strength could cure anything. Before huntsmen set out, the dance would imagine and predict success for them—sometimes in the deer dance, with men garbed in deerskin and hunted down by other dancers as heroes; or the antelope, the elk, the buffalo, all costumed accordingly, and full of respect for the habits of the beloved adversary and victim who would be brought to death in order that the people might live. In the animal dances, little boys sometimes went costumed as bobcats and coyotes, jogging under the dancing bodies of men who impersonated deer or buffalo. Sometimes a boy dancer was a turkey, bridling and flaring with a suit of feathers.

To imitate was to induce, in gesture, sound, and article.

To impersonate was to become.

To endure ordeal was to know not exhaustion but refreshment.

For when evening came the dancers, the singers, and drummers were not tired. They were stronger than ever. They were lifted up. In giving they had received. The great ranks ended their slow stately evolutions, and the men retired to the kiva. The women sought their houses. The chorus broke formation and entered the kiva. The clowns went trotting lazily over the town. They capered benignly now. Dwellers came forward from their rooms and, breathing upon corn meal, dusted it into the air before the clowns, who took the tribute with a kindly bend of painted nakedness. The spectators drifted to their rooms.

Such a pueblo typically sat on an eminence above the river, and near to it. The river was a power which, like the light of the sky, was never wholly lost. It came from the north beyond knowing, and it went to the south nobody knew where. It was always new and yet always the same. It let water be taken in ditches to the lowest fields. Trees grew along its banks—willows, cottonwoods, young and old, always renewing themselves. The water was brown, as brown as a body, and both lived on earth as brown. The river was part of the day's prayer.

Evening came down over the west, like thin gray smoke pulled over color, and the evening star stood like a great trembling drop of water on the soft darkness of the sky.

Before daylight was all gone, the pueblo was silent but for the little sounds of ordinary life—voices lost in narrow walls, a dog, someone breaking branches for firewood, children. The twilight was piercingly sweet and clear. The river went silent and silken between its low banks where grasses grew and saplings and little meadows sprung up out of mudbanks. Sky and town and valley were united in deep peace after the hard wonders of the dancing day. And at that hour the men of the dance came through the sapling groves to the river. The deepening yellow dusk put color on the water. The men came in their ceremonial dress. They took it off and went naked to the river's edge. There they breathed upon the pine boughs which they had worn, and the baldrics of rabbit fur, and sometimes the gourd rattles, and cast them upon the sliding surface of the water. They sent their prayers with the cast-off branches and the skins which, wherever they were borne by the river wherever it went, would go as part of that day's pleading will. Then, entering the river, the men bathed. The brown water played about them and over them and they thanked it and blessed it. Silken as beavers they came out and dried. Now their voices rang and they laughed and joked and gossiped about the long hard day, for its ceremony was over, and its make-believe, and could be talked about quite ordinarily. They felt strong and refreshed. It was good to have such a river, and such a town, and to have done such a work as that of today. Everything about it told nature what to do; everything was done in exactly the right way; all the ways were right, because, said the men, "they came up with us."

So the idea of creation, and so the ways of propitiating the creators.

There in that long stretch of New Mexico valley (which even so was but one seventh of the whole length of the river) the Pueblo Indians ordered the propriety of their life to the landscape that surrounded them. This act was implicit in all their sacred beliefs. It recognized the power, nearness, and blaze of the sky; the clarity of the air; the colors of the earth; the sweep of mountain, rock, plain; and the eternity of the river. Environment directly called forth the spirit and the creations of the people. The weather had direct effects upon vegetable growth, and the life of waterways, and the change in land forms. It had equally direct effect upon the human personality and its various states and views of life. The presence of mountains; the altitude of the very valley itself; the outlying deserts beyond; the effects created by the interchange of influence and response between that particular land and that particular sky—all had effect and expression in the Pueblo world.

The natural forms rising from a landscape created by surface-water action, the wind, and volcanic fury—that is to say, river, desert, and mountain—bore intimate fruits in their imitation by the forms of Pueblo life. The cave became a room. The room became part of a butte. The butte, joined with others like it, resembled a mesa, terraced and stepped back. The Pueblo town looked like a land form directly created by the forces that made hills and arroyos and deserts. Daylight upon the face of a pueblo looked the same as daylight upon the face of a cliff. Who knew how much this was accidental, and how much devised by the Indian in his sense of propriety in the natural world, his reverence for all its aspects, and his general application in imitative symbols of all the living and enduring forms he knew about him? Even where his town stood above the river, the river dictated his farming methods; for the irrigation ditch leading from the river to the fields below the town was in itself but a tiny river in form, with the same general laws of flow, and reach, and structure as the big river. People not too long the owners of such a concept would not find it a naïve one, to be taken for granted. It would instead be a grave and reassuring fact, to be thankful for along with all of the other energetic expressions of the landscape, among which the Pueblo Indian prayed passionately to be included as a proper part—not a dominant part, not a being whose houses and inventions and commerce would subject the physical world until he rose above it as its master; but as a living spirit with material needs whose modest satisfaction could be found and harmonized with those of all other elements, breathing or still, in the dazzling openness all about him, with its ageless open secrets of solitude, sunlight, and impassive land.

So every act and relationship of Pueblo life included the intention to find and fulfill such harmony. The whole environment found its way by spiritual means into all Pueblo life. Works of art captured the animal and vegetable and spiritual world—always in objects meant for use, never display for its own sake. The work of art, in the sense that all elements were brought together—colors, emotions, ideas, attitudes—in harmonious proportion and mixed with fluent skill, the work of art was the act of living, itself. No one part of it had significance alone, just as each feature of the landscape by itself meant less than what all meant and looked like together.

Worship entered into every relation between the people and their surroundings. The mountains were holy places; temples standing forever which held up the sky. Gods lived in them, and other supernaturals. The priests of the people went to the mountains to call upon the deities of the four points of the compass. The various pueblo groups identified their sacred mountains differently. For one of them, the northern one was Truchas Peak; the eastern one was the Lake Peak of the Santa Fe range; the southern one was the Sandia range, which they called Okupinn, turtle mountain; the western one was Santa Clara Peak of the Jemez Range, which they called the mountain covered with obsidian. All of them rose far back and above the Rio Grande, into whose valley they all eventually shed water.

The action of the river upon land forms was recognized at times by the Indians. Near the pueblo of San Ildefonso is a great black mesa on the west of the river, faced across the river on the east by high ground. This place they called P'o-woge, "where the water cut through." In the midst of supernatural explanations of natural conditions this was suddenly a cool and observant conclusion; not, however, to the disadvantage of another idea, which was that in the great cave on the north side of the black mesa there once lived (they said) a cannibal giant. His cave was connected with the interior of the vast, houselike mesa by tunnels which took him to his rooms. His influence upon the surrounding country was heavy. Persons did the proper things to avoid being caught and eaten by him.

Lakes and springs were sacred, too, and natural pools. They were doorways to the world below. If everything originally "came up" with the people through the sacred lake Shi-pap, the same action could be imagined for other such bodies of water. Many of these were springs which fed the river. Gods and heroes were born out of springs, and ever afterward came and went between the above and below worlds through their pools. Every pueblo had sacred springs somewhere nearby. There was every reason to sanctify them—physical, as life depended upon water; spiritual, as they had natural mystery which suggested supernatural qualities; for how could it be that when water fell as rain, or as snow, and ran away, or dried up, there should be other water which came and came, secretly and sweetly, out of the ground and never failed?

Some of the rivers that went into the Rio Grande dried up for months at a time. In the Pueblo world, the most important tributaries were Taos, Santa Cruz, Pojuaque, Santa Fe, and Galisteo creeks on the east, and on the west, Jemez Creek, the Chama River. Of these only the last one had perennial flow. Its waters were red in melting season and colored the Rio Grande for many miles below their confluence. But the courses of them all bore the valley cottonwood. It was the dominant and most useful tree in all the Pueblo country. Its wood was soft and manageable, and it supplied material for many objects. Its silver bark, its big, varnished leaves sparkling in the light of summer and making caverns of shade along the banks, its winter-hold of leaves the color of beaten thin gold lasting in gorgeous bounty until the new catkins of spring—all added grace to the pueblo world. The columnar trunks were used to make tall drums, hollowed out and resonated with skins stretched over the open ends. The wood was hot fuel, fast-burning, leaving a pale, rich ash of many uses. Even the catkins had personal use—eaten raw, they were a bitter delicacy in some towns. And in that arid land, any tree, much less a scattered few, or a bounteous grove, meant good things—water somewhere near, and shade, and shelter from the beating sun, and talk from trifling leaves.

The feeling, the sense, of a place was real and important to the people. Almost invariably for their towns they chose sites of great natural beauty. The special charm of a place was often commemorated in what they named it. On the river's west bank stood a pueblo called Yunge, which meant "Western mockingbird place." The name was a clue to the sense of the place, for above its graces of flowing water, rippling groves, and the high clear valley with its open skies would rise the memory of the May nights when the prodigal songs of the mockingbirds year after year sounded all night long in the moonlight. The birds sang so loudly as to awaken people from sleep. Night after night a particular voice seemed to come from the very same tree with the same song. It was like a blessing so joyful that it made an awakened sleeper laugh with delight, listening to that seasonal creature of the river's life. In the daytime little boys on rooftops caught moths, which also appeared in

May, and, whistling to the mockingbirds, released the moths which the birds in an accurate swoop caught in midair with their bills.

Everything in the landscape was sacred, whether the forms of nature, or those made by people—altars, shrines, and the very towns, which were like earth arisen into wall, terrace, light, and shadow, enclosing and expressing organized human life.

iii
Community

It was an organized life whose ruling ideas were order, moderation, unanimity. All ways were prescribed, all limits set, and all people by weight of an irresistible power took part in the town life. Examples of such controls elsewhere suggested that they must come from a ruler, a presiding head of state whose decrees could only be obeyed, on pain of despotic gesture. But the Pueblo people had no ruler; no despot. The irresistible power which ordered their communal life was the combined and voluntary power of the people— all the people, in each town, giving continuity to inherited ways by common agreement.

Everybody, together, in a pueblo, owned all the land, all the religious edifices and ritual objects. Assignment of use was made by a council of elders. Heads of families were granted the use of portions of land, which could be reallotted every year, according to change in families through marriage or death. Religious properties were assigned to proper organizations.

Crops grown by families upon their assigned plots belonged to them alone. Families owned objects which they made for their own use. Families were given permanent possession of rooms in the pueblo for as long as the family existed and could build additional space as needed. When a family died out, its apartments were abandoned and went into ruins.

Since property was entirely for use, and not for sale or trade within the pueblo, everybody lived upon the same scale. Their rooms were alike. Their holdings in food, clothing, furniture, were about the same. Living closely together, they interfered very little with their immediate neighbors, though within the family there was no privacy and no desire for any. Outbursts of feeling, emotion, violence, were bad form, and so was indulgence in authority for its own sake, instead of for the propriety it was meant to preserve. Nobody was supposed to stand out from everyone else in any connection but that which had to do with official duties. Everyone understood that certain work—official or religious—had to be done by someone who was given, by common consent, the authority to do it. But nobody was supposed to propose himself for the job, or go out after it. If he was chosen for it, a man, with real reluctance but equally real obedience to the wishes of his associates, accepted it and did his serious best while in office. If anybody in such a position showed the wrong attitude, or indeed, if anyone at all transgressed against the accepted way of things, he was shown his error in the ridicule he received from other people. He did not like to be laughed at in the town, or made sport of by the clowns in the dances, and he would mend his ways if he had gone too far out of line. There was no excuse for him to feel differently from anybody else, and to behave accordingly. As there was a proper way to perform all acts, everyone not only understood ritual but performed it. United in gesture, the pueblo had a strong sense of its own identity. Everyone agreed how things were and had to be and should be. Understanding so, there could be few disappointments in life, and few complete bafflements.

Certain towns had thin, narrow, long stones which rang with a clear song when struck. They were hung by deerskin thongs to the end, outdoors, of a roof beam. The singing stones could be heard in the town and the nearby fields. To summon men for meetings, the stones were struck. Meetings were held often, for the town had many organizations, each with particular work to do.

In some towns, all people were divided into two cults—the Summer, or Squash, People; and the Winter, or Turquoise, People. Other towns knew four seasons of the year, and organized accordingly. All towns had secret societies with particular social duties, all religious in form. At the head of the pueblo, as guardian of all spiritual lives, was the cacique. He served for life. He had many duties, for no important act was ever done without ritual, and it was he who blessed and approved all ceremonies. In his own life he invoked holiness with fasting and prayer. That he might be free entirely for his sacred offices he was relieved of all other work. His house was built for him. Other people planted for him and cultivated his crops and made his harvests. In his shrines he kept fetishes which had to be fed with rabbit meat. Men went on special hunts to bring him rabbits, and the sacred food was prepared by his appointed helper, who cooked the rabbits and also kept his house for him, making fires, sweeping the packed earthen floor, and ministering to his needs.

The cacique made important appointments to the priesthood. Two of these were the war priests, named for the twin boy-gods Masewi and Oyoyewi. They held office for a year. Part of their duty was to observe the cacique in the performance of his duties, and to admonish him if he was negligent. Each year he appointed ten assistants to the war priests. His influence was great, his position among the people that of the fountainhead of all spiritual belief and practice. He was both father and mother to them, a living analogue of the source of their lives. Upon his death his successor was chosen by the war priests from his own secret society.

The cult was a medium through which the people could formally take part in the religious life of the pueblo. Everyone belonged to one or another of the cults in the town. Membership was hereditary, except that a girl who married entered the cult of her husband. If she was widowed, she could choose between remaining in the cult of her husband or returning to that of her father. The cult had a head who was in charge of all its activities. The most sacred of objects were the masks used in the kachina dances—those great group prayers in which the gods of rain were believed by women and children to be actually present in the dance. These masks, and the costumes that went with them, and the miniature carved figures representing the godly kachinas, were kept by the cult leader as his own personal duty. He alone could mix the turquoise-green paint used in decorating masks. Not everyone could have masks. Only married men of mature experience could have them. With the mask came powers—the wearer turned into someone else. His real person was hidden not only from the spectator but delivered from himself. Behind the mask he was the godlike being which the people saw. He escaped into a new and sacred dignity, leaving behind him the weak man of every day to whom he must return when he doffed his mask again, but surely with some lingering joy and a new strength.

The cult had its ceremonial home in the large chamber of the kiva, sacred to its own members. It was usually circular, sometimes underground, generally above ground. Here was the very house of power and ritual. It was entered through a hatch in the roof, by a tall ladder which leaned down to the floor. A small altar stood in the room, sometimes against the wall, sometimes free. Before it was a small round hole. This was called by the same name as the original place where the people came up into the world—Shipapu. A shaft built into the wall brought air to the altar, and with it would come and go the spirits addressed in prayer. Smoke from fires built before the altar was carried out through the entrance hatch in the roof by the spirits of the kachinas. On another plane of experience and discovery, the air descending through the shaft made the fire draw, and set up circulation which drew smoke to the roof and out into the air through the hatchway. At about the height of a kneeling man, a deep shelf or seat ran around the wall of the interior. The wall was sometimes painted with sacred images and symbols of weather, animals, birds, plants, and human actions, all with ritual purposes.

The whole kiva itself was a powerful symbol. It was like a small butte with a flat top, a land form often seen. In its interior it gave passageway to the two worlds—the earth-world above, through the hatch to natural life of land, creatures, and sky; and the netherworld below, through the portal of the world's womb from which all had come so long ago. Both worlds were made to join in the kiva. Here the holy pigments were prepared, and the costumes for the dances. Inherited rituals were studied and learned here. Sacred objects remained in the kiva when not in use out of doors. Fetishes were fed there. Boys were initiated there into knowledge and power of which they had known only animal intimations. There dancers painted and dressed for their outdoor ceremonials and, when readied, came in a crowding line up the ladder through the hatch, over the roof and down to the ground. To perpetuate the kiva in filling vacant kiva offices, there the members met in conclave. There in the significant number of four times—invocation of the whole world through its four quarters—ceremonies were prepared during four days of vomiting and other purifications.

Each kiva group was dedicated to the ceremonial work of one of the seasons. Since ritual and its texts were elaborate and long, and transmitted only by memory with no written records, and since every phase of community life was accompanied by its ceremonial observance, no one cult could learn and execute the liturgy for all occasions. Yet certain events, like the great corn dance, called upon two or more cults to perform in the plaza, alternately throughout the day-long invocation of the spirits of fertility and growth, when one group would dance while the other waited to take its place, with all joining at the end.

So the religious life of the people was formalized in groups that separately represented neither the whole town nor a single clan, but drew symmetrically upon the population until all were included, empowered in the same terms, and actors of the same myths. Religion was not a thing apart from daily life. It *was* daily life, a formalization, an imitation of nature, an imagined control of the elements, and of what was obscure in the spirit of men and women.

In addition to the major divisions of the kiva groups, which cut boldly through the whole company of the town for organized religious acts, there were smaller groups with specialized missions whose members were not chosen along the lines of kiva organization. These were the secret societies. Each had its unique purpose. There was one in charge of war. Another appointed all holders of major nonreligious offices. Another comprised the koshare, the clowns of the dances who served also as the disciplinarians, through censure or ridicule, of individuals who offended against the unspoken but powerful sense of restraint and decorum that governed behavior. Several others were curing societies, and together constituted the medicine cult. And another embraced the hunters of the town. All selected and initiated their own members throughout the generations.

Of the secret societies those which did battle on behalf of the people against illnesses of body and spirit had the largest number of members. Their work was highly specialized and in much demand. Almost everywhere there was reason to call upon them, for even a suspicion of illness was enough to invoke the powers of the curing societies. All such response was related to what the people said was behind illness—any illness but the little commonplace ones that came and went in a day. No, there were other kinds that came from nowhere, lasted a long time, and had strange effects. They were not accounted for in ordinary ways. Something was at work, something wicked, something unseen, and clever, and dangerous because it might be right here, anywhere, abiding for the while in a bird, or an animal, or a person, or a rock, none of whom knew it. Possibly an ant, or a toad, or a buzzing insect contained the responsible thing. One day well, the next day sick—the invalid, they said, must have received the sickness in his sleep when nobody was watching, and the awful thing had its chance to happen. Once again they had struck, those powers of evil and illness, of whom everybody knew, and sooner or later encountered. They were witches, male and female, who were invisible, who put themselves into innocent creatures and objects, and who did their worst work in all success because people could not recognize them and prevent them from creating harm and havoc. All witches worked upon the same purpose—to make people sicken and die. Sometimes they put spells also upon useful animals to make them die. The danger was so real and so prevalent that everyone kept a sharp watch for suspicious behavior on the part of persons, animals, and things. And yet much else had to be done, daily, and so the people gave to the curing societies the special responsibility of keeping vigil against witches, and of taking proper action when the blow fell.

It was, they said, most fortunate that the doctors of the medicine societies were able to receive extraordinary powers from the real medicine men of the spirit world—the ones who were animal-gods and heroes, whose benign influence reached to all the quarters of the world, and to the zenith and the nadir, too: the mountain lion, the bear, the badger, the eagle, the wolf, and the shrew. Thanks to these powers, the doctors were able to recognize witches where no other person could possibly do so. Once identified, the witches could be unmasked and worked against. It was hard work, calling for exactly learned methods, and sadly enough there was always the possibility of failure. Still, everything possible had to be done, and if in the end the doctors lost their patient, the people did not hold it against them, but realized that in this case the opposing powers were the stronger, and could not but prevail. Witches were powerful; that was just the point of being so careful about them, and working so energetically against them. Witches especially tried to destroy the young men. It was particularly evil of them thus to strike against the strength of the present and the seed of the future.

When a person was bewitched into sickness, great forces went to work to save him. His people sent for a doctor of a medicine society who came to the house. Family and friends were there. The prevalence of witches was of much concern to everyone. The doctor followed a procedure known to all, for it was established long ago. He removed his clothes, returning to his animal estate naked. He examined the patient with thorough care, feeling him all over his naked body to determine the location of the malevolence which had invaded him. He prayed. If there was a fracture, he made splints and set the bone. If there was lameness, he massaged. If there was an eruption, he lanced it with a flint knife. If no visible ailment showed, he administered medicines brewed of herbs and water. He anointed the sick body with his curative saliva. He was disembodied from his daily self. The patient and the people knew him as a power in tune with greater powers, and as he worked, they felt in themselves the energy he brought and the conviction of recovery he carried. Hope arrived with him. Witches might be strong, but here

was strength too, in every curative gesture, word, and thought. At
the end of the treatment, the doctor resumed his clothes and left,
with instructions to summon him again if the patient did not improve rapidly.

If he was needed again, he then assembled all the other members
of his own medicine society and, unless the patient was critically ill,
the doctor worked with them for four days in ritualistic preparation
for the major cure which they were to undertake together. If the patient seemed to be dying, they proceeded at once to final measures.
Otherwise on the evening of the fourth day (the people said great
virtue resided in the number four) they returned to the house to
exert extreme powers. The doctors undressed as usual. Now, to
frighten the witches they painted their faces black. Over their heads
from ear to ear they each fastened a band of white eagle-down, and
around their necks hung necklaces of bear claws. Each doctor held
two eagle-wing feathers and a gourd rattle. The whole medicine society was ready to go to work.

The doctors in turn came to the patient and felt over his body to
determine the seat of illness. When they found it, they would know
into what member the witches had shot their evil, and what was its
nature. The whole cure led to the extraction of the evil object from
the patient's body.

Meantime there were prayers and chants. Paintings of colored
meal were laid upon the swept floor by a medicine priest. He sprinkled grains of color through his fingers, drawing lines with delicacy.
He aimed the dropping meal with his thumb that sifted it, to compose in flax yellow, turquoise blue, berry red, skin brown, black, and
white, a design full of magic power against sickness and witches.
Before he changed from one color to another, he cleaned his fingers
by twiddling them in a little pile of clean sand, like the sand that
was spread down as the general background of the painting. It was
almost hypnotic, to see the curative design come to being out of the
little pouring streams of colored motes. Where nothing was, now
power dwelt. How fortunate to know that it came manifest on the
side of good, against evil! And then medicines were mixed and administered. The doctors partook of them along with the patient.

The proceedings were dangerous, they said, because such a gathering of virtue and opposition would in itself attract witches who
would do their utmost to defeat the forces of good. Therefore, the
war priests Masewi and Oyoyewi, also attended, to defend the doctors at their hopeful work. They stationed their assistants outside

the house of illness with bows and arrows with which to shoot the witches if they came close. Nobody was in any doubt—the witches were there, and the last act of the curing drama was soon to come, after everything proper had been done in the sickroom. It was sober and urgent in feeling—so many personalities, so much gesture, such powerful singing, all the medicines—and the patient alone and bare in the midst of it felt these forces pulling at him and empowering him to recover. The doctors labored mightily. Feeling the flesh of the patient, one of them found what they had all searched for—the place of illness, and the physical cause of it: turning to the assembled powers, he indicated the place, and then he bent to it and sucked upon the skin, or he operated with his hands until he was able to come away from the sufferer and show everyone the cause of the trouble which had been stricken into the sick man by the witches. It was sometimes a thorn; again, a little snake, or a lizard, or piece of rag, or a pebble; any small foreign substance might turn out to be the seat of trouble. Only a trained doctor, they agreed, could ever find it, and bring it forth for everyone to see.

And now it was time to do battle directly with the witches who lurked outside. Already they had been partially defeated with the discovery of their projectile in the flesh of their victim. The doctors would finish the cure by physically punishing the witches so they would hardly dare to repeat their wickedness soon again.

Each taking up a sleeve made of the skin of a bear's leg (the power of the deity of the West), the doctors covered their left arms and took flint knives in their right hands. Linking arms, they went out into the dark of the night in the open air before the house, and there as they knew they would they came upon the witches, who were invisible to all but them. A fearful struggle followed, as the people could hear in the sickroom. The patient could hear how mightily he was being avenged and—all hoped—freed of his trouble. There were shrieks and thunders, blows and wounds and imprecations without, as the doctors fought in the dark. The whole town was aware of the battle. The witches were strong and terrible. They might lead the doctors away. The sounds of the fight came and went. Now and then there was a human scream as a witch killed a doctor, who fell down dead, in proof that the enemy was formidable and the cure hazardous. Gradually all sounds whimpered down to nothing, and the guardian war priests went to look at the evidence of the struggle. On the ground they found the dead doctors. The other doctors who survived on their feet helped to carry the dead ones back to the curing chamber. There, with measures known to the doctors as part of their powers, the dead men were revived.

But the witches were repulsed. Sometimes a witch was killed by a shot through his heart with a flint-tipped arrow. Witches were known to have escaped the very grasp of a doctor, leaving only their clothes in the doctor's hands—but that was proof, anyway, of how close the battle was. There was much to talk about when the whole thing was over. The medicine meal had to be swept up, the pictures destroyed, the ceremonial equipment taken away. The Masewi always stood up, at the end of the curing labor, and told all how the patient had been cured. How strenuous the efforts; how huge and powerful the witches; how deep-seated the disease, and how wise the doctors to find it; how satisfactory the way in which all had participated; how fortunate the patient.

Then, with the luxurious thoughts of the aftermath, the people went home. Now and then for the next several days one or another of the doctors would call informally upon the patient until he was well entirely, or dead. If it was death instead of cure, everyone, however saddened, knew where it came from and sighed over the awful power and strength of the witches, whose thundering blows and calls and general tumult they had heard through the darkness several nights before in the town. No wonder the doctors had not prevailed. If it was cure, that was not surprising, they said, for who did not recall the fury of the encounter with the witches, the valor of the doctors, the expertness of their ritual? No wonder witches could not endure such powerful attacks.

Thus comfort through organized observances.

The whole year had its cycle of them.

All winter the river ran shallow and lazy from the faraway north, and deep against the sky of the whole valley the snow was locked on the peaks by cold air. The fields by the pueblo were dry and the irrigation ditches which ran to them from the river were overgrown with the dry golden stalks, the pink brush, of the past year's weeds. In March* it was time to clean the ditches and then with prayer, dancing, and prayer sticks, open the ditches to bring the river water in upon the spring plantings. The masked gods came from the otherworld to attend. They were seen right there in their masks among the dancers.

* For convenience I have used modern calendric names, which of course were not accessible to the Pueblo Indians of the Rio Grande in the period before recorded history.

In April, with four days of preparations, the assembled kiva groups of pueblo held a dance for the blessing of corn, which would come to summer harvest. Water, rain, were the greatest of blessings, and all was asked in their name, and in their image, gesture, and sound. The curing societies during this month went into retreat for purification and for prayer, again invoking rain, upon whose coming the lives of plant and person and animal alike depended. They retreated to their houses which they called, during the retreat, Shipapu, the same as the place of origin, through which everyone had come up. The retreat over, dances followed, again with the gods in their masks, who also had spent the same time in retreat at the real Shipapu. Well into the summer, retreats and emergence ceremonies continued.

In early summer the ceremony was held by the curing societies to pull the sun to the south, where his hot light would make long days and help things to grow.

In full summer they danced again for corn. Sometimes they started out in clear day, with the kiva groups in fullest magnificence under a spotless blue sky which gave back heat like stone near fire. Rain could never come from such a sky. But all day they pounded the prayer into the ground and showered the sound of falling drops of rain from the air to the earth while the heat grew and grew and the shadows of the houses stood like triangles painted on pottery in black paint; and presently they might see without giving any sign what loomed in the north and the west against the ringing blue—dazzling white thunderheads marching slowly and powerfully over the sky toward this town, these fields and seeds. The blessings were vast and visible; and late in the day, as the prayer still beat its way into the ground, the light might change, and the clouds meet over all, and brown color of the bodies and the town and the earth all alike would turn dark like the river, as rain came and fell upon them and answered them and the sparkling green shoots of the corn in the fields. Sometimes it rained so hard and long that the earth ran and the gullies deepened, and new cracks appeared leading to them, and rocks rolled scouring new ways to the river, and the river rose and flowed fast carrying unaccustomed things sideways in the queer sailing current of flood.

In September, as the border of summer and winter was reached, the Summer People and the Winter People both held dances. Autumn brought hunting dances too, and some of them were given later in wintertime. In November came the feast of the dead, when all the ancestors came back to the pueblo to visit for a day and a night. It was a blessed occasion and a happy one. And before long it was time to urge the four curing societies to watch the sun, and call it back to the north before it went too far southward.

In midwinter the kiva groups chose their officers for the next year, and held dances to honor them, to bless them, and to make them know the right ways. The curing societies now frequently in the winter held general cures for everyone. People could come to the curing ceremonies with their ailments and have them included with the other ills against which the doctors gave battle. They purged everyone, the whole town, of evil spirits. Again they cried out and struck blows against the witches, while all heard the encounters, and were reassured.

In February the koshare danced, the clowns, the critics, who hazed the people, sometimes to laughter, sometimes to shame, the spirit of irony and perversity thus accounted for and made useful.

And it was by then observed that the sun was safely on his way north again, and there was a ceremony to confirm this and give thanks.

Then the winter's weeds stood thick again in the ditches, and the path of life from the river to the fields had to be readied. Once again it was time to burn the weeds away, clean the ditches, let the river in, and set the plantings of another year.

It was an organized life based upon the desire for peace. The Pueblos rarely went to war unless they had to resist attack. The war society with its chief captains Masewi and Oyoyewi maintained the magic necessary to use in times of crisis from without the town. The war society was also a medium for the forgiveness of killing. Its members—all men—were those who had brought upon themselves the danger of having killed someone. This danger was the same whether the killing was accidental, murderous, or in sanctioned conflict. If there was blood upon a man, he had to join the war society to wipe it out. He then became a defender of his people. He was confirmed with ceremony. After his initiation he went—like all boys and men after initiations and dances—to the river to bathe his body and his thoughts.

As for thoughts, when grave matters were in the air, requiring the judgment of the cacique and his council, these leaders fasted. They did penance, the better to make wise decisions. Their fasting was known about. At home they abstained. In the kiva they abstained. They spoke to no one of what lay heavily upon their thoughts, but their concern was plain to all. Soon there was wonder, and gossip, worry; something was brewing. What would it be? Was there anywhere to turn but once again to blind nature?

But at last the council would speak to them. At evening, the town crier went to his rooftop. Perhaps the sky was yellow behind him and the house fires sent their smokes upward in unwavering lines of pale blue above the earth's band of twilight. The murmur of talk was like the sound of the river beyond its groves. Facing four ways in succession, the crier told four times what the council had decided and what it wanted of the people. On their roofs, or by their walls, or in their fields, the people heard him, and gave no kind of response; but they all heard and in proper order and time did what was asked of them.

iv
Dwelling

When the Pueblo builders came to the river,* they found dwellers in little shelters built of upright poles stuck in the ground with brush woven among them and covered with dried mud. The walls of the cliff cities which had been left behind were of chipped flat stone anchored with earth. Now by the river there was no stone to be had, and the outlines, the terraces, the pyramids of the cliff towns were reproduced in the river valley material—earth, mixed with brush or straw from dried grasses native to the valley. At first even the upright poles of the scattered *jacales* along the river were used, in modified design. The poles were set close together in double rows. Between the rows wet earth was poured. The faces of the walls, outdoors and in, were built up with earth scooped together a handful at a time and patted, puddled, into place. Layers were allowed to dry, and new layers for strength and thickness were added. When a wall was thick enough, it could support beams; cross branches could be laid on the beams and plastered over, to make a ceiling, and a roof. Once a smooth level was managed on the roof, it could serve as a floor for a second story, which in turn could support a third, and a fourth, until the great hive with all its cells had a porous strength shared by all its supporting uprights and laterals. There was no entrance at ground level. Ladders took the dweller from ground to all levels above.

The cities were much alike in form, varying most in color. The Rio Grande long ago cut down through different layers of buried color, revealing each at widely separated places along its course. The

---

* c. the thirteenth century, possibly earlier.

local soil made the walls, and gave them their color. The prevailing hue was pale, the Indian tan of dried river mud, wherever the pueblos sat on or near the river course in its most pastoral character. Where lava still showed in the soil in spite of centuries of weathering after forgotten upheavals, the earth, and the town had a gray look, as at San Ildefonso. Up the Chama River, the ancient pueblo of Abiquiu had a dusty vermilion earth, taken from the red hills and cliffs. A faint pink earth went into the pueblos of the Piros farther down the Rio Grande near Socorro.

The form of the pueblos was not found only on the Rio Grande. Those cities, and the typical life they showed, were common to great areas and long gaps of time. Just as certain tribes of Pueblo Indians came to the river to resettle, so others went westward and grew their cities in northwestern New Mexico and northeastern Arizona. Even deep in Mexico, and long before them in time, the Rio Grande Pueblos had their counterparts among the Aztecs, whose houses, temples, rituals, and organization suggested theirs. Much came northward with the seed of corn and of ways to cultivate, invoke, and protect it.

In the community house each family had a room. It was private, for its only entrance was through a hatch in the roof, entered by a long ladder. It was low-ceilinged and small—barely a body's length in reach. The walls were painted with gypsum and water whitewash. Much gypsum was available in the river country. The beams overhead were brought from forests far away. The length of the timbers determined the size of the room. Smoke from fires built on the floor went up through the hatch in the ceiling. Little openings in the walls let a draft in and gave a view outward, and in times of trouble served as a hole through which to fly arrows. Blankets of cotton and yucca-fibre mats made beds and places to sit upon. There were also drum-shaped stools carved out of cottonwood trunks, and hollowed out on top.

If the family grew, a room next door was built, connected by a low opening to the first room. Each family prepared its own food. Food and water were kept in pottery vessels, and cooked in them. Pottery bowls were used to eat from. The pots were more than just receptacles. They were works of art, and more, they were made as acts of devotion, just as the poetry and song and drama and design of the dances were. All imaginative creation and skilled craftsmanship went to fulfill a direct purpose which was partly religious, partly esthetic, and always utilitarian. A pot was made in a certain size and shape for a certain purpose; beyond that it was decorated with designs which spoke of the potter's desire for blessings from the natural world and its gods. By representing the forms of life associated with fertility, rain, and growth, the Indian painter called them into being on his own behalf. Handling pots decorated with such symbols, the family had daily communion with the powers. The designs were without meaning for their own sake. Their value was not inherent in their lines, masses, and colors, but dwelt in their spiritual message. They were outpourings of wish, not of artistic pleasure. As all forms of art and craft went to express the unanimous belief and observance of the people, so every person was in some degree an artist or a craftsman. The arts like all other phases of Pueblo life were communal in their purpose and realization.

The ancient people of the Rio Grande had no metal crafts. Their products were all made with stone or bone tools, and with fingers. Raw material and finished object remained close to each other. What was inherent in the one determined the form of the other.

Pueblo symbols for bird, or cloud, lightning, or rain, animal, or man, or mountain, were used by all makers. There was a common graphic language in each tribe. Its designs were not meant to be realistic, nor were they purposely grotesque. They were stylized images hallowed by long usage and accepted as descriptive. The typical Pueblo pot carried around its circumference bands of design combining specific symbols with abstract lines and spaces. Even these last had a suggestive power. Though they represented nothing, they seemed to recreate the spaces and the angles, the sweep and line of the Southwest, the shafting of light in the sky, the bold mesa, the parallels of rain, and the dark spots of juniper on hills otherwise bare. There was a genius common to all Indian artisans— a tepee recalled a pine tree, a pueblo was a mesa, a clay cist was a seed pod. Whatever its conscious motive, however symbolic its style, the impulse to record life was an ancient one; and in any degree of its fulfillment always respectable as art.

The needs of daily use called forth in the Rio Grande town Indians a profuse and vigorous creation of pottery. They took the same material of which they made their houses and with it made their vessels, and somewhat by the same method, building up surfaces of moist earth, letting them dry, adding more, and exposing the final form, in the one case, to the baking sun, and in the other, to the fire of the kiln. The decorations of the pottery were rich, often using two or three colors, some of which had a glazed finish. Black, white, red, and natural clay color were the most common. A syrup of the yucca fruit was used with paint and water. The designs were painted with a brush made of yucca leaves. The line was flowed firmly, the sense of balance and proportion was exquisite, and the use of color was both strong and delicate. In such artistry there seemed to be an impersonal obedience to laws of harmony and grace which dwelled deep in the common spirit of the people. They said that life existed in everything; and that when they made a pot, they gave personal life to it, just as all creatures, places, and things had personal life. Believing so, they knew a responsibility not to art and its abstract aims, but to life and its hope of perfection. They dared not make even a pot with less than their utmost skill if it was to live a good life. Allowance was invariably made for its spirit to breathe and come and go in the painted design on its surface. Somewhere in the decoration there was always left an opening in the design, a gap, a space not closed, so that life might enter there or flow from it. Wherever decorative design appeared—on textiles, walls, or on the half-sections of gourds fashioned into ladles—the ceremonial gap was represented.

V
Garments

The pueblo people wove cloth and wore it hundreds of years before they came to the river. They made thread from the native cotton, and used a true loom, but whether they invented it or acquired it from Mexico* no one can say. Cloth came from yucca fibres, too. On their clothing they painted or embroidered designs, much like those which they used in making baskets and pottery. Their costumes were rich and complete, according to the season. In summertime the children went naked, and the men and women wore as little as necessary. In cold weather they had plenty to cover themselves with, some of it magnificent. They domesticated the wild turkey for the use of his feathers. Turkey tail feathers were part of the dance paraphernalia, and the soft little feathers of breast and body were tied with yucca fibres to make rich, warm blankets that could be worn as cloaks or slept in. Turkeys evidently had no other use, for the Pueblos did not eat them; but a glaring and straining bunch of live turkeys tied together by the legs made a ceremonial gift to visitors who came to the pueblo.

The people's clothes took their prevailing color from the natural

* For the reader's convenience I have used post-Spanish geographical terms for a ready sense of locality.

hues of cotton and yucca fibre. Designs were added in colors taken from the earth and plants. There was a rich red from clay. Mustard yellow came from rabbit brush, and a soft golden yellow came from ochreous earth. Larkspur and the blue bean yielded a delicate blue stain, and copper sulphate gave again the brilliant blue-green dye which prevailed in the kachina masks.

A man dressed himself in a breechclout of cloth when he wore no other clothing. Otherwise, he wore a broad kilt wrapped about his waist. His shirt was a square of cloth with a hole cut for the head. Around his head he wore a cloth bandeau. His legs were sometimes covered by the superb buckskin leggings which he imitated from those of the hunting Plains Indians. The leggings were not joined, but hung separately from the sash or breechclout by leather thongs, from the crotch to the ankle. They were often gathered at the knee with ties of rawhide. On his feet he wore soft skin moccasins. Over all he wore a robe or cloak, now of turkey feathers, again of rabbit fur cut in strips and laced together with yucca thread. Tied to interesting points of his costume he wore, if he was fortunate, a number of the little copper bells and beads made far away in Mexico, and very rare in his river country. But some of the bells came northward in trade, and possibly some were made by wandering metalworkers from far to the south who came to the river and used local metals, but without leaving their skill behind them, for the Pueblo people had no metal crafts in ancient time. Such an ornamental bell was about an inch long, open at the bottom, and had a pebble strung on a thread for its clapper. The beads were an inch long and shaped in tight little cylinders. The bells seemed to be cast by some lost method and the beads were hammered. The man wore jewels, too, as many as he could contrive out of strings of turquoise, bone inlaid with bright stones, black, red, or blue; and bits of shined rock in any beautiful color. He wore strings of precious color about his neck, and hung them from his ears, and wrapped them about his arms. Finally, on many occasions, he used paint on his skin as decoration, whether in the dance, in ceremonies for the sick, in rites of the hunt, or in war.

A woman wore a mantle four or five feet long, and about three feet wide, which she wrapped about herself under the left arm and over the right shoulder and held together with a long decorated belt that went several times around her waist. She wore nothing on her head and, except in bad weather when she used moccasins, nothing on her feet. Like her husband she wore as much jewelry as she could get, and in her uses of the dance and other ceremonies, she wore paint, but only on her face.

As among people anywhere, the children wore miniature imitations of adult costumes except in hot weather, when they wore nothing at all.

The skins of the people were the color of moist river-earth. Their eyes were black and so was the thick hair of their heads. In general they were not tall. The men, from the exercises of their rituals, the ordeals of work, were lean and muscular. The women early lost the figures of maidenhood and grew heavy, moving modestly and calmly about their duties, fixed in their pivotal positions as the bearers of life, the holders of all that brought stability to the family.

vi
Man,
Woman,
& Child

For in the analogy of woman as the repository of continuing life, it was the wife and mother who was custodian of the family dwelling and all communal property. Growing up among her relatives, she was courted by her suitor, who sometimes played to her upon the flageolet in the evening on the hills at a little distance from the town, when the fading light was still clear and the day's sounds were dying away. If she heard him with favor and took him as her husband, he joined her in the circle of her blood relations, who helped her with materials to build new rooms for her own life. She herself made the walls out of earth long ago laid down by the passage of the river. She received her husband in the shelter of her own life, with her person, her house, and her years. It was hers to make all the enfolding and conserving gestures of life, whether as maker of shelter, of children, or of pottery. She took her husband for life and he understood that he was to have no other woman. A daughter born meant that the mother's family was increased, for the child would in her time bring a suitor to the same family premises; while a son meant that one day he would leave and find his mate in another settled family bound together by its matron. From mother to daughter the home was passed on, not from father to son.

The father and mother rarely separated from one another; but if it came to pass that the marriage must end, it was the man who was removed, leaving the dominion of the family secure with the mother and her relations. He would one day find his few personal possessions set out upon the doorstep of his home by his wife, whereupon he would weep, take up his things, and return to the house of his mother, for it was there that he went at important times. If his mother was dead, there he would find his sister, to whom he gave his ancestral allegiance.

A woman in her house produced the clothes worn by her husband and children. She prepared the food and cooked it. The staple of the diet was corn, and she ground the meal, often before sunrise. While her husband sang to her a song which celebrated the act of grinding corn, or beat upon a drum, she worked the kernels in time with his rhythm. She put the corn upon a large flat stone and ground it with a smaller bar of stone, and in time the first was hollowed out like a dish and the second was rounded off at the edges by the work. Her hands grew hard and big and her fingernails wore down as she labored. For each batch of meal she used several different stones, going from coarse to smooth, always refining the flour and roasting it after each grinding. Sometimes several women ground corn together at night. If a woman wanted to make a gift to a man, she would give corn bread or any cooked food.

She kept her house immaculate and the roof above it and the space before it. Her broom was made of slender branches of Apache plume (or poñil) bound to a willow stick. When she swept her floor, she first sprinkled it with water or blew a spray of water from her mouth. Her soap was made from yucca roots. To make cord or rope she boiled the succulent leaves of the yucca and when they cooled, she chewed them until they were soft, and then drew out the stringy fibres which she worked together.

Her day was busy and her duties were serious. Much depended upon her; not only what needed to be done, but also how. From her mother she had learned the proper ways of life, and it was now her obligation to transmit these to her own daughters. Even hopes and desires had their proper gestures, to be made in the image of what she wanted. If she wanted a son and had none, she went to find a stone that had the shape of a man's generative member. From this she scraped a little stone dust and put it into water and drank. She prayed. She deeply knew her animal womanhood and enacted its appointed nature in harmony with what she saw of life all about her.

A man's purposes and duties were likewise all plain.

If he owned no house, anyhow he governed the town. He explained life through religion and ordered, preserved, and executed the ceremonies which he said kept the year and its seasons in their proper passage. He provided raw food by farming and hunting. Like the seed for childen, the seed corn belonged to him. All the powers latent in the fields were his, and so was the rubble after harvest. Harvested food and stored corn was, he said, "my wife's." If he wanted to make a gift to a woman, he gave the products of his work—game, firewood, embroidered or woven cloth, which it was his to produce. He ruled the river and brought its water to the fields for irrigation. And in times of danger from other peoples, he made war.

The Pueblo people were peaceful. They said they never carried war to others, but gave battle only in defense of their own lands, towns, and families. One Pueblo tribe sang a traditional song of war which told of no glory, no brag, no zest for a fight:

> So we have bad luck
> For we are men.
> You have good luck
> For you are women.
> To Navaho camps we go
> Ready for war. Good bye.

Bad luck—but ready, they sang, with realism and a larger bravery.

The Pueblo warriors painted themselves, for there was power in paint, and to go out to save their community life was in itself a ceremony. The surface of their bodies, perceptive of touch, caress, and wound, was beautified with designs that came alive with movement —the lift and fall of breathing, the haul and suck of the belly in exertion, the climb and pound of limbs. Flesh became a living temple of esthetic and spiritual feeling. In an act of both art and religion, the warrior's mortal humanity, his bodily stuff dear because it was not immortal, became the very material of his craft. Using the colors of the earth itself, the great source and repository both, the act of devotion combined in tragic wholeness the Pueblo man's concepts of himself and his gods. Upon his own nakedness he used his earth in the symbols of what he believed in.

First he put on his skin a layer of tallow. Over this went the colors—gypsum white that clothed but did not conceal his legs; red, from clay or crushed amaranth blossoms, on arms and chest; lines of soot black edging designs; yellow from the dust of sunflower petals. He ceremonially washed his hair in yucca suds. Wearing only invocations as armor, he went to the enemy carrying his loins wrapped in buckskin. A buckskin baldric hung over the left shoulder, and above the same shoulder peered the bow case and the quiver, from which arrows could be slipped with the right hand, the left holding the bow. From a tight belt were slung a stone knife and a club, a pouch of sacred objects to bring power, and a little bag of ground meal to be used with water as food on the campaign. Bad luck—but ready for war. The Pueblo men were devoted to their soil. Their towns rose from the river earth like shapes of nature. Their fields were cunningly cultivated. The seed corn secured them life. Their wives gave houses to live in to generation upon generation. There was every reason to stay at home and live well. But their most powerful enemies came from the plains where nothing grew but food for the wandering herds of buffalo, whose flesh made meals for the marauders, whose droppings gave them fire, whose vast seasonal whims took them drifting like cloud shadows over the exposed prairies. The invaders had little to lose and much to gain. But the Pueblo people had everything to lose and they fought for it and kept it. Their ways came up with them from a long time ago, and gave them strength.

They lost few of their reluctant prehistoric wars, though perhaps a town here, a scatter of houses there, might suffer and be abandoned. They could come home and make sacrifices of thanksgiving with ceremonies, smoking clay pipes filled with red willow bark, and telling of battle. They had earned their ease. When they wanted to relax and gossip, and be purified, the men took sweat baths together, putting heated stones in a closed room, and pouring water upon them, and finally going to the river to bathe. The river always purified. It seemed to bring some thoughts from far above, who knew from where, and carry others far downstream, who knew whither. Using the river, a person could dream awake, like a child.

The people treated their children tenderly, from the time of birth to the entrance into adult societies. Ceremony and symbol accompanied the child into the world, and at every stage of life thereafter attended him.

The mother unbraided her hair and wore her clothing unknotted that her unborn child might learn to come easily without stricture into the world. A midwife delivered him. In slow or dangerous deliveries, medicine priests might be sent for. They had measures. With invocations, they would hold the laboring woman up by her hips. Again, they would burn pine-nut shells on live coals in a medicine bowl, placing it under her blankets to sweat her. They would massage her belly and call forth the child.

When a baby was born, the midwife cut its cord and wiped its eyes. If a boy, she put his legs and feet into a black pottery bowl so that he might have a heavy voice, and then handed him to his maternal grandfather. If a girl, the midwife put her in the grinding bin for a moment to make her a proper woman, and handed her to her maternal grandmother. The midwife took the afterbirth to the river and threw it into the water, which took it away in purification. For her help she received a gift of fine meal.

The paternal grandmother or aunt took up corn meal and with it sprinkled on each wall of the room four little parallel lines, saying to the infant, "Now I have made you a house, and you shall stay here." In his blankets the baby was laid between two unblemished ears of corn that would guard him until he was given his name. His mother chose a woman to name him, which would be done after four sunrises. Before dawn on the fifth day the sponsor came to the baby's house. Taking him up, and accompanied by the mother, she went outdoors just before sunrise and as the sun rose, she presented him to the light and spoke his name. The sun was his spiritual father. All then returned to the house and feasted. The sponsor was given a gift of meal. The child was given an ear of corn so that he might always know plenty. Then he was put upon his cradleboard and was so carried on her back by his mother for the first year of his life. Thereafter he was taken from it and taught to walk. Young girls and old men helped to take care of him in his infancy. Through him, the one could learn motherhood, the other could contemplate the cycle of life.

A girl grew up learning the ways of the household from her mother.

Between five and nine years of age, a boy was taken by the men for schooling in the man's duties of government and ceremony. He was initiated into a kiva. He was too small to learn anything of the ritual or to understand the revelations which awaited him later, and which in their stunning force would bring him almost at one stroke from the sweet useless thoughts and illusions of boyhood to the purposeful impostures used by men. As a little boy in the kiva, he was brought into direct relation with the spirit powers, and given strength. He learned through fear and pain, for the masked kachinas came to his initiation bearing yucca whips with which they whipped him until he cried. Their lashes drove out the badness in him and made him ready for a good future. His elders nodded and approved as he cried under the punishment of his innocence. Now he had his allegiance, and though understanding nothing of what he did, perhaps he might impersonate an animal in one of the dances, and trot cleverly among the legs of the dancing men.

At adolescence, ready with new powers and desires, the boy was again the victim of a kiva rite. Again the masked gods came and whipped him, harder than before. He venerated them. He felt that the greatest power in the world was chastising him directly. He knew the gods, for they danced in their masks at all the great ceremonials. He knew they came from the sacred lake far underground to the north, where all life had come up. He knew the gods had come down to be about him on this day. It was terrible to be so near to the gods and to receive punishment from their own hands. But he bent himself under the painful honor and valiantly endured what he must.

And then more horrifying than any of the blows he had taken, more shocking than any other discovery of growth, an incredible thing happened to him. The masked gods who were savagely whipping him suddenly stopped, faced him, and lifted from their heads and shoulders their bright copper-green wooden masks with feathers and designs, and showed themselves to be men—neighbors, or uncles, people whom the boy had always known and taken for granted.

The boy was stupefied with terror and amazement.

Then the dances? Who were the gods there?

They were the same men who here, at the kiva ceremony, now removed all their masks. All were men. None was a god. But only men knew this. Women and children still believed that it was the real gods who came masked to the pueblo. Here: let the boy learn how mortal the masked figures were; take this whip. The boy was made to whip the unmasked gods who had whipped him. They put a mask on him and he knew how it felt to be the impersonator of the god from the sacred lake. When he learned enough, he would be able to act out what all the other people believed of the gods. He now owned a tremendous secret which he must never, never betray. They spoke of one boy who had told, and what had happened to him. It appeared that they had cut off his head and then, using it like a ball in a game, had kicked it to the sacred underworld.

There would be much learning and several years to go through before they were men; but boys passing the stage of discovering the gods were no longer children. There were other stages. They could not smoke until they had qualified in the hunt, killing deer, buffalo, rabbit, and coyote. If before this anyone found them smoking, they were thrown into the river, in punishment. Though punishment played less part in the lives of children than fear.

Unless children behaved well, they would be in danger from giants and bogeymen who knew all. Once a year the bogeymen, wearing fearful masks, came to the pueblo and knew exactly which children to visit and scold. They knew all the bad things that parents had been harping on. They appalled the children, who had heard of one giant, for example, who went every day to a pueblo near the black mesa in which he lived, and stole children, took them home, and ate them. The bogeymen made threats. The children shivered. And then their parents in anguish begged the bogeymen not to take the children or hurt them; they were sure the children would be better boys and girls from now on. Wouldn't they, children? With sobs and shudders the children promised. The bogeymen rattled their masks. No, who could be sure? Threats and horrors were renewed. The parents pleaded. Promises were repeated. At last the dreadful visitors consented to go, for this time. But remember and beware!

Happier children were favored with the protection of the masked gods, the kachinas, who rewarded their goodness.

In the morning, waking up, one of the children in the family was sent out to make a prayer, sprinkling sacred meal or pollen to the sun. Then came duties, and then play. The boys tried all the games played by the men. They practiced the kick-race, which the men ran on a course sometimes as long as forty miles, circling out by landmarks and back to the pueblo. Two teams played, each kicking a lump about five inches in size made of hair stuck with piñon gum. The men could kick the ball twenty yards. The boys tried. They also played a game using a curved stick with which they knocked a deerskin ball filled with seeds. The winner was the one who broke the ball. They liked to run relay races, wearing tufts of down to make them light as birds. All running games were valuable, they said, because they kept the sun running in its course. The boys pitched little stones at a larger target stone. They threw darts and practiced with bow and arrow. Boylike, they discovered things to do with things. They took the fruit of the ground-tomato, which had a puffy envelope over it, and, by smacking it against their foreheads, made a fine loud pop.

Children were desired and cherished and given all that their families could give of things and powers and certainties. The blessings of life came from the parents, the ancestors, to whom gratitude and veneration were due. On the hot afternoons of the summer, when the sky blue had golden shimmers over it from heat, and the cotton-woods were breathless and the river ran depleted in and out of their shade, there rose on the hot silver distance the big afternoon rain clouds, with their white billows and black airy shadows. They had promise and blessing in them—rain and life. The people pointed to them and said to the children with love and thanks, "Your grand-fathers are coming."

vii
Farmer &
Hunter

The people did not consider that the cloud that made the rain that fell on the mountain thus made the river. Long ago, when they lived on the mesas and plateaus, far from the valleys, they needed water direct from the clouds to make their crops grow. In dry times they took water out to the plants in jars and spilled it carefully on the roots. Sometimes when heavy rain brought fast floods, they channelled the runoff to their fields. Running waters took usually the same channel, deepening it, widening it, turning its soil over. The people began to use such places in which to plant so that their crops would receive the water that fell and ran.

When they came to the river and through generations settled their life along its farming plain, they saw that if water could run into the river from all the uplands, then on the immediate floor of the valley it was in many places possible to run water out of the river to the fields. Nearly a thousand years ago Pueblo people were irrigating their fields through well-laid canals and ditches. The river had in some places sharp, steep, deep walls of rock which ran for many miles. But most of these hard-buried canyons opened out as the river went downstream into wide, flat valleys whose floor on each side of the riverbed was lush with growing grasses, plants, and trees. In such places the people placed many of their towns. The river was accessible. They used it and it sustained them.

There were thirty thousand people living in at least thirty, per-haps up to seventy, towns on the Rio Grande of central and north-ern New Mexico. They cultivated in all about twenty-five thousand acres, through irrigation from the river and its tributaries, and by the use of controlled floodwater. They grew corn, beans, pumpkins, gourds, and cotton. They said it was the leaves that made the plants grow, because when the leaves dropped off, the plants stopped grow-ing. The leaves could be watched. Roots were below ground and could not be watched. But even things that could be watched might mean nothing. Pollen from corn was sacred and used in many a prayer; it was part of the great plant which gave life; but nobody noticed what pollen did to make more corn.

Seed corn was kept into the second season before it was planted. Each town used its own, and refused to plant that of other towns, for, they said, the corn was the same as the people. Sowing was assisted by much prayer. Under the waxing moon of April the corn was planted so it would grow as the moon grew, for under a waning moon the corn paused in its growth. Each farmer made his own prayer, and conducted his own ritual. One said this:

> Mother, Father, you who belong to the great
> Beings, you who belong to the storm clouds,
> you will help me. I am ready to put down
> yellow corn and also blue corn, and red corn
> and all kinds of corn. I am going to plant
> today. Therefore, you will help me and you
> will make my work light. You will not make
> it heavy and also you will make the field
> not hard. You will make it soft.

The river water was let into the ditches to run to the fields. As the sluices were opened, the farmers prayed and threw feathers upon the first, seeking ruffles of the muddy water in the dry ditches whose winter reeds had been burned down. As plants grew, the farmers cultivated them with sharpened sticks. Each plant had its own little crater of shaped earth to conserve water. The fields were laid in long narrow strips touching at their ends to the river course so that each would have access to water. The farming lands were owned by the town, and each family man's share was assigned to his use by the cacique's council.

The growing plants had enemies that had to be watched out for. So, in a place commanding a good view of the fields and the country beyond them, the old men who could no longer do the work of irrigating and cultivating served as guardians of the fields. For this duty a lookout was built, eight or ten feet square and two stories high. Four posts held up the deck of the second floor and a brush roof over the top. There were no side walls, for the view had to be clear. But brush was sometimes set along one side as a windbreak. Under the platform, in the ground, there was a first floor made of a shallow pit with a fireplace and food storage. The guard sat up on top. Women came and prepared his food in the pit below him while he kept up his watch against enemies. Sometimes they were

Navahos, Apaches, Comanches, who grew no food for themselves but knew where to find it all done for them. Sometimes it was birds who came to flock through the tender new plants and strip them clean. Small riverside animals sometimes found a crop to their taste and had to be scared away. The watchman often had with him a dog who could give chase, or bark an alarm, or simply doze and scratch companionably and affirm by his devoted presence how suitably things were arranged, with one to lead and one to follow, and behind both, the need, the power, and the responsibility of the earthen town whose life came from the river.

As crops matured, the people danced for rain in late spring, full summer, and early fall. Then came the harvest. First the melons were taken in and stored, and then the corn. In many towns the ground was swept clean before the corn was brought through the streets from the fields. Everyone—men, women, and children—took part in the harvest, which lasted for several days. It was a happy time, full of social exchange and pleasure. Neighbors helped one another. The storage bins were ready. The year's hard work was over for a spell. Peace and plenty repaid virtue. The winter was coming when nothing would grow. The days would be bright, the nights cold; sometimes there would be ice on the river. The cottonwoods would turn golden and keep their dried leaves. The stalks and grasses by the water would be rods of rusty brown and black and pink and pale gold. In the fields, the cornhusks would dry and crackle in the wind. The ditches would be clogged with withered weeds. Vegetation did not rot. It dried up. A seed planted then would be lost. But it did not matter, for now in harvesttime there was enough food to last through the coming months, and people could live.

If the summer was the man's season, then winter was the woman's. For the harvest was hers, and she knew what to do with it to make all its produce into good dishes to eat. There were two meals a day to prepare, the first in midmorning, when everyone had already been at work for several hours; the second in late afternoon, when smoke from cooking fires stood plain against the setting sunlight. The mother and her girls prepared the food. They had to have enough on hand in case anyone appeared at mealtime. This often happened. Brothers and sisters, aunts and uncles, grandparents, felt free to go visiting and to take a meal in the family at any time. Friends sometimes came, too, with the unspoken question: What do you suppose she is going to serve this evening? They would find out, and whatever it was, they would know it represented the best the family could offer, for the news would travel fast if the guest found any evidence of poverty, carelessness or clumsiness in the meal. The company sat in a circle on the floor. The tone was one of gaiety and good humor, for it was not good manners to be gloomy or disagreeable while dining. The room was small, the air smoky, the floor hard, but with much to say, and plenty to taste, they all enjoyed themselves.

The staff of life was maize. It was prepared in many ways. It was boiled in the whole ear, or the ear was toasted over charcoal fire, and the corn was eaten off the cob. It was ground into meal and cooked as a mush and eaten hot. For anniversaries and dances and weddings, corn bread was made in fancy shapes called flowers, with fluted designs, or shell coils, or petals, or little hunks pinched out into spikes. Thin large wafers of corn dough mixed with fine cottonwood ashes were baked into tortillas. Corn meal, ground fine, and toasted three times, was carried by travellers, who needed only to add water to it to have a nourishing dish called pinole.

Roots of wild onion and mariposa lily were cooked for green vegetables. Milkweed was eaten raw or boiled. Seed pods were boiled, and seeds often made into dumplings with corn dough. The berries of the ground-tomato and nuts from the oak and pine were eaten raw. Pumpkins were given as presents, and served uncooked, and also could be preserved. The housewife cut off the rind, opened one end of the pumpkin and scraped out seeds and pithy fibres, and put the pumpkin to dry overnight. The next day she tore it carefully into long, spiral strips, and hung each strip to dry on a cottonwood sapling, which she had trimmed as a drying rack. When the pumpkin meat was dry, it could be bundled together and stored until it was wanted for stewing and making into pies.

The people had meat on special occasions. They liked mountain sheep, deer, squirrel, prairie dog, mountain lion, badger, fox, and the fat field mouse. Meat was cut into little strips and, unsalted, hung out in the sun to dry, after which it could be stored without spoiling. Fresh meat was cooked on sticks held over a fire of coals, or included in a stew with vegetables. Fat and marrow were the tastiest parts. When the ducks came down the river in the fall, or went back up in the spring, the Pueblos snared them and cooked them between hot stones. They did not eat fish, for this reason: they said that two pueblos faced each other across the Rio Grande near the confluence of the Chama and the main river. The towns belonged to two groups of the same ancestry. Desiring intercourse, they said they would see that a bridge was built over the river between them. Their medicine men built it, reaching out from one bank with parrot feathers, and magpie feathers from the other. When the feather spans met, people used the bridge until evil witches one day overturned it, causing people to fall into the river, where they became fishes. The people said they must not eat their own bewitched relations.

They made tea from the leaves of coyote plant, coreopsis, mistletoe, and thelesperma, and if they wanted the bitter brew sweetened, they used corn syrup. Young girls, whose mouths were pure, were chosen to make the sweet syrup. For days before they worked, they kept spurge root in their mouths to clear their breaths. Then they chewed fine corn meal until it became a paste. This was added to a mixture of water and corn meal, and the cornstarch and the saliva of the maidens combined to make sugar. There was no alcoholic drink.

The people took much of their food from wild nature. After the corn harvests they went to the mountains to gather the little sweet nuts from the piñon tree, and crops of acorns and wild plum. Men and women, young and old, went on the expeditions, and for the young, these were occasions of love-making and courtship. To the children who stayed home in the pueblo the elders would bring back sticky juniper boughs loaded with frost-purple berries.

The Pueblos never domesticated animals for food. One tribe did not even have a word meaning animal. Each kind of animal had a specific name, and each creature had its own identity, like a living person. The dogs they lived with, perhaps the domestic mouse, the turkeys they kept for feathers, could no more be eaten than a person (for it was a long time since human sacrifice had taken place among them, even though to the south in Mexico it still was performed daily in untold numbers). But the wild animal was fair game, and the hunt was one of a man's glories. It made him not only a provider, proud to bring home that which kept life going. It gave him a challenge, and it told him of his own animalhood, which he must use with all his craft and power if he was to succeed over other creatures. The mountain lion was his hunting god, a symbol of the killer who saw with a piercing yellow stare, who moved as softly as cloud, and who killed with claws like lightning. On a mountaintop above one abandoned plateau city, hunters had long ago carved two stones into the likenesses of the mountain lion,

and later hunters carried little images of him in clay or stone when
they went out.

Some useful animals were found near home—the prairie dog,
whose bark the men could imitate to perfection; the beaver along
the river, whose meat was good to eat, whose fur was needed in
dance costumes. All the animals they hunted had many uses—food,
hides and fur for clothes, bone for instruments, sinew for stitching
and for bowstrings, leather for drumheads, pouches, bags. They said
in one of the towns to the north that the animals of the hunt lived
together far off to the west in a great kiva, and when the people
needed them, they were sent out to be hunted. They were clever,
and every skill had to be shown by the people and by their dogs. Before a good hunting dog went out with his master, he was given
food containing powdered bumblebees which would buzz and sting
inside him and give him power.

Some hunts took place far away and lasted several days, some just
for a day, nearby.

The deer hunt was often sacred if the meat was to be used in a
ceremony. The deer was hunted by many men, who scattered until
they could surround him. They closed toward him. They forced
him to a trap, made of a great snare of yucca fibres, sometimes over
two hundred feet long. They took him alive, and smothered him to
death so that his blood would not be spilled and his meat contami-
nated and made useless in the rites for which they took him. If the
deer was captured for food and other use, he was killed with a
knife. So with other animal victims too. When they came back dead
with the hunting parties, they were received in the pueblo with
great respect. Many more animals would be needed for food, and if
they heard from the spirits of those already taken and killed how
gentle the people were, how respectful of the loved creatures whom
they had killed out of need, then, when the hunters went out again,
the wild quarry would be kind and come to be captured and killed
and given honor. So they laid bodies of the deer and the other animals on fur rugs, and covered them with blankets, and hung precious ornaments on them of turquoise and shell. The animal dead
lay for a little while in pathetic splendor before being put to many
uses.

Deer hunts were held in fall and spring, rabbit hunts many times
a year, and for several different purposes. The ceremonial treasures
of the kiva had to be fed—the kachina masks, the scalps collected in
warfare, the sacred fetishes made by the medicine priests. Rabbit

meat went for that, and the hunts were held in spring and fall. Other rabbit hunts were held in honor of the cacique and the war captain, to supply them with food and fur. The men alone hunted for these. In the fall, when harvesttime brought high spirits and symbolized sharp change in the year's life, rabbit hunts were held for the girls, in which they were permitted to join. The koshare were in charge of the hunt and, holding authority from all the people and the gods, performed without resistance from the people whom they mocked, chastised, and humiliated. They seemed to act on witless impulse, and they also gave freedom to the spirit of the perverse and the sardonic, which lived somewhere in everyone, and never otherwise escaped into comic mockery of life and its origin. The power of the koshare was absolute when they took charge. They called the girls and men and boys to the hunt, telling them the time and place to assemble. Woe to them if they were late. What happened to them was the worst kind of punishment—they were made objects of derision. The koshare watched for those who came late, had them lined up in the presence of all the other hunting men and girls, and ordered them to show their sexual parts to everyone. The victims were half ashamed, half satisfied at making a sensation, and all went on the hunt in high spirits.

The men were armed with throwing sticks with which to kill rabbits. The girls did not kill. They all walked to the hunting place. Girls brought food along for lunch. When a man killed a rabbit, all the girls broke loose in a run and each tried to be first to pick up the dead game. Whoever touched it first could keep it, and take it home. At lunchtime she was the one who had to feed the man who killed the rabbit. The koshare watched to see that all was properly conducted. After lunch the hunt was resumed. The party spread out and drove the rabbits within an always contracting circle. Now and then someone—a man, a girl—would be far out on the circle, and might disappear together behind a protecting bush or rock. If they were certain they had not been noticed, they had forgotten the koshare, who came to see what they were doing. If they were coupled together carnally, the koshare broke them apart, and took them back to the party in captivity for the rest of the day. News of the arrest, and what for, would spread, and everyone, with amusement, would wait for what came next, for all knew what must follow. At the day's end, when the hunt was over, and the whole party gathered together to return to the pueblo, the koshare produced their prisoners and had them resume and complete before everyone the act which had been interrupted. After this, all went home. The girls took their trophy rabbits with them, and cooked them for their families to eat.

On the hunts they encountered members of the reptile creation, but did not fear them. The rattlesnake was the only poisonous snake in that part of the river world, and though the people knew of its dangerous nature, they did not regard it with horror. Some of them used the murderous snake in ceremonies as messenger to the cardinal points of the world. The swift, a little gilded lizard, was the supernatural of the sixth, or downward, point of direction. Turtles sometimes lay in their path. They saw many of the harmless horned lizards, or horned toads, and blue and green racer snakes, brown bull snakes, little water snakes with black and gold stripes running the length of their bodies. Deep and dim was the memory of past life which came stepping down the generations in talk; the people knew of a curious mixture in nature between snake and bird, each of whom was born in an egg. They made prayers to their image of the feathered serpent, and believed prodigies of a bird that could crawl and a snake that could fly. Land and sky with all their separate mysteries were brought together in that god, and in thread and paint the people made his picture again and again.

To find a certain game the hunters had to go far away from home. For the big bear they went deep into the mountains to the north, and for the bison whose robe was so rich, whose meat was so good, and whose head and horns were such mighty ornaments for the dance, the men of the pueblos went to the eastern plains. Out of their own valley of the Rio Grande, they followed a pass eastward to the valley of another river, the Pecos, which began its life between high mountain walls. But the eastern wall ended more or less due east from the central Rio Grande world, and the hunters came up a grand escarpment to the plains not long after crossing the Pecos. They had to go carefully in some years, for the plains people sometimes came that far west, and not always for peaceful purposes. But with care and good fortune, the Pueblo men could advance to the immensity of flat land and hunt the bison. They could see, it seemed, forever, as if time and distance there became one. The horizon was clear and flat and the light was stunning. Stiff grass grew everywhere, and in dry years was brittle and yellow. From time to time they would see far away what looked like a grove of trees. But there were no trees on that plain. Those tree trunks, rising to dark blurs of joined treetops, were actually the legs of bison against the white lower sky, and the heavy tree crowns were their bodies—all optically enlarged in the shining air. The bison at first were not afraid. Sometimes they moved off in answer to scents on the wind. Sometimes they watched the hunters approach. When the attack came, they would heave and run away together. The hunters had their plans. They set great snares and then, as in the rabbit and deer hunts, they separated and began to drive the bison inward to the trap. They set fires around the circle they made and the big herds ran against them in confusion and were turned back as the burning circle narrowed. In high weather, the sky was blinding blue and the sunlight white. Strenuous bison-colored smoke blew upward in rolling clouds. Fire in daylight at the edge of the hunt showed yellow and red and brighter than the air. There were yells and commotion. Silvery waves of heat arose. The bison stormed from side to side. Their eyes glared sidewise in terror as they fled to their doom. Behind them came the naked hunters, shining with sweat and triumph, making calls and motions of menace. Blue, black, straw, curly smoke and pelt, running flame and figure—the picture ended with the capture and the kill.

It was a different picture when they hunted bison in the winter. They found the great herds black against the snow and searched until they found deep drifts piled up on unseen obstacles by the hard north wind that made storm on those plains. Spreading out on the white flat land, in a thin line of dark dots, the hunters began to drive the herd toward the drifts of snow. In the end, the animals got in deeper and deeper, until at last they could flounder no more and were caught for red slaughter on the white drift.

There were years when plains people, the Comanches, came west bringing bison furs and horns to the river people to exchange for corn, corn meal, and other precious things. Products and stories, habits and words, beliefs and wonders—there was much to trade.

viii Travel & Trade

The Rio Grande pueblo world had corridors to other worlds. Mountain passes to the east gave upon the great prairies. Deserts and mountain parallels to the west finally led to the sea. The river's own valley led south to Mexico through a pass which opened on a vast plain just as the river turned southeastward on the course which finally took it to the sea. With these roads open, the people yet did not travel them very far, and only the hunt took them away from their pueblo world. The river towns knew one another, and exchanged visits, and took part in one another's dances, and showed, and sometimes traded, curious rare objects that had come from nobody knew just where, or by what crawling pace, through what perilous distance. A stranger now and then appeared, walking, moving into the sight at first like a fleck of dust that bobbed on the glaring distance and seemed to come hardly nearer. He would be noticed. Someone saw him and told. Without seeming to, many people watched, as they went on with their work. Where was he from? What would he want? What did he bring? Was he alone? Perhaps he finally arrived half a mile away and sat down and stared at the pueblo for a while and rested. And then moving gradually so as not to be noticed, he came closer, and was at last where people could hear him, and see his ingratiating nods as he unpacked his pouch and revealed bits of color.

Perhaps he came from northern Mexico, where he obtained from another man, who got it from another farther south, who in turn had it from a hunting party in the jungle, a bundle of macaw feathers—sunflower yellow, scarlet, sky blue, copper green. For their rarity, beauty, and sacred meaning, they were wanted for ceremonial use on masks, headdresses, robes. Sometimes the trader brought with him a live macaw with its feathers still in place. That was a treasure. The bird changed hands and after an honored lifetime of yielding its blazing feathers to the needs of ritual, was buried in the pueblo with ceremony, prayers, and fetishes.

Perhaps he came from the deserts to the west, bringing a rare red paint, chips of agate, and fine baskets which had come to him through many hands.

If he came from the plains, the trader might have with him not only the useful products of the bison, but also worked buckskin, moccasins, odd foods.

The pueblos were a thousand miles from the sea, with every danger of weather, distance, time, human and animal conflict, desert and mountain between. Yet the trader, walking—for there was no other way to travel—might have with him a pouch of little sea shells that came either from the ocean to the west or the gulf to the southeast. The trader may never have seen the sea; but others had, and what they found came slowly and through many relays to the upper river whose origin and whose end, in relation to its populated part, none of the people knew. The shells were acquired and made into necklaces, pendants, fringe. From the western sea came over sixty species of shells, and from the gulf, nearly a dozen. Red-coral beads came through tribe after tribe, from the seacoast inland.

The trader may have brought stone tools to offer, or a few pots to exchange for the kind made by the women here in the town.

And beyond all that, there was much to tell about and to hear.

The walking trader might come alone, but often he had company. Even so, in such a wilderness, reaching so far and open without forest and with little water, it took an intermittent multitude, toiling on foot in tiny, scattered bands across rocky space, immeasurable time to make their mark. But they made it. Trails were established, first in relayed knowledge of landmarks, and then in barely worn but visible pathways that were like the first tributaries of communication struggling to feed a stream of knowledge.

The incoming traders looked for things to take back with them when they left. News of what was to be had always took people to country strange to them. In the river towns, traders saw the accumulated produce of the pueblo farms. There was corn meal to be had, either coarse, or ground fine in pinole. Dried pumpkin seeds, squash were bartered. Irrigation ditches ran to cotton fields, and picked cotton was made into cloth, and cloth could be carried away in bulk, or in the form of shirts, kilts, sashes, or shawls. Mineral and vegetable dyes were used to decorate such garments. The traders might trade for the knowledge of how to use such colors.

There was one color and substance they wanted most, for the river Pueblos had much of it and prized it dearly. It was turquoise, and the people knew of a place, the only place in the river world, where it could be found in the earth. South of the site of Santa Fe, they mined turquoise for centuries in undisputed ownership. They made necklaces and ear pendants of the rich green-blue stone, usually carving little discs which they pierced and strung on yucca fibre. It was their principal jewel, and as such it was given to the gods in costumes, vessels, masks, fetishes with sacred meaning—and sometimes with magnificence: in one ancient town there was a superb basket, made in the shape of a cylinder, paved with 1,214 turquoises. If the people had treasure to bury, it was turquoise, and bits of red coral, which they put into large jars and hid in the earth.

Not only trade from far away made trails. The river people themselves went travelling to fulfill their needs, one of which was salt. They knew where to find it, in great deposits across the mountains to the east of the Rio Grande, and about in a line with the southernmost of the river pueblos. There, across that mountain range from the river valley, lived other town people who spoke a different language. They occupied ten or more communities, and their life faced out across the great plains to the east. Mountains behind them divided them from the river world. Precariously they survived the wandering fighters of the plains who came periodically to make

war. Their bleak riches were the salt deposits which lay in a series
of shallow, white lakes surrounded by low curving hills whose sky-
line seemed like the idling path of a circling and banking vulture.
In some years the lakes were dry, and the salt glistened dry at the
sun. In others, a milky water filmed over the beds and rippled like
cotton cloth when the wind came. Little vegetation grew about the
lakes. They were like part of the underworld exposed. Nobody
stayed by the brackish water for very long, but gathered up salt, and
made whatever trade was necessary, and returned on the trail
through the mountains to the river.

They saw much along the way. There were long-abandoned
towns here and there, and from the ruins the travellers could learn
something about the vanished inhabitants. Wanderers sometimes
came to the pueblo world from down south on the river where, they
said, there once flourished life in river caves that was long since
gone. The river went more or less straight south as you left the
pueblo cities, and for the most part, the best—though not very good
—trails were along the west side, for on the east, mountains came
very close to the river and made travel difficult if not impossible.
But finally after its usual succession of canyons and flat, fertile valleys, and after finding a pass between the ends of two mountain
ranges, the river turned southeastward across a hard desert. Travellers had little reason to go there. They said that as far away as
many days of walking, the river entered mountains which no man
could enter, and disappeared between high rock walls into deep
shadow. There were few people there.

But news of the other people who had once lived in river caves
far away drifted with the wanderers. (These were the caves of the
Big Bend and below.) The Pueblo dwellers listened, though the
facts were scattered and few. Still, they could recognize by their
own ways what other people must have been like.

The caves were in a great rocky wall of a river far to the southeast. (Was it the same river? It might be. And yet it was very far
away. Rivers came from many places. Who could be sure?) The
rocks were marked with lines like the flow of water. Water once
made the caves and filled them and then left them as the gorge
deepened. People came to live in them for part of the year, passing
the rest of the seasons on the flat plain above the river cliffs. On the
cave walls and on nearby rocks they made pictures by scratching
with hard stone. They drew animals and the four directions and
made marks to show time passing, and more often than anything

else they drew hands in outline on the rock. There: hand, meaning a person was here; the thumb spread, the fingers straight. On a wall, hand. On a flat stone up on the plain, hand. I, long ago, hand now, and forever, said the rocks, without saying who.

From the river they took smooth large pebbles the size of the palm of your hand and painted upon them various yellow, blue, and gray lines and made certain spaces which sometimes looked like a man, sometimes like nothing to see but like something to think. They carried these, or made offerings of them in ceremonies, or buried them. They took their colors from rock and berry. With a hollowed bone from a deer's leg filled with color that could ooze from a little hole in the end, they drew their shapes and spaces.

They had no corn, but near their places up on the plain above the cliff they gathered berries and yucca and ate of them. In time bushes and stalks grew nearer to the cave entrances, as seeds were dropped near the shelter. Paths and toe holds—the only way to the caves—led from the plain above. The men fished in the river where they could get to it. They used hooks made from bent thorns of devil's-head cactus, and yucca-fibre nets weighted with round stones, and stone fish-knives. With a throwing stick from which they discharged spear and arrow they hunted running animals. With bone daggers they struck a wounded animal to death.

There were not many caves—fewer than a dozen, and only one family lived in each, at a time. They built fires under the overhang of rock, using long slender wooden drills which they palmed to spinning against a wooden hearth to make smoke, spark, and flame. From the dry, hard brush of the plain they gathered little bundles of kindling.

Like many people they wore few clothes in warm seasons, when the men went bare, and the women wore skirts made of yucca fibre that was corded and woven into matting. In cold times, they all wore blankets of lechuguilla fibre twisted with strips of rabbit fur. Traders rarely came their way, and so they had no turquoise, no red coral for necklaces. Instead, they strung together something that made beads, that was fairly hard to get, even dangerous, and was therefore valuable and not entirely commonplace. It was the vertebrae of the rattlesnake.

What they used more than anything else were baskets and other articles woven from fibre or straw or tender twigs. They made no pottery. But baskets served to cook in and eat from. The children had toy baskets to play with. Even bracelets were made of basket-work. They came to know, as anyone might, how to make baskets from watching birds. The parent birds brought little twigs and bits of grass to make a nest, twining them in and out until a little cup-shaped wall was made. There the nestlings were safe as they grew. A woman of the river caves in time would have her nestling and must carry him with her and keep him. If she wove a nest for him out of fibres, she might make other things in the same way.

As children grew within each family, they met new times of life during ceremonies which told them fearful things and made them able. The gods lived in the sun, in fire, and in the snakes of the can-yon and the plain. People of the river, and those far away to the south beyond the river in Mexico, prayed to the same powers. Shaped stones and modelled clay represented other powers to help men make and keep life through the day's hard work of providing shelter and food—coyotes, bears, lions, frogs, wolves.

All about them, on both sides of the river, ranged other people who hunted everywhere, never staying to live and worship and grow in one place; but always prowling to kill. They were Coman-ches, Apaches, Lipans. Lipantitlan was the rippling name of the do-main where they roved. They came to the caves, perhaps many times, and in the end, they finished forever what was trying to fix its life there above the river in the rocky walls. It was like much life in many other places of the desert and mountain land. It did not last very long, but it made signs, even in death.

A body was buried in rock shelters or under piled rocks in the open. Its limbs were gathered against itself and bound. A few of its meagre possessions were placed with it—things to work with and to pray. Woven fibre matting was wrapped around all, and where at last it lay, a blanket of cactus leaves, thick and bristling with sharp needles, was put to protect and cover all. On a flat rock face nearby was a picture that said "Hand," and meant "Forever."

Below, in its rocky trough, the river went on and presently—not very far off—was joined by another big river from the north—the Pecos of today. The two streams came along the flat sides of a great rock wedge that ended sharply, like a stone hatchet. They went on as one river when they met below the hatchet edge.

All along the river there were wandering people, even at the coast where the brown water went into the green sea. People travelling inland followed rivers, and those by the sea followed the shore. Out of Mexico went travellers up along the coast, coming to the mouth of the river, crossing it, and going on beyond to see what they could find. The travellers met trouble at times, for the people who roved the great vaporous sea-plain were hostile. They were naked hunters, always moving, and they attacked not only animals but people, and when they made any kill, they ate of it. Otherwise on the sandy plain where the sky all day long changed from thick to thin and back again, there was little to be had except roots in the sand and food from the sea. They snatched the white crabs of the beach and fished in the surf and in the end-waters of the river that passed through empty wilderness to meet the tide.

In news that came to the river Pueblos from travellers who had seen, or heard, all of it, there was little of any other cities that lived anywhere else along the river. Towns at the river's mouth were made of sand grasses that blew away in hurricane or fell down dry if the rovers left them for long. A few dug-out pits roofed with yucca stalks clung to the river in the middle desert (southeast of the site of El Paso) whose people grew corn and went to the buffalo plains to hunt. But it was much harder country than the pueblo valleys up north—rockier, hotter, barer, dryer. Sometimes the desert part of the river failed to run. Its mountains were too far away to renew it. It was, there below, a river to cross, not to live along. The Pueblo people were the only ones, with their many towns up and down the green, gold, blue, black, and pink valley of their world, to whom the river through a thousand years gave continuing life and connection with one another.

People from the farthest north pueblo, Taos, which was on a plateau too high for the growing of cotton, came south to the central towns below the volcanic canyons of the river, where the land forms stepped down immensely and the farms lay two thousand feet lower in altitude, and traded for cotton cloth.

During November men from the red rocks and plains of the West came on travels to see dances and to make trades, and went home again to their own towns, that were made of shale and mud plaster.

Other travellers, the Navahos, wandered with the seasons, and sometimes reached the western edge of the river world. If fixed with the spirit of war, they struck, thieved, and fled. If at peace, they threw up their mud cells, like wasps' hives, and dwelled in them awhile. If someone died in a Navaho hut, it was fearfully abandoned and a new one built by the survivors. The house meant nothing in itself. Thus, neither did a town, or a place. The Navaho moved, always just ahead of his hunger and his fear.

Stable, relatively secure amidst all such movements and motives, the river people received the trails as they were made, and maintained themselves at home by their work, their search for harmony with the visible world, and their endless propitiation of forces of whose existence they dreamed but whose nature they did not know.

Imprisoned in their struggle with nature, the people sought for an explanation of the personality they knew in themselves and felt all about them, and came to believe in a sorcery so infinitely distributed among all objects and creatures that no act or circumstance of life was beyond suspicion as evil or destructive. Neighbors might be trusted; but they had also to be watched in secret, for who knew who among them might finally turn out to be a witch? If every object, every animal, every man and woman quivered with the same unseen personal spirit, to whom prayers might be said, and of whom in anxiety blessings could be asked, then they could also and with terrible swiftness turn out to be agents for evil. Long ago, they said, the young war gods Masewi and Oyoyewi, the powerful twins, lived amongst the people and protected them by killing witches and giants. Nature was vast and people were little and danger was everywhere. But (in the universal canon of faith which brings to every Goliath his David) there was the very cast of hope in the people who imagined their survival and triumph in the midst of menace, then willed it, and even by implausible means achieved it.

But at great cost.

Anyone suspected of sorcery was put to death, often in secret, often by individuals acting without formal sanction. What would identify a witch? A vagrant idea in someone's head; a dream (for dreams were always seen as truth, as actual life encountered by the spirit freed from the sleeping body); a portent in nature; perhaps a conspicuous act, aspect, or statement; anything too unusual, too imaginative in unfamiliar terms; persistent misfortune or sickness among the people, which must be blamed upon someone—the notion could come from anywhere. If only one or two people knew of the witch, he might be secretly killed. If everyone suspected him and knew about him, he would be accused and pressed to confess. In their search for a victim the people sometimes fixed upon an ancient person who had outlived his family and, obtaining a confession through torture, exiled him to another pueblo or simply killed him. Sometimes people in one town would discover in another town

*ix
Personal-
ity &
Death*

a witch who was causing them grief, and would murder him virtuously. Retaliation, inspired by the highest motives, would follow. The killings of witches at times reached such numbers that whole towns were nearly wiped out by it.

Otherwise believers in peace, and calm, measured life, the people sanctioned their only outbreak of violence in connection with punishment of witches, whose machinations, they said, threatened the communal safety of life. Was that very communality itself an expression not so much of the dignity of men and women as their fear —a fear which put them always on guard, created a propriety of the commonplace, and held as its core a poisonous distrust of one another? The old people told the children that no one could know the hearts of men: there were bad people—witches—everywhere. Evil resided in them, and never came from the gods. The gods were exempted from doubt or blame. All believed so and, believing, all followed the same superstitions in the same strength of mind. Such strong beliefs, laced through with such compelling fears, created a personality common to the people as a whole.

Men went out during the night to encounter the spirits at sacred sites. They went in fear and returned trembling, whatever their experience, for they went to garner omens for themselves. Going home from the shrine they must not look behind them, no matter what might seem to be following them. They would consider gravely before they would tell what they had encountered, for what had been gained could be lost if not kept secret. It would not be a sin to tell—there was no guilt in the people since they were not responsible for what nature did to them—but in telling a secret, new power against menace might be lost. Ordeals were spiritual rather than physical. Endurance of torture was demanded only of witches.

The personality had many private faces, each with a new name. A man had his name given at birth as a child of the sun. When he joined a kiva, he received another, and another when he entered any organization, and he was nicknamed after his various duties and kinds of work. The personality was renewed and purified by ritual acts, such as vomiting. Before all ceremonial dances, all taking part were required to vomit in the early morning for four days (four was a powerful number in all ways). They said that those who vomited breathed differently from those who had not. "After you vomit four days, you're changed." A man thus purged left the daily world and entered the supernatural.

The personality was clever. A man prowling in hostile country wore sandals made of wooden hoops wound with thongs of rabbit-skin. His footprints were round; from them, he was sure, nobody would tell which way he was coming or going.

The personality could be shared: images of men or animals were made in gestures of menace, to frighten trespassers away from property.

And the personality was vain, for the people of this town looked down upon the people of that town, saying that those others did not hunt so well, or farm, or fight, or sing, or dance, or race, so well as we do, the poor crazy things, with their silly ways, and their bad imitations of what we do, which they stole by watching us secretly. But this was a pitying superiority, without anger or quarrel.

The most immediate medium of personality was talk. The people of the river world did not all speak the same language, but were divided into two general groups, Keres and Tewa, each of which had its localized variations. But all derived from the same mother tongue long ago far in Mexico, and ventured northward with the farming people and their maize. In spite of differences in language, the river pueblos with their local variations lived under much the same beliefs, customs, and ways of work. Their language was expressive and exact. The men spoke it with voices that seemed to try to escape from smothering. They formed some words deep in the throat. Others were framed lightly on the lips. Some ideas were given through little pauses in a series of sounds, and a tiny round-mouthed silence became eloquent. Their words were never written, even though in Mexico the mother tongue of the Aztec people was used in written form. The Pueblo people taught all their knowledge by word of mouth. The greatest body of it had to do with ceremony and ritual. "One who knows how"—that was a man of power who remembered all that had been told to him. For the dances those "who knew how" had to memorize tremendous amounts of ritual, word-perfectly. Such men showed great powers of mind which their life in other directions hardly equalled. The great movements of time and the seasons, the acts of life and work, the inherited stories of the gods, the forms of prayers, all had to be stored in mind, along with their many variations and combinations, until a vast body of knowledge rested trembling and precarious on the spoken thread of the generations that was spun from elder to youth. Thus even the act of literary creation was not individual but co-operative, since it took one to tell, and another or more to listen, and remember. Much of what was so recorded in memory was to be kept secret among those "who knew how." If a man betrayed them, he was punished. The war captains put him naked within a circle drawn upon the ground. He must not lie down, but stand or sit. If he moved to step across the circle, he was shot with arrows by the captains.

People within a language group visited one another's towns. Before he went, a man had his hair washed by the women of his family before sunrise, and his body bathed in yucca suds. They gave him a new name for his venture. At the end of his journey, if he found a friend awaiting him, he took his hand and breathed upon it, and clasping it with both hands lifted it toward the sky without words, for joy muted his speech.

"May I live so long," prayed the people, "that I may fall asleep of old age." The personality ended with death and had to be exorcised from living memory, and become one with all ancestry, impersonal, benign, and beyond fear. When a man lay dying among his relatives, they sent for the doctors of the curing society that combatted witches. Then doctors came and undressed the dying man to examine him carefully. If he was already dead, they put a cotton blanket over him. His people brought all his clothes to the doctors who tore little holes in each garment to let its life, too, escape and leave the dead cloth. They folded the arms of the dead across his breast, tying his wrists together. His legs they closed up against his body. They wrapped him in this huddled position with cotton blankets. His clothes were included. A feather robe was folded about him next, and lastly, a yucca matting was bundled over all, and tied with a woman's sash. Crouched in silence within its wrappings the body was a restatement of the attitude of birth, when the unborn infant was folded within the womb; and bound by a mother's cincture to the womb of all it was now returned. The doctors rinsed their mouths and washed their hands, saying to each other:

"Now he is gone."

"Yes, he is gone back to Shipapu."

"The place from where all emerged."

"He is gone back to Shipapu."

The family took the body out of doors to burial in the open ground, or in a rocky crevice, or in a midden. With it were placed water and food. The food was cooked, so the dead could feed on its aroma. The dead man's turquoises, his weapons, his tools were buried with him, for he was now about to set out on his journey to the underworld from which all life had come, and his spirit would need the spirits of all such articles to use in the life that awaited him. He was on his way to be one with the gods themselves. At the end of his journey he would take up again what he did in the world, whether as hunter, farmer, priest, or dancer.

Four days after his burial, his personality was finally expunged with ceremony. The doctors returned to his house and arranged an altar on which they laid sacred ears of corn, bear paws, a medicine bowl, and kachinas. They sang songs and ceremonially cooked food for the ghost to smell. They made a painting on the floor with colored corn meal. He was gone, and to confirm this and help him where he now would be forever, they made a bundle of offerings containing moccasins in which he might journey, a dancer's kilt, and turtleshell rattle and parrot feathers and necklace, which he might use to start rain from the ghostly world. They buried this out of doors. Underground, he would find it. Doctors then dipped eagle feathers into the medicine bowl on the altar and sprinkled the meal painting, the sacred implements, and the people. They swept the walls of the dead man's room with the eagle feathers to brush away his spirit, and they went to other houses where he had last been seen and did the same. Returning to the house of the ghost, they sang again, and all settled down to a feast provided by the family. A few morsels were thrown aside by the doctors for the spirits. At the end of the repast, the doctors arose and were given finely ground grain for their services. They destroyed the painting and took up its colored meal in a cloth, which they gave to a woman who carried it to the river. There she threw it into the water which for all his life had flowed by the dead man, had sustained him, purified him, and which now took away his last sign forever, through the shade of cottonwoods and into the sweet blue light of distant mountains beyond the pale desert.

So the Pueblo people agreed without exception in their worship, their work, their designs for making things in the largest to the smallest forms, their views of property, the education of their children, the healing of their sick, and their view of death.

A clear and simple, and within its limits, a satisfactory plan of living together was understood by everybody, and complied with. But essentially it lacked the seed of fullest humanity. Mankind's unique and unpredictable gift was not encouraged to burgeon in Pueblo society. Individuality, the release of the separate personality, the growth of the single soul in sudden, inexplicable flowering of talent

X
On the
Edge of
Change

or leadership or genius, were absent. In harmony with all nature but individual human nature, the people retained together a powerful and enduring form of life at the expense of a higher consciousness —that of the individual free to unlock in himself all the imprisoned secrets of his own history and that of his whole kind, and by individual acts of discovery, growth, and ability, to open opportunities that would follow upon his knowledge for all who might partake of them. It was costly, that loss of the individual to the group. The essential genius of humanity, with all its risks, and yet too with its dazzling fulfillments, was buried deep in the sleeping souls of the Indians by the Rio Grande.

They solved with restraint and beauty the problem of modest physical union with their mighty surroundings.

But only to their gods did they allow the adventure, the brilliance, the gift of astonishment that came with individuality. Those mythic heroes, those animal personifications ranged sky and earth and underworld performing prodigies, releasing dreams for the dreamers, perhaps beckoning inscrutably toward some future in which the people too might find freedom before death to be individuals in nature instead of units among units in a perfected strict society whose loftiest expression of the human properties of mind and soul was an invisible tyranny of fear that bent them in endless propitiation before inanimate matter.

The deep alien sadness of such a life was born with dignity. They lived like figures in a dream, waiting to be awakened. Possibly if left to their own time and development, they would have awakened by themselves to discover another and greater environment than the physical one to which they were already accommodated with economy and tenacity. The inner environment of the conscience, the responsible and endlessly replenished human soul, the recognition of God within mankind above a multitude of gods without—these might have come as their own discoveries to those people who already had climbed far from forgotten antiquity.

But men of another order were making ready to come to the river as ministers of enlightenment and shock and the strongest necessity of their epoch.

BOOK THREE

Latin

Conquering Spaniards &
Their Mexican Sons

1·Collective Memory

Brown plains and wide skies joined by far mountains would always be the image of home to them, the image of Spain, that rose
like a castle to inland heights from the slopes of the Mediterranean,
and gave to the offshore wind the fragrance of ten thousand wild
flowers that mariners smelled out at sea.

The home of the Spanish spirit was Rome. When Spain was a
province of the Caesarian Empire, her promising youths went to
Rome, to make a name for themselves, to refresh the life of the capital with the raw sweetness of the country, and to help form the
styles of the day in the theatre, like Seneca of Cordoba, and make
wit acid as wine, like Martial of Bilbilis, and elevate the public art
of speech, like Quintillian from Calahorra, and even become Emperor, like Trajan, the Spanish soldier. Rome gave the Spaniards
their law; their feeling for cliff and wall, arch and cave, in building; and their formal display of death in the arena, with its mortal
delights, its cynical esthetic of pain and chance. Martial said it:

> *Raptus abit media quod ad aethera taurus harena,*
> *non fuit hoc artis sed pietatis opus. . . .*

A bull, he said, taken up from the center of the arena rises to the
skies, and this was not an act of art, but of piety. . . . It remained
an act of passion when Spanish piety turned to Christianity.

It was an empowering piety that grew through fourteen centuries,
the last eight of which made almost a settled condition of life out of
war with the Moslems of the Spanish peninsula. It was war both
holy and political, striving to unify belief and territory. Like all vic-
tors the Spaniards bore lasting marks of the vanquished. Perhaps in
the Moors they met something of themselves, long quiet in the
blood that even before Roman times flowed in Spanish veins from
Africa and the East, when the ancient Phoenicians and the Cartha-

i

Sources

83

ginians voyaged the Latin Sea and touched the Spanish shore and seeded its life. From the Moslem enemy in the long strife came certain arts—numbers, an ancient astronomy, the art of living in deserts, and the virtue of water for pleasure, in fountains, running courses, and tiled cascades. That had style: to use for useless pleasure in an arid land its rarest element.

Hardly had they made their home kingdom secure than the Spaniards put themselves and their faith across the world. They fought the infidel wherever they could find him, they ranged toward the Turk, and the Barbary Coast, and for them an admiral mercenary in 1492 risked sailing west until he might fall over the edge of the world and be lost. But however mockingly he was called a man of dreams, like many such he was a genius of the practical, and as strong in his soul as in his heart; for he believed as his employers believed.

*ii
Belief*

They believed in God, the Father Almighty, Creator of heaven and earth; and in Jesus Christ His only Son their Lord, Who was conceived by the Holy Ghost, born of the Virgin Mary, suffered under Pontius Pilate, was crucified, died and buried. He descended into hell; the third day He rose again from the dead; He ascended into heaven to sit at the right hand of God the Father Almighty from thence to come to judge the living and the dead. They believed in the Holy Ghost, the Holy Catholic Church, the communion of saints, the forgiveness of sins, the resurrection of the body, and life everlasting. Amen, they said.

So believing, it was a divine company they kept in their daily habit, all, from the monarch to the beggar, the poet to the butcher. The Holy Family and the saints inhabited their souls, thoughts, and words. They believed that with the love of God, nothing failed; without it, nothing prospered. Fray Juan of the Cross said it for them:

> *Buscando mis amores,*
> *Iré por esos montes y riberas,*
> *No cogeré las flores,*
> *Ni temeré las fieras,*
> *Y pasaré los fuertes y fronteras.*

Thus seeking their love across mountain and strand, neither gathering flowers nor fearing beasts, they would pass fortress and frontier, able to endure all because of their strength of spirit in the companionship of their Divine Lord.

Such belief existed within the Spanish not as a compartment where they kept their worship and faith, but as a condition of their very being, like the touch by which they felt the solid world, and the breath of life they drew until they died. It was the simplest and yet most significant fact about them, and more than any other accounted for their achievement of a new world. With mankind's imperfect material—for they knew their failings, indeed, revelled in them and beat themselves with them and knew death was too good for them if Christ had to suffer so much thorn and lance and nail for them—they yet could strive to fulfill the divine will, made plain to them by the Church. Relief from man's faulty nature could be had only in God. In obedience to Him, they found their greatest freedom, the essential freedom of the personality, the individual spirit in the self, with all its other expressions which they well knew —irony, extravagance, romance, vividness and poetry in speech, and honor, and hard pride.

If they were not large men physically, they were strong, and their bodies which the King commanded and their souls which God commanded were in harmony with any task because both God and King gave the same command. It was agreed that the King held his authority and his crown by the grace of God, communicated to him by the sanction of the Church. This was clear and firm. Thus, when required to serve the King in any official enterprise, great or small, they believed that they would likewise serve God, and possessed doubled strength from the two sources of their empowerment.

But if the King was divinely sanctioned, he was also a man like all; and they knew one another, king and commoner, in the common terms of their humanity. To command, to obey; to serve, to protect—these were duties intermixed as they faced one another. The King was accountable to the people as well as to God; for they made the State, and the State was in his care. *Del rey abajo ninguno,* they said in a proverb. Between us and the King, nobody. So they spoke to him in parliaments. Representative government began with the Spaniards. All, noble or commoner, had equality before the law. They greatly prized learning and respected those who owned it, such as lawyers. Indeed, the law was almost another faith, with its own rituals and customs, and even its own language, closed to uninitiated eyes and ears. Learning being scarce must also have seemed precious, and beyond the grasp of many a hungry mind. Yet with other peoples of the Renaissance, the sixteenth-century Spanish had intimations of world upon world unfolding, and they could not say what their children would know except that it would be greater than what they the fathers knew, watching the children at play with their little puppets of friars made from bean pods, with the tip broken and hanging down like a cowl, and showing the uppermost bean like a shaven head.

iii
The Ocean Masters

The year after the astounding first voyage of Admiral Christopher Columbus came the Bull of Pope Alexander VI, giving the King and Queen of Spain for themselves, their heirs and successors, almost all the lands of the New World known and still to be known. Given the unexempted belief of all western society in the reality of the Pope's spiritual and temporal power, this was an act of unquestionable legality. Thus the Americas came to belong to Spain, and to reach those lands she became a great sea power, for a time the greatest in the world. Schools of navigation and piloting were founded at Ferrol, Cádiz, and Cartagena. Universities maintained professorial chairs in cosmography. The great lords of Spain were given command of the fleets that plied to the Indies, though some had no qualities for the ocean but rank and magnificence, like the old marquis, a certain governor of the Armada, who through gout could not take off his own hat or feed his own lips, but had to have his courtesy and his food handled for him by servants. But still the Spanish sailed, and sailed well, and their fleets were prodigious at their greatest, like the one that bore the King to marry the Princess of England—gilded carving on the stern galleries, and sails painted with scenes from ancient Rome, and fifteen thousand banners at the masts, and damask, cloth of gold and silk draping the rails, and the sailors in scarlet uniforms, and all the ships standing to one another in such perfect order as to remind those who saw it of the buildings of a city, and the music of silver trumpets coming from the ships as they sailed.

To recruit the Indies fleets, a public crier and his musicians went from town to town, mostly in Andalusia that bordered on the sea. The drums rolled in the plaza, the fifes whistled a bright tune, calling a crowd. Then the crier bawled out his news. He told the sailing date of the next fleet, how great the ships were, some of one hundred twenty tons burden and sixty feet long, how skilled the captains, what opportunities overseas awaited the able-bodied young man between twenty-five and thirty years of age with a taste for adventure and good pay. And many a youth saw in his mind the great lands lifting over the ocean, with their Amazons who invited and broke men, and the golden treasuries waiting to be shipped home, and shapeless but powerful thoughts of how a fortune waited only to be seized, and a fellow's excellence recognized, his body given content, his pride matched with hazard, his dearness to himself made dear to all whom he should newly encounter. Many answered the fifes, the drums, and the crier. But if the recruitment was not great enough under the regulations which forbade signing on heretics and foreigners, then the merchant marine took on Jews, Moors, Frenchmen, Italians, Englishmen, Scotchmen, Germans, for the fleets had to sail and men had to sail them.

They sailed twice a year from Seville, in April and August, after three inspections held in the Guadalquivir. Crewmen signed on in the ship's register, took an oath of loyalty to the captain or the owner, and were bound for the voyage. Some were paid by the month, some by the mile, some with shares in the cargo. A sailor could not go anywhere without the commander's consent and, unless in port for the winter, could not even undress himself without permission. If he did so, he was punished by being ducked in the sea three times at the end of a rope from the yardarm. The crew's rations left them hungry enough at times to catch rats and eat them. The ship provided beef, pork, rice, fish, spices, flour, cheese, honey, anchovies, raisins, prunes, figs, sugar, quinces, olive oil, and wine, but in poor quantities, and very little water. The officers fared better, dining apart.

The passengers prepared their own meals out of the stores they had brought along, mostly hardtack and salted beef. They were almost always thirsty. Some slept on deck, some in little cabins five feet square, on mats stuffed with a thin layer of doghair, and under a blanket of worked goatskin. Below decks all day it was nearly dark. They could hear cockroaches and rats at restless work, and feel lice multiplying. There was no place in which to walk around. They could only lie down or sit, day and night. In storm the alcázar at the stern swayed as if to fall off the ship, and the blunt prows under their heavy castle shook like shoulders burrowing into the deep. The pumps at work spewed up bilge water as sickening as the air below decks, and all remained above whenever possible—the pilot navigating, the captain inspecting the artillery and other defenses, the master of the treasure that was packed in the hold, the cargo-master, the barber-surgeon, the caulker, the engineer, the cabin boys, the seamen.

But on open days when the weather was blessed, the company was busy with interest. So long as they lasted uneaten, cocks were set to fighting on deck for an audience that took sides and made bets. A young fellow would become a bull and another would pretend to fight him with cape and sword. Clever people got up plays and gave them. Others sang ballads to the music of the vihuela. Others read poetry aloud or improvised rhymes about the people on board. There were always some who brought the latest books printed by the Crombergers of Seville, and sat reading by the hour. The fleet might be becalmed, and then boys and men went over the side to swim near the ships. And when the wind came alive again, the painted sails swelled out, and the hulls leaned, and their sodden timbered breasts pushed heavily against the waves, while the cabin boy sang out the devotions of praise and thanks, "Amen: God give us a happy voyage, may the ships make a good passage, captain, master, and your lordships, good day my lords, from stern to prow," and at evening they cried, "Evening chow, ready now," and "Long live the King of Castile on land and sea," and all bowed and said, "Amen."

So they sailed and were sailed, taking two to three months to come to New Spain, where, like Juan Ponce de León, when he saw Florida, they said, *"Gracias le sean dadas, Señor, que me permites contemplar algo nuevo,"* giving thanks to God that He granted them to see the new.

And some amongst them feeling, if they could not speak, the wonder of the New World, where dangers and hardships in the end bound them more closely to her than easy victories ever could have, exclaimed in their hearts, with love, in their various ways, "Oh, Virgin of the World, innocent America!"

That the Spaniards take her lawfully, with care, and with conscience, the Spanish kings of the Golden Age worked without cease.

iv
*The King
& Father*

Not all Spaniards had seen the King, but in every large company there was always one who had seen him, or knew someone who served him closely, and remembered much to tell. Anything they could hear of the King was immensely interesting and important. He was their pride even as he was their master. He commanded them by the power of God; and yet, as they were, so was he, a man, their common image, but with the glory and dignity of the crown over his head, and so, over theirs. What he was had greatly to do with what they were, as in all fatherhood. So his image passed through them to the Indies, wherever they went, beyond cities and maps, however far along remote rivers. Even the gossip about great kings created the character of their subjects.

King Charles, who was also the Holy Roman Emperor, lived and worked in hard bare rooms with no carpets, crowding to the fire in winter, using the window's sunshine in summer. The doctors of medicine stated that the humors of moisture and of cold dominated his quality. His face was fixed in calm, but for his eyes, that moved and spoke more than his gestures or his lips. His face was pale and long, the lower lip full and forward, often dry and cracked, so that he kept on it a green leaf to suck. His nose was flat, and his brows were pitted with a raised frown that appeared to suggest a constant headache. He held his shoulders high as though on guard. He would seem to speak twice, once within and fully, and then outwardly and meagrely. But his eyes showed his mind, brilliant, deep, and always at work. He loved information for its own sake, was always reading, and knew his maps well. They said he saw the Indies better than many who went there, and held positive views on all matters concerning the New World and its conquerors.

But if his opinions were strong, so was his conscience. He said once that it was his nature to be obstinate in sticking to his opinions. A courtier replied that it was but laudable firmness to stick to good opinions. To this the Emperor observed with a sigh that he sometimes stuck to bad ones. Much contemplation rested behind such a remark. He was in poor health for most of his life, and as a result considered himself in many aspects. In his young days he was a beautiful rider, with his light legs and his heavy lifted shoulders. He once liked to hunt bear and boar; but illness and business put an end to it. He worked all day and much of the night, until his supper at midnight, at which he received ambassadors, who were amazed at his appetite. Matters of state went on even there, by candlelight, as the platters were passed, and the baskets of fruit, and the water bowls. He wore his flat black cap, his black Flemish velvet doublet and surcoat with the collar of Germany-dressed marten skins, and his chain of the Golden Fleece. The letters of Cortés from New Spain had good talk in them, and the Emperor later had them published in print.

Whether or not America, so far away, was a matter of policy instead of feeling, Charles required justice for the Indians of the New World. Before 1519 he was sending people to the Indies to study and report to him upon the conditions of the natives. Uppermost was his desire that their souls be saved through Christianity. It was of greater moment that Indians became Christians than that they became Spaniards. So, as the conquerors made cities in the New World, they made schools, colleges, and universities for the Indians, in which to teach them—often in Latin but more often in the Indian tongues which the friars learned rapidly—salvation in Christ. The Emperor held that through such salvation all else of life must naturally take its course and would come. He strongly supported the missioners in the Indies, and inspired them and many laymen to build the Church in the New World even as ominous cracks ran up its walls in the Old.

But from the first, and increasingly, another spirit worked against the Indians. The military, the landowners, the civil officials believed that conversion was a proper thing, but once out of the way, let the natives be useful to them in labor and arms. But the priests meant what they preached, just as much as the men of the world meant what they ordered. Both said they served the Crown as it desired to be served. Both appealed to the King.

His Holy Caesarian Catholic Majesty (for so he was addressed in documents) wished to know an all-determining truth. Was the Indian a man, as many claimed? Or was he an animal, as many others insisted? Could he understand Christianity? Did he deserve better than the yoke of slavery?

Commissions investigated, passions rose, and humanity triumphed. The Cardinal Adrian in Spain preached that the Indians were free and must be treated as free men, and given Christianity with Christian gentleness. The Emperor acted, and the laws for the Indies were decreed in that spirit. The Crown gave its approval to the ideals of the missionary priests, who ever afterward, over new land, went with the armies not only to convert but to protect Indians.

When the Emperor left Spain for Germany, and after his retirement from the throne in mid-century, he kept the problem in mind, for he wrote to his son Prince Philip to caution him that he must be vigilant to prevent oppressions and injustices in the Colonies, saying that only through justice were sound business and prosperity possible. It was a cold and impassive statement of policy, but in it (as in the brilliant black and white flash of those eyes in his pallid face that found it so difficult otherwise to express itself) true humanity shone behind expediency.

When the Emperor abdicated to become a country gentleman at Yuste near Placencia, there was still much to hear about him, even as he invented ways to pass the time. He made a garden. He designed and fashioned mechanical works, including a hand mill to grind meal, and a marvellous set of little clockwork soldiers that performed military drills. Visitors brought him watches and clocks upon which he delighted to work. The joke went around that one time, when he complained of his food, he was told by the major-domo that the only thing that would please his palate then would be a stew of watches. He laughed heartily at this.

From his early days in the Italian campaigns he loved the arts of music and painting. In his military travels, even to Africa, he took along his choir—the best choir in Europe—and pipe organs. His ear was true, he remembered music as well as he did facts, and he loved to sit and listen to a French air, *Mille regrets*. At Placencia he had his nine favorite paintings by Titian with him.

With a few guests in his party, he would go wandering through the woods with his harquebus in hand, watching for game. But the joy he took from this sport in his old age was more that of watching birds and little animals, and their quick mysterious commerce, than that of killing them. He would shoot now and then, but his friends said that the pigeons pretended out of courtesy to be frightened of his blasts, and perhaps he was an old man hunting for life, not death.

But his piety kept death before him. He was read aloud to from the *Confessions of Saint Augustine,* and he could nod in recognition of anybody who turned sharply away from the great world to lead a modest life of outer trifles and inner mysteries of faith and conscience. It was talked of everywhere, for thousands were there, when he had a Requiem Mass sung to rehearse his own funeral. It was just as though it were the actual funeral. There before the altar was the catafalque swept in black draperies and silver lace, with thousands of candles burning at all the altars and shrines, and the prelates and priests singing at the pontifical Mass, and the Emperor's wonderful music in the stalls with the organ, and there in the middle of it, wearing a black mantle, was the Emperor himself, praying for the repose of his soul before it left his body.

The Spaniards knew the same thing in themselves—the strength and the countenance to stare upon contrition and death. For, in their belief, what could anyone do enough to mortify himself, if he was to be worthy of salvation by the sufferings of the Son of Man upon the cross? The Emperor had a flail with which he would whip himself so hard that the thongs showed his blood. After his death it became known that in his will he left this flail to his son Philip, for him to prize all his life and in his turn to pass on as a beloved heirloom, a relic of the blood of the father. . . .

Philip II spared himself no less, and left his image no less in the Indies, though in somewhat different manner. People missed the occasional humor and grace of the Emperor, even though under him they had had to work just as hard as under his son. But there was, as it were, a darkening of life that came when the Emperor retired and, dying in retirement, left all power to the new King. But the King demanded more of himself than of anyone else. New Spain and all the other Indies became greater, quieter, richer, and as the conquests receded, the work of government grew enormously. The whole world wrote to Spain. Her ships carried not only the treasure of the New World, they took also reports, contracts, budgets, petitions, court records, confidential intelligence, complaints, and all manner of papers to Madrid. And there, the King himself read them, all of them, and marked his wishes upon the margins.

Secretaries came to him in the morning as he dressed, and after dinner at mid-day, and again to spend the long evening, while he dictated, initialed, weighed, decided; held in abeyance, revived for discussion, or postponed again; examined for policy or referred for further study dozens, and hundreds, and tens of thousands of papers through a lifetime of late-working nights. Besides all that, there were the endless committees to receive, who sat through hours of *giving all aspects proper consideration*. Minutes of such meetings were kept and, doubling the ecstasy of administrative indulgence, could always be referred to later. It was a poor business if anyone sought to relieve the King of any small details of his official burden. Some of the best men in the land were called to court for appointment to important posts, and then denied the use of their faculties of originality and initiative. No detail was too small to interest the King. If he was King and was to sign, then what he signed must be exquisitely proper and he would put all the power, weight, and style of his office into a debate upon the nicety of a word to employ in a certain phrase to be written down in a state paper. He would refuse to be hurried, but would spend himself twice over on a matter rather than settle it out of hand. Don Pedro Ponce de León wrote to the King from Mexico, asking for the command of the entry into New Mexico to colonize the Rio del Norte, and as the ocean passage of letter and reply would take eight months more or less, he expected to hear nothing for a while. But time passed, and no answer came to him from the King, whereupon he wrote again, begging in all respect for a reply to his earlier petition. The reply, when it came, said, "Tell him it will take a year to decide."

There was much to decide at home. The King saw with sorrow the disorderly and frivolous nature of the populace, and, asking less actually of them than of himself, issued decrees of prohibition upon conduct, possessions, and belief. It was unseemly and therefore forbidden by royal edict to wear luxurious dress; to live amidst lavish surroundings; to use private carriages or coaches except under certain stated conditions; to employ courtesy titles; to seek education beyond the frontiers of Spain; to open the mind to the inquiries of science; or otherwise fail in proper humility and self-discipline. It was a grief to Philip that, despite his endless efforts to guide his great family of subjects in ways of piety and decorum, all manner of license grew and continued. Rich and clever people found ways to evade the laws, while poor people could not even qualify under them to commit the crimes of indulgence they forbade. Orders might come in a stream of papers from the palace, but Madrid remained a mudhole, the filthy streets choked with carriages and palanquins, bearing rich ladies who accosted men unknown to them, and of whom they invited proposals of shame. How could this be in a land where women were previously sacred and guarded within the family walls as the very Moors had done before them?

How could it be when any man worked so hard that he should be visited with so many sorrows and reverses? The King bent his head and spoke of the will of God. There were endless tales of his natural piety that sustained him in the hours of humiliation that came to Spain. The Dutch wars went against the Spanish forces. They were defeated in France. The English under an infidel Queen broke Spain's greatest fleet and a year later raided, burned, and robbed Cádiz, Spain's richest city. Spanish ships were attacked homeward bound from the Indies. The King suffered all with courage, determined to be an example to all in adversity, that they might keep their faith. He declared that it was better not to reign at all than to reign over heretics. Of these there were not many, then, and those few learned or vanished, though the question remained whether the delicate seed of faith that could grow to such mighty power could truly prosper through the habits of brutality of all agencies of discipline, such as the army, the constabulary, the office of the Inquisition, and the law courts alike. And still the King worked, writing orders to govern how many horses and servants a man could maintain with seemliness; how funerals should be conducted, and how weddings; what public amusements might be countenanced and what not. And while he slaved at concerns so alarming and dear to him, there went unanswered pleas from his ambassadors overseas and viceroys desperate for Crown policies ("Tell him it will take a year . . ."), and groaning supplications from fiscal officers who expected mutinies unless the armies were paid.

How could a man's goodness be so crushing?

Those who saw him come to the throne saw his father's son, in the tall forehead, the vivid black and white eyes, the lower lip permanently outthrust. Even then, as a young man, there was no mark of humor in his face, which was furrowed beside the nose and under the cheekbone. Yet it was a head of grace and distinction, lean above the ruffed collar of Brabant linen, and the puffed doublet worked in gold. His beard and hair, that had a little wave in it, were a golden brown. And then those who saw him long later saw a heavy face, with sallow color, and sacs about the eyes, now smaller and heavier-lidded. His dress was different; he wore a tall black cap and black garments relieved only by the starch-white of his collar. His spirit was heavy, too, and sallow, if souls had color. The feature most unchanged in his face was the deep cleft between his eyes that made a scowl of abnegation natural to him in youth when he first renounced so much for himself, and that cut deeper in age when he renounced so much in their own lives for others.

An image of his quality was the palace of the Escorial, which he built on the sweeping plain outside Madrid, below the mountains. It was as big as a palisaded mesa. The plain was as barren as a desert. In New Spain and New Mexico was much country of which that was the miniature. The palace rose in a great square of ochreous gray walls. It was so vast that human silence seemed a very part of its design. What no man could see, but what the profuse flocks of little martins and swallows could see as they circled over it, was that within the great square stood inner walls, crisscrossing one another in the form of a gridiron or grill. It was believed that this was built in imitation and endless reminder of the grill upon which St. Lawrence met his death. Thus Philip could have constant point for contemplation. Within the palace the long corridors that followed the lines of the grill were low and narrow, showing the bare granite of their walls. The floors were of unfinished stone. Coming in from even a hot summer's day the courtier met indoors the chill of the tomb. The palace was so made that a great portion of its internal volume was taken by a dark church, whose dome and towers rose above the enclosing walls. The King's own bedroom, a cell, was placed so that he could look out from it through an indoor window and see the Mass at the high altar, which was just below. Church, monastery, palace, and tomb, that tenebrous heart of the Empire expressed in all its purposes the sacred and profane obsessions of the King, its builder.

And if the monarch had his palatial rack designed after a saint's, the soldiers, the traders, the shopmen, the scholars, the voyagers of Spain each had his Escorial of the soul, where to endure the joys and the pains of his spiritual exercises he entered alone and in humility.

Perhaps the deeper a man's humility in the privacy of his soul, the more florid his pride in public. All Spaniards, high or low, could use a spacious manner. Its principal medium was the Spanish language. Not many could read; but all could speak like lords or poets. The poorest soldier in the farthest outlandish expedition of New Mexico might be a chip floating beyond his will on the stream of history, but still he could make an opinion, state it with grace and energy, and even, in cases, make up a rhyme for it. He spoke his mind through a common language that was as plain and clear as water, yet able to be sharp as a knife, or soft as the moon, or as full of clatter as heels dancing on tile. Like Latin, from which it came, it needed little to say what it meant. It called less upon image and fancy than other tongues, but made its point concretely and called forth feelings in response to universal commonplaces rather than to flights of invention. With that plain strength, the language yet could show much elegance, and such a combination—strength with elegance—spoke truly for the Spaniards and of them. The Emperor once said that to speak to horses, the best tongue to use was German; to talk with statesmen, French; to make love, Italian; to call the birds, English; and to address princes, kings, and God, Spanish. In the time of Cicero the Spanish town of Córdoba was famous for two things, its poetry and its olive oil. Cicero said the poetry sounded as though it were mixed with the oil.

A passion for study filled the century of the Golden Age. In Spain, thirty-four universities were at work, and others were founded in the New World within a few years of the conquest. The German Jacob Cromberger and his sons established their printing

V

Arts

house at Seville in 1500, reading became an indispensable part of living, and all because a complicated machine held together many rows of reversed little metal letters and pressed them into damp paper, again and again, until many copies of the same words and ideas were at hand. Because her language went everywhere with Spain's power, printers in Italy, France, the Netherlands, and the Indies printed books in Spanish.

Everything found its way into print, even the ballads that previously passed through generations by word of mouth. People made them up in inns and on travels and marching in wars, telling droll stories or love stories or wicked scandals; and the rude narratives were sung wherever somebody had an instrument to pluck. Seeing how such efforts looked in print, men of letters began to write ballads in the style of the old popular ones, that had gone always changing as one man's memory revised the residue of another's. The new poetic ballads sang of the courts of chivalry; imaginary histories that revealed Spanish ideals of noble kingship, knightly valor, reverence for womanhood, and death to monsters. True histories were also written in rhyme, long chronicles of heroes, as when Captain Pérez de Villagrá, the alumnus of the University of Salamanca, sat down to write the history of Oñate's first year on the Rio del Norte, in New Mexico, he wrote it in heroic verse. The Spanish world grew not only in range but also in meaning as the people saw its likeness in all that was made by writers and artists.

As his father the Emperor admired Titian of Venice, so King Philip admired and employed Domenico Theotocopuli, known as The Greek, who came from Greece by way of long studies and labors in Venice and Rome. He was a learned man and a pious one, and for the Escorial and churches elsewhere he painted many pictures that swept the eye and mind of the beholder upward to heaven. Often even the very eyes of the kings and saints he painted were gazing heavenward and shining with great diamond tears of desire, and seeing them so, the beholder cast his desires upward also. The skies of his pictures of martydoms and sufferings and triumphs were like the skies of Good Friday afternoon, torn apart and blowing aloft in black and white clouds through which the Spanish temperament could see the immortal soul of Christ as it flew to His Father from the cross. The Greek painted many likenesses of people of circumstance, who without their starch and black velvet and swords, their armor and ribbons, or their violet mantelletas and trains, would have looked very much like everybody else in the

Spanish populace, even those on the northern river of the latest and farthest Crown colony in the New World. All countenances which he limned were grave and melancholy, even that of the Madonna in the Nativity. The Spaniards were a people who did not often smile, but more often laughed outright or possessed their faces in calm, when most faces look sad. The Greek was much seen at Toledo, where he painted the town many times, making odd changes in exactly how it looked, yet by so doing, making the city's image combine with the beholder's feeling to produce a rise of the soul.

It was the same rise that Spaniards knew from music in the High Mass, when the dark high vaults of the church where candlelight never reached would be filled with the singing of choirs, plain, without instruments. They heard the masses composed by the great Tomás Luis de Victoria of Ávila, and Cristóbal of Morales, and Francisco Guerrero. The voices of boys came like shafts of heaven, and in the polyphonic style, the voices of men rose under them and turned with melody, and the two qualities met and divided, the one qualifying the other, now with one long note held against several notes in a figure, again with highs against lows, and again with syllables against whole words, and loud against soft, so that in heavenly laws known to music alone an experience of meaning and delivery struck all who truly listened, and the stone arches and the drift of incense and possibility of divinity in mankind and the Mass at the altar all became intermingled with the soul that rose. How, lost in dark choir stalls under lofting stone, could boys, having yet had so little of life, strike so purely to the darkest self with their shining voices that seemed to come from beyond all flesh?

And there was other music that used the very flesh itself, spoke to it, enlivened it, cozened it with coarse jokes, and pulled its nose and made the hearers laugh and clap and stamp their feet. It was heard at the inns, in public squares, and in the theatres, when ballads were sung or skits and plays given by actors and dancers. They came out on a stage, bringing sackbuts or dulcimers, harps, lutes or vihuelas, or combinations of all these, and struck up a tune to which they sang a story with many verses. They plucked, beat, blew, and nodded together, and often repeated with each verse a clever effect in which one musician gave a little variation at the same place each time, so that the audience listened for it in following verses. Such players entertained anyone who called for them and displayed a coin. They went from one tavern to another, ready to stand in a half-circle facing a table and play to a private party much to the advantage of any others in the place. Their music went with the Spaniards wherever in the world they might go.

If popular balladry was the poor man's comfort, there was much to sing about as the world moved and poor times befell Spain in her might. Great fortunes shrank, and the high state of many nobles lost its quality because it could not be paid for, and wage earners found their coins worth very little, and poor people lived always hungry. It was the very outpourings of wealth from the New World that caused such trouble. When so much more gold than usual came to be circulated, each little coin or bit of gold spent in trade was worth much less than usual, as gold itself became too common. In giving civilization to the New World, Spain seemed to give up its own strength as the new land found the lusty power to grow by itself. In the home kingdom, while all graces were maintained, the substance behind them shrank, and for great numbers of Spaniards the graces which they aired came to be pretensions and little else.

vi
Style &
Hunger

And yet there was that in the Spanish spirit which made of each Spaniard his own castle, and it was very like them all that as the wealth that sustained public nobility began to shrink, and as every hidalgo by birth disdained to reveal his poor estate, so many another man who had no title or claim to nobility adopted the airs and styles of the hidalgo, until the land became a parade of starving lords, real and false, who the lower they fell in wordly affairs, the more grandly they behaved. Going hungry, they would loll against a wall in public, picking their teeth to convince the passer-by that they had just dined on sweet carrots and turnips, sharp cheese, pungent bacon, fresh eggs, crusty roast kid, tart wine from Spanish grapes, and a covered dish of baked gazpacho, that was made out of wheat bread, olive oil, vinegar, onions, salt, and red peppers hot enough to make the eyes water.

There was little else for such a gentleman to do. If he had talents that could be employed, there was hardly anybody to pay him for them. He was a man of honor and to make a living could not stoop to improper ways which, no matter how hard the times, seemed always to prosper. If his shanks were thin and bare, and his sitting bones almost showed in his threadbare breeches, and his belly was puffy with windy hunger, then he still had his ragged cloak to throw about such betrayals. Within his cloak he could stand a noble stance, and at a little distance, who was the wiser? As the proverb said, "Under a bad cloak there may hide a good drinker," which gave comfort to fallen swagger; and to comfort the dream of impossible valor, there spoke another proverb, saying, "Under my cloak I kill the king."

But no patch ever failed to show, however lovingly stitched, even a patch on a man's pride. To cloak his spirit, the mangy gentleman had another sort of possession left to him from his better days. This was the high thought of chivalry that gave to human life, all human life, so great a dignity and such an obligation of nobility on behalf of all other persons. There was a poor sweetness in this extravagant spending of spirit, that the more a man lacked simply to keep him alive, the more he disdained his own trouble and grandly swore to demolish the trouble of another. In his ironic self-knowledge the Spaniard knew such men, and smiled at the antic capers they cut in their hungry pretensions. And yet he bowed to their spirit which stated that "he is only worth more than another who does more than another." It was no surprise to him that a champion should vow the rescue of anyone in distress, without reference to rank or station. If there were different levels of life, then one man in his own was worth as much as another in his, and was free to state as much and act accordingly. And as every soul originated in God, and so was equal to every other in worth, so its sufferings on earth deserved succor without discrimination. The Spaniard knew that the grandeur of God did not disdain the humblest surroundings, and could say with Saint Teresa of Ávila, *Entre los pucheros anda el Señor*—"God moves among the kitchen pots."

But all came back to hunger. Private soldiers who went to the Americas were experienced in that condition. It was a marvel how far they could march, how hard they could fight, and how long they could cling to unknown country on empty stomachs. Nuñez Cabeza de Vaca, Coronado's soldiers, Castaño de Sosa pillaging at Pecos, Zaldívar crawling over deserts toward the river, all gnawed on traditions when rations were low. Certainly the adventures did not enlist for the pay, for the pay was meagre and always in arrears, even that owed to the commanders in silver-gilt armor. Nor did they venture forth for commerce as it could affect the ordinary individual, for the risks were too great for uncertain profits, and in any case the Spanish gift for business fulfilled itself not in the largest but in the smallest affairs, face to face with another man. For the pleasures of business were firstly social—little exchanges of desire and deceit, indifference and truth, the study of human nature, the flourish of bargaining, the satisfaction of the righteous swindle, in buyer and seller alike. Nor was it inordinate love of adventure that took Spaniards past oceans and shores, and up the river, for adventure could be had anywhere, even at home. Perhaps more than any one other motive it was a belief in their own inherent greatness that took the men of the Golden Age to their achievements in geography and colonization.

For to them it was finer to make greatness than to inherit it; and after they made it, they could in all justice cry with the True Chronicler of the conquest of Mexico, "I say again that I—I, myself —I am a true conqueror; and the most ancient of all . . . and I also say, and praise myself thereon, that I have been in as many battles and engagements as, according to history, the Emperor Henry the Fourth." In such spirit, what they did with so little, they did with style.

vii
The
Swords

Even the swords that were extensions not only of their right arms but also of their personalities came out of humble means through fire and water to strength and beauty. Ovid sang the praises of Toledo blades, the best of which were made of old used metal, such as horseshoes. The Spaniard's sword was born at nighttime, through fire, of a river and the south wind.

In the city hall of Toledo the master steelworkers—Sahagún the Elder, Julian del Rey, Menchaca, Hortuño de Aguirre, Juanes de la Horta—kept their metal punches when these were not in use to stamp the maker's name on a new blade. Every blade had its *alma,* and this soul was the core of old iron on whose cheeks were welded new plates of steel. Standing ready were the two gifts of the river Tagus that flowed below the high rocks of Toledo. These were its white sand and its clear water. The blades were born only in the darkest nights, the better to let the true or false temper of the steel show when red-hot; and, of the darkest nights, only those when the south wind blew, so that in passing the blade from fire to water it might not cool too rapidly as a north wind would cool it. The clumsy weld was put into the coals where the bellows hooted. When it came red-hot, the master took it from the fire. It threw sparks on meeting the air. Casting river sand on it, which extinguished the sparks, the master moved to the anvil. There, with taps of hammer and sweeps of the steel against the anvil, he shaped the blade, creating a perfectly straight ridge down the center of each side until, squinted at endwise, the blade looked like a flattened lozenge. Now the blade was put again into the fire and kept there until it began to color again, when the master lifted it into the darkness to see if it showed precisely cherry-red. If so, it was ready for the river. There stood handy a tall wooden pail filled with water from the Tagus. Into this, point down, went the blade for its first immersion. To keep the exact right time for each immersion, and to bring blessings, the master or one of his boys sang during the first one, "Blessed be the hour in which Christ was born," and then the blade was lifted out. Heated again, it was returned to the water, and they sang, "Holy Mary, Who bore Him!" and next time they sang, "The iron is hot!" and the next, "The water hisses!" and the next, "The tempering will be good," and the last, "If God wills." Then once more the blade went to the fire, but this time only until it became dull red, liver-colored. Then with pincers the master held it by the tang which would later fit into the hilt, and had the boy smear the blade with raw whole fat cut from the sac about the kidneys of a male goat or a sheep. The fat burst into flame. They took the blade to the rack and set it there against the wall, point downward. The fat burned away, the blade darkened and cooled through several hours. In daytime they sharpened and polished it, and if it was to bear an inscription, it went to the bench of the engraver, who chiselled his letters on one of the flat faces, or perhaps both, spelling out a pious or patriotic motto, like one on a sword found in Texas, not far from the Rio Grande, that read, on one side, "POR MY REY," and on the other, "POR MY LEY," thus swearing protection to king and law. The hilt, with guard and grip, then was joined to the tang, and those for plain soldiers were of well-turned iron, but without inlays of gold or silver, or studdings of smooth jewels, or wrappings with silver-gilt wire that variously went on to the swords of officers and nobles.

And at last the maker sent for his stamp from the city hall and let his device be punched into the blade at its thickest part near the guard, and the proud work was done, and the Spanish gesture could be sharpened and elongated across the world.

viii

Soul &
Body

Both within the Spaniard and without him lay the country which Lope de Vega called "sad, spacious Spain." If Spaniards enacted their literature, it was because, like all people, they both created literature and were created by it. So it was with memories and visions in the colony of the river wilderness. Their hopes of what to be were no less full of meanings than their certainties of what they had done, and both found their center of energy in a moral sense that gave a sort of secret poetry to the hard shape of life. The Spaniard was cruel, but he loved life, and his melancholy brutality seemed to issue forth almost involuntarily through the humanitarian laws and codes with which he surrounded himself. If his nature was weak, his conscience was strong, and if he sinned, his first act of recovery must be to recognize his guilt. When one of the most brutal of the conquerors of the New World was dying of wounds given to him by Indians, he was asked where he ached, and he replied, "In my soul."

So the baggage of personality brought by the colonists told of their origin, their faith, the source of their power, the human types by which they perpetuated their tradition; and forecast much about how they would live along the river.

But in that very summer of 1598, when the newest colony of the Spanish Empire was settling on the Rio del Norte in northern New Mexico, the Empire was already ailing. Its life stream carried human tributaries to the river, but already at its source, in Madrid, the springs of Spanish energy were starting to go low. It was an irony of history that, just as the American continent was being comprehended, the first great power that sought it began to lose the force to possess it. It would take two more centuries for the flow to become a trickle that barely moved and then altogether stopped. But the Spanish effectiveness in government, society, and commerce began to lose power in the New World with the failure of life in the last of the kings of the Golden Age.

Laboring inhumanly to govern his world-wide kingdoms for goodness and prosperity, Philip II left them a complicated legacy of financial ruin, bureaucratic corruption, and social inertia. After a dazzling conjugation of *to do,* the destiny of Spain seemed to turn toward a simple respiration of *to be.* One was as true of the Spanish temperament as the other.

If Philip left to his peoples anything in the way of a true inheritance, one that expressed both him and them, and that would pass on through generations, it was his example in adversity, his patience facing a hideous death, and his submission to the will of God.

He lay through the summer of 1598 in the Escorial, holding the crucifix that his father the Emperor had held on his own deathbed. The son, in an agony of suppurating tumors, repeatedly gnawed upon the wood of the cross to stifle his groans. His truckle bed was run close to the indoor window through which he could look down upon the big altar of the Escorial church. In the early mornings he could hear the choir singing in the dark stalls and watch the Holy Sacrifice of the Mass performed for the repose of his soul, whose liberation was nearing. But it came slowly. On August 16 he received the pontifical blessing from Rome. A fortnight later he took the last sacraments, and afterward spoke alone to his son and heir on the subject of how reigns ended and crowns passed and how instead came shrouds and coarse cinctures of rope in which to be buried. For days and nights the offices of the dying were chanted by priests in his cell. If momentarily they paused, he whispered, "Fathers, continue; the nearer I come to the fountain, the greater my thirst." Before four in the morning on September 13 he asked for a blessed candle to hold. Its calm light revealed a smile on his face. His father's crucifix was on his breast; and when he gasped faintly three times, and died, and was enclosed in a coffin made of timbers from the *Cinco Chagas,* a galleon that had sailed the seas for him, the crucifix was still there. By his will the blood-crusted flail left to him by his father now passed to the new ruler, King Philip III. In the austere grandeur of such a scene the deathly luxuries of the Spanish temperament, as well as the dying fall of the Empire, found expression. At San Juan de los Caballeros, in the valley of the Rio del Norte, near the junction with the Chama, in northern New Mexico, where willows and cottonwoods along bench terraces of pale earth all imaged the end of summer, the Crown's new colony was at work on a matter of enduring importance to their settlement. By order of Governor de Oñate they were already building their church.

2 · The Desert Fathers

An early Franciscan on the Rio Grande said that its human life seemed to show on a map the shape of a cross. The upright stem, north and south, was the river itself along which clustered the great house-towns, and the arms reached east and west to settlements of other Indian people. It was an approximate image, but it expressed the dedication of the friars to their inner and immaterial motive. Their spirit and their flesh were one in purpose. They came to take nothing and they brought with nothing that could be measured. Like the founder of their order, Saint Francis of Assisi, they could have said that they "had been called to the way of simplicity," and that they always "wished to follow the 'foolishness of the cross,'" by which they meant the innocence that made worldly men smile. Certainly it was the act of a fool, in terms of shrewd mankind, to go into barbarian wilderness, at times alone and unprotected, to preach the love of Christ. The Castilian Saint John of the Cross said, "Where there is no love, bring love and you will find love." The martyrs of Puaray, and Fray Juan de Padilla in Quivira, had made their ultimate demonstration. "They killed him," said another Franciscan of Fray Agustín Ruíz, "and threw his body into the Rio del Norte, which flows along the edge of this pueblo." And at Taos, when Fray Pedro de Ortega came to offer his faith to the Indians, he was refused a place to live, and to eat was given tortillas made of corn meal and the ground-up flesh of field mice, mixed with urine. These he ate with words of relish, remarking that for "a good appetite there is no bad bread." The Indians marvelled. "They go about poor and barefoot as we do," said Indians elsewhere, "they eat what we eat, sit down among us and speak to us gently."

In one respect the Indians and the friars were close together from the beginning. Both had profoundly religious character, and saw life's essentials best explained through the supernatural. But as the friars believed that their faith enclosed all faiths and purified them in the fire of divine love, until God's relation to man shone forth in the image of Christ Who was the Son of Man, so did they think to bring love to replace the fear that animated all objects, creatures, and forces in the Indian's pagan world. The gift they sought to give the Indian was the sense of his individual human soul, and the need, and the means, of its salvation.

But if the friar in himself was poor and managed with very little, his work in the aggregate required extensive organization. The friar's immaterial mission was enclosed in a system that rested on a rigid hierarchy and showed itself in massive monuments. At the pueblo of El Agua de Santo Domingo, that stood on the banks of Galisteo Creek a short way east of the river, the Franciscan order established the religious headquarters of the whole kingdom of New Mexico. There resided the Father President, and there he held his yearly chapters when all his friars would come from their lonely posts in the outlying missions. Santo Domingo was a little Rome, the seat of an authority that bowed to no secular power in matters

of the spiritual welfare of men and women. In the mountains to the
northeast was the new political capital of the colony at Santa Fe,
founded in 1610. Between the river pueblo and the mountain capital
much was in dispute throughout the seventeenth century and would
be composed only in slowly gathering tragedy.

Meanwhile the work of the religious reached into the river towns
to the north and south; into the pueblos of the west, and to the sa-
line towns over the eastern mountains. Nominally, even the Apache
nations, who roamed the plains and alternately traded with and attacked the settled Pueblo people, were part of a missionary parish.
The Apaches, wrote a Father President in his report, "are very spirited and belligerent . . . a people of a clearer and more subtle understanding, and as such laugh at other nations that worship idols of
wood and stone. The Apaches worship only the sun and the moon.
. . . They pride themselves on never lying but always speaking the
truth." It was an optimistic vision of mass murderers of whole
towns. To such peoples went "missions of penetration," consisting of
a travelling friar who preached, converted where he could, and if he
lived, returned to Santo Domingo, or to the settled "mission of occupation" to which he was assigned; for many of the outlying missions in Indian towns were organized as field headquarters from
which faith and civilization were carried to other towns that had no
permanent pastor. Such other towns were designated *visitas*.

Fifty churches were built in New Mexico by twenty-six friars in
the first quarter of the seventeenth century. First came the word of
God and the conversion of the Indians; and then, with no other
power but example and patience, the solitary Franciscan father led
his parishioners in building a church. In choosing the site for his
church he considered many things. He looked into the hearts of the
Indians and, seeing all that mankind was capable of in good and
evil, he felt that a church surrounded by the town was subject to
being overwhelmed from within. He looked at the country beyond
the town and he saw that the strongest fortress should stand first in
the way of invaders. Considering ceremony, he saw how a church
must have approaches for processions; and remembering functions,
he knew it must be close to community life. Accordingly, at the
edge of the pueblo he marked out a site for the church where it
could stand by itself, yet be tied to the walls of the town.

He had large papers scratched with drawings. The people looked
from these to his face and then to the straggled marks on the baked
ground. He was all things: architect, engineer, carpenter, mason,

foreman, building master to apprentices who themselves were masters of a building style. He did not scorn their methods or their designs. He saw their perfect economy of material and purpose in what they built. Remembering vast vaults of stone, the flutings of arches and echoing heights, sombre color in glass and every intricacy of grille and recess and carved screen, he saw that, reduced to essentials, even the great churches of Europe and Mexico had a plain strong purpose, which was to enclose the attention of men and women in safety and direct it toward the altar. Here were wanted walls and roof as soon as possible. They must be made of materials already used and understood by the people, and to them must be added new methods understood by the friar. He had with him, assigned by the Father President at Domingo, and paid for by the King of Spain, ten axes, three adzes, three spades, ten hoes, one medium-sized saw, one chisel, two augers, and one plane; six thousand nails of various sizes, a dozen metal hinges, two small locks, several small latches, and one large latch for the main church door. With him, too, he brought the principle of the lever, the windlass, and the block and fall. Out of his belief and his technique, combined with native materials and the Indian's reproduction of earth forms in building, a new style was ready to come, massive, stark, angular, and powerfully expressive of its function.

Until they worked under Spaniards, the Indians built their walls of puddled clay and rock. Now the first lesson of the friar was to teach the making of adobes—earthen bricks. Clay was disintegrated rock. The adobe was a restoration of clay to coherent form—a sort of return to rock. With their new hoes, people went to work mixing water and earth in an excavated tray. Only Indian women did this work, for as theirs was the ancient task of enclosing life, so they had always made the dwelling rooms of the family. Men, as craftsmen of arms and tools, learned carpentry, and made wooden moulds after the friar's instructions. Into the wet clay, straw was mixed as a binder, and the clay was then pressed into the moulds to take the shape of large bricks. A brick weighed sixty pounds, and measured ten by eighteen by five inches. It was about all the load a man or a woman could carry over and over, as the rows of drying bricks grew longer.

Sometimes foundations were dug and filled with loose stone footings, sometimes the walls rose directly from unopened ground. The walls were deep—six to nine feet thick—and one side wall was several feet thicker than the other. The people wondered why this was as the width was marked out on the ground, and as the walls rose, they discovered why; but meanwhile the dried bricks were brought by a long line of workers, and laid in place. The entire pueblo worked on the church. While women mixed earth, and men moulded bricks, other men and boys went to the mountains to bring back timbers. With rock and chisel they shaped these. The friar drew patterns for them to follow and out of the wood came beams, corbels, door panels, doorframes, window embrasures. If someone knew where deposits of selenite or mica were to be found, men were sent to bring in a supply so that thin layers of the translucent mineral could be worked into windowpanes. The days were full and the walls rose slowly, but all could see progress, and it made them one in spirit. The church was from twenty to forty feet wide, and sixty to a hundred feet long. Its ceiling was to occur at about thirty feet. On one of its long flanks, against the thicker of the two walls, were laid out living quarters for the friar and his Indian staff in a row of little square rooms with low roofs. These formed one side of a patio, the other sides of which held more rooms or a covered cloister. In certain towns the walls of the convent quadrangle took in a round sunken kiva previously used by the Indians. Rooms in the patio were planned for teaching classes, for cooking, dining, and storage of grain and other supplies.

Nowhere in the church or its convento, excepting an arched doorway at Pecos, was there a curved wall line, or arch, or dome. As the walls rose to their limit, the purpose of the wider wall became plain. Down on the ground the great tree beams were about to be hoisted up to span the church. Their weight needed a heavy support, and the dozens of men on top of the wall, working to bring them up, needed room to stand. The wide wall made a fulcrum for the great levers of the beams, and served as a broad platform on which men could work. Scaffolding was little used. Indians had ladders by which to enter their houses and kivas from the roof, and these were put to work too in acts of building. As the church walls achieved their height, carved wooden corbels were laid into the bricks to support crossbeams. Oxen dragged one timber at a time to the base of the walls and men hauled it upright, tipping it against the massive fulcrum at the top, and laying it across the nave. Such beams, or vigas, were of unequal length. Their ends projected beyond the walls and were often left so. Now between the beams were placed branches of uniform size to close the ceiling, and above these rose the parapet of the walls high enough to hide a man. Crenellations were let into the parapet for sighting with musketry or arrows. Over the whole roof went load after load of loose earth, which was packed down by feet, and hardened by water and sun.

The river churches followed two designs. One was that of a long, narrow, straight box; the other that of a cross, with shallow transepts. Where the transepts occurred, the builders lifted a higher roof over them and the sanctuary in a gesture of grace; for where this higher portion rose above the long nave, they placed a clerestory window, reaching the width of the nave, that took in the light of the sky and let it fall upon the altar, while the rest of the interior remained in shadow. The only other occasional windows were two or three small, high openings in the thinner of the long side walls.

Entering by the main door, anyone had his attention taken to the altar by many cunningly planned devices of which the first was the pour of wide and lovely light from the clerestory whose source was hidden by the ceiling of the shadowy nave. The builders used the science of optical illusion in false perspectives to make the nave seem longer, the approach to heaven and altar more august and protracted. The apse, tall and narrow, tapered toward the rear wall like the head of a coffin. Where there were transepts, the body of man was prefigured all evidently—the head lying in the sanctuary, the arms laid into the transepts, and all the length of the nave the narrow-ribbed barrel and the thin hips and the long legs inert in mortal sacrifice. Many churches added one further symbol and illusion: the rear wall of the sanctuary was built upon another axis than that of the nave. It suggested two things—the fall of Christ's head to one side as He hung on the cross; the other, a farther dimension to the house that honored Him. All such variation of symmetry, and modification of perspective, combined with inexact workmanship and humble materials, resulted in an effect of spontaneity and directness, like that in a drawing made by a child to fulfill a great wish. The wish, the emotion, transcended the means, and stood embodied forth in grave impersonal intimacy.

Over the adobe texture was placed by the women a plaster of mud. They applied it with the palms of their hands and sometimes smoothed it with a patch of sheepskin, bearing fleece. The outer walls in time bore the same marks of the weather as the ancient natural forms of earth all about—little watercourses that ran, making wrinkles which, when dry, came to resemble the marks of life in an old sun-browned face. And yet, with even such sensitive response to the elements, an unattended adobe building weathered down only one inch in twenty years. In any proper town the walls were replastered after every rainy season. The walls were renewed so long as human life used them. Some stood for centuries after being abandoned, and still stand in part, above talus of their own yielding as they go ever so slowly to the earth.

The interior walls received a coat of whitewash and on this in pure colors the people painted designs, as though they were decorating great unrolled surfaces of clay pots. Scrolls, parrots, columns; flowers and cornstalks; symbols of sun, rain, lightning, thunder, and the oblique slantings of terraced forms that took an impression of the landscape receding from the river. Many of the frescoes had not only an Indian but also a strangely Byzantine air, as though a new hybrid culture must turn back to relive all the stages of its various influences.

Finally, before the front of the church, a walled enclosure was completed where the blessed dead could lie, and where, against the façade an outdoor altar could be set in a sort of atrium to accommodate large crowds on feast days and Sundays.

From a little distance, then, the finished building gave its purpose with hard grandeur in its loom and weight, its grace of plain angular shadow, and the wide sunlight on its unbroken faces, where the shadows of the vigas bladed down the walls, making a sundial that told not hours but centuries. The whole mission with church, convento, cloister, and walled burial field seemed like a shoulder of earth emerging out of the blind ground as a work of living sculpture. To see the true beauty of those structures it was necessary first of all to love and to believe in their purpose.

With the establishment of the "missions of occupation" came the need of a train to bring supplies from Mexico every three years. An invoice of 1620 showed, aside from common tools and builders' supplies, a variety of foodstuffs, clothing, and articles of religious use. The Father President at Domingo received for distribution many boxes of salt pork, cheese, shrimps, haddock, dogfish; lima beans, lentils, frijoles; rosemary and lavender; white sugar, salt, pepper, saffron, and cinnamon; preserved peaches and quinces and sweetmeats; noodles, Condado almonds, Campeche honey, Castile rice, cloves, ginger, and nutmeg; and wine, olive oil, and Castile vinegar. On his lists he checked frying pans, brass mixing mortars, tin wine vessels with pewter dishes, and leather wine bags. To clothe his friars he noted Córdoban shoes, Mexican sandals, leggings, kidskin hats with cords, sackcloth and Rouen linen in bolts; and to work these materials, papers of pins, sixteen hundred needles, twenty-four pounds of thread, and fifty-two pairs of scissors. To take the missioners on their visits he issued travelling bags for bedding, and leather saddlebags and saddles and heavy Michoacan cloth of tents, and tin boxes in which to carry the Host. For the infirmaries he checked one hundred and seven Mexican blankets.

To furnish the altars he distributed frontals of Chinese damask, with borders of brocatel and fringes of silk, and lined with Anjou linen; figures of Christ on crosses four and a half feet high; pairs of brass candlesticks and snuffing scissors; an octagonal wooden tabernacle over six feet tall, lined with gold leaf and its panels painted in oil with sacred likenesses; several large paintings framed in gold; a pall of red damask edged with brocade; vessels of tin, silver, and copper for water and wine; and handbells for the consecration. He bestowed silver challices lined with gold plating, and gold patens, and bound missals "recently revised," and tin chrismatories, and processional candelabra of gilt wood, and choir books, and a brass lamp. For sanctuary floors he sent Turkish carpets. The Father President assigned vestments to the missions—chasubles, stoles, maniples, dalmatics, and copes, of various materials: velvets from Granada and Valencia; brocades from Toledo, enriched with designs by the embroiderers whose craft came long before from the Netherlands; "small shirts of Chinese goods to be used as surplices" by altar boys; and for the friars albs and surplices of Rouen linen and lace. He gave them rosaries and breviaries and little iron moulds in which to make the wafers of the Host. For the towers he sent bronze bells, and for High Mass sets of musical instruments—flageolets, bassoons, and trumpets; and incense, and wax, and four quires of paper, and oddments like a gross of little bells, and macaw feathers, and twelve bundles of glass beads, and ecclesiastical certificates on which to record the large stages of life, and twelve plowshares with steel edges to help all become self-sustaining on their riverside fields. The Father President's catalog was a history in itself.

And when the mission was built and furnished, it was both fortress and sanctuary. When outside its blind heavy walls a wind rose, there within were peace and security, where the many candle flames never wavered as they shone on flowers of colored paper. "It all looked very holy," remarked a friar of such a church in 1634. And yet, if he knew Spain and its sacred treasures, he perhaps looked upon his mud walls and his rough-chiselled timbers and bitterly told himself that here he had contrived no beauty or splendor, re-

membering such an altar vessel as the monstrance of Toledo that
took nine years to fashion out of three hundred and thirty pounds
of silver, until it was eight and a half feet high, with two hundred
and sixty small statues amongst jewelled pillars, so that in its exposi
tion the Blessed Sacrament appeared to hover in midair surrounded
by a shining cloud. He could only say to himself that there was
work to be done as well as possible with the materials at hand. End-
ing his day only to dedicate the morrow, he recited the prayer written by his founder Saint Frances that said ". . . grant that I may
not so much seek to be consoled as to console; to be understood as
to understand; to be loved as to love; for it is in giving that we receive; it is in pardoning that we are pardoned; and it is in dying
that we are born to eternal life."

And when the morrow came, there were many tasks to guide.
The convento and the church were staffed by Indians—a bell ringer,
a cook, two or three sacristans, a porter, two boys who kept order in
the friars' cells, some women to grind corn, an old man who
scratched at the beginnings of a garden within the clay walls of the
patio. Without seeing themselves so, the Franciscan priests of the
early river were great artists of community life. If they desired to
bestow and maintain the standards of civilization in their wilderness, they had first to show the Indians the whole image of the cultivated life that came from Europe. Many of the friars were extraor-
dinarily versatile, and most of them were wholly without that pride
of learning which, in the universities and coteries of the day, often
allowed both the scholar and his knowledge to die unused by life.
The friars put their learning to work.

Lessons were organized and conducted with discipline. At dawn
every day but Sunday the bellman went to ring the church bell for
Prime. The pupils, young and old, came to the classrooms, which
they at once swept out. They then took their places and the pastor
came to teach.

He was quick at languages, and for immediate understanding of
the Indians, learned the native tongues rapidly, and taught the
Christian story in the people's own words. The earliest book to be
printed in the New World appeared in Mexico in 1539 under the
imprimatur of Zumárraga, the first Bishop of Mexico. It was a catechism in Spanish and Nahuatl. Some of the friars came to the river
after preaching for years in Mexico in the native dialects. Once having reached the understanding of the Indian, they developed it with
classes in many subjects. They first taught Latin so that the re-

sponses at Mass and vespers could properly be made. Eventually they taught Spanish so that daily life might link the wilderness people to the all-powerful source of national life in Madrid. The Indians learned to speak and to write in those new ways, through which such amazing information came to them. The past found a way to exist in the Indian mind.

Along with words, the Indians learned music. Boys were formed into choirs and trained in the sacred chants of the Church. In one pueblo, out of a thousand people who went to school the pastor chose and trained a "marvelous choir of wonderful boy musicians." In another, the singing boys "with their organ chants . . . enhanced the divine service with great solemnity." Winter and summer, in the river dawns and twilights, the heavenly traceries of the polyphonic style rose to the blunt clay ceilings of the coffinlike churches; and the majestic plainness of antiphonal chants echoed from sanctuary to nave as the people together stolidly voiced the devotions composed by Fray Geronimo Ciruelo and shipped north to the river in 1626. A little organ with gilt pipes went to Santa Fe in 1610, and a few decades later eighteen of the kingdom's churches had organs. The friars taught how to play them, and how to make and play stringed musical instruments, and flutes, and bassoons, and trumpets, after the models shipped in from abroad. On great feast days, the level Indian voices were enriched by ardent stridencies from pierced cane, hollowed gourd, and shaped copper. A tradition lasting centuries had an imitation of nature at work in the worship of the Mass. From the choir loft over the main door of the church came first softly, then mounting in sweet wildness, the sounds of a multitude of little birds calling and trilling in controlled high spirits. On the gallery floor a dozen little boys lay before pottery bowls half filled with water. Each boy had a short reed pierced at intervals which he fingered. He blew through one end while the other rested in the water, from which rose the liquid notes of songbirds adoring God. At the elevation of the Host or other moments of high solemnity it was proper on great feast days to fire a salute of musketry amid the rolling of the bells.

The Franciscan school taught painting. Indians learned not so much how to hold a brush or use color—they knew that—as how to see, look, formalize a representation. A whole new notion of what the world looked like came to the Indians; yet without greatly affecting their decorative styles, for they continued to draw more the spirit, the idea of a subject, than its common likeness.

Joy and laughter were praised by Saint Francis, and there was no
reason why the river fathers should not by these means as well as
any other reach into the minds and hearts of their taciturn children.
The Spanish delight in theatre, scarcely a hundred years old, was already a deeply rooted taste; and the friars, like the lay colonists,
gave plays on suitable occasions. In the pueblos, the comedies were
meant to instruct as well as entertain. Ancient Nativity stories were
acted out by well-rehearsed Indians, who not only took the parts of
the Holy Family and their ecstatic attendants but also represented a
little party of Indians in their own character. When in the play it
was asked who were these strangers come to attend the birth of the
Infant Savior, the answer said that they too were men for whom the
Son of God was born on earth that He might save them. A dignify-
ing love reached out to the Indians in the audience. Sometimes the
plays were hilarious, and all could laugh at the embarrassments and
defeats cleverly visited upon Satan, whose exasperation would know
no bounds. Any play telling the story of people brought a sense of
community and self-discovery.

The Franciscan teaching turned everywhere, lifted up the soil,
planted new seeds, and put the soil back. Among the first new crops
was one directly related to the Mass. Cuttings of fine grapevines
were brought across the sea from Spain and sent up the long trail
from Mexico—a light red grape and a purple one, from which the
fathers made sacramental white and red wines. New fruits were set
out in orchards—peaches, apples, pears, plums, cherries, quinces,
figs, dates, pomegranates, olives, apricots, almonds, pecans, walnuts.
Later, when the missions rose by the river at the gateway to Mexico,
lemons and nectarines were planted to thrive in the mild winters,
and oranges, which had first been planted in the New World by
Bernal Díaz del Castillo landing with Cortés. Together with the
fields of newly introduced vegetables, the orchards were irrigated
from the river with improved methods long known to the friars
from their Mediterranean culture. With the foundation of horses,
cows, and sheep brought by the colony, the friars taught the Indians
how to herd and how to breed the animals for improvement of the
stock. There were workable resources in the kingdom observed by
the well-educated priests, who said that with patience and labor
much could be done with the ores in the mountains. The treasure
hunters had come and gone, unwilling to work for what they
wanted. New Mexico was officially reported as a poor country. But
a Father President of the Franciscan province in 1629 disagreed:

"As for saying that it is poor, I answer that there nowhere in the world has been discovered a country richer in mineral deposits." He listed the very localities of the river kingdom where he had seen deposits, and went on scornfully to say that all such news meant nothing to the Spaniards in Mexico, who, if they had merely a good crop of tobacco to smoke, were content. It seemed odd to him that they should be so indifferent, when Spaniards "out of greed for silver and gold would enter Hell itself to get them."

But the chance and toil of the freight trains to and from Mexico could not be lightly ignored. The regular service to supply the missions was established in 1617. Trains left for the north every three years, and took the better part of a year to complete the journey. Escorted by a handful of hard soldiers and driven by Mexican Indians, about thirty cottonwood carts drawn by oxen came over the gritty trail in movements as slow as the high turns of astronomy by which, like ships at sea, they made their course. They passed among enemies and at the Northern Pass (the site of El Paso, Texas), came to the Rio del Norte, whose source, they said, was at the North Pole. This was easy to believe, in the absence of maps visualizing the unknown country above New Mexico, for the river had an arctic character, "during the months of November, December, January and February . . . frozen over so solid that iron-bound wagons, heavily laden," crossed on the ice, and "vast herds of cattle" went over it at full gallop. "To the same extreme," they noted, "this land suffers from the heat during the months of June, July and August, for even in the shade of the houses tallow candles and salt pork melt."

The freighters saw the Manso Indians about the river at the Pass, who ate their fish and meat raw and bloody, not even cleaning the entrails, but devoured it all "like animals." With mineral powders of different colors rubbed on their nakedness they looked fierce, despite their "good features." As the years passed, and the trains came and went in their crawling regularity, these people about the ford at the Pass came to know the Franciscans and in them grew the desire to be Christians. In time they were taken farther north on the river, near to the Piro pueblos, which were the first of the river towns reached by northbound travellers, from Nuñez Cabeza de Vaca to the supply trailers of the seventeenth century; and there they found their missions. It was the policy of the religious province wherever possible to bring together compatible Indian peoples, the better to instruct large numbers, and to insure common defense. Pueblos

grew. Ways were traded. New dimensions of human life reached
out from the river. Tucked away in the lumbering carts were richly
printed little gazettes and random news sheets from the printing
shops in Mexico. So came news of the great world, the gossip of
government and religion and Spanish bulletins in science and philosophy, to the remote fastnesses of spirit and education in the river
kingdom of the north.

Knowledge, a full mind, made a companion in the empty wilds
when the friars went forth from their clay citadels to preach among
the Indians far east or west of the river. They might be accompanied by a dozen soldiers "more," as a Father President said, "for the
pious sentiment of not abandoning such a sacred enterprise than for
protection or defense, which would have been very limited considering the large number of people they were to meet, all as skillful at
arms as they were tenacious in their wars." The friars, he said,
"know much hardship in crossing the river each time their ministering demands it, since the river is very swift and subject to bad
floods." But all was endurable in the natural world for the sake of
that which came to pass in the spirits of those whom they sought in
simplicity and love. An Indian cacique came to a father missioner,
bringing him a marvelously tanned buffalo hide. Unfolding it, the
friar saw a painting that showed a green sun and a gray moon, and
above them each a cross.

"What does this painting mean?" he asked, and the cacique replied:

"Father, until now we have not known other benefactors greater
than the sun and the moon. They light us and warm us, and make
our plants produce and the flowers germinate. Thus because of so
many benefits we have worshipped them as the arbiters of our lives.
But since we heard you tell us who God is who created the sun and
the moon, in order that you may know that we now worship only
God, I had these crosses, which are the emblem of God, painted
above the sun and the moon."

And there were other simple evidences of the new reach of spirit
and understanding. If once the Indians were creatures of blind destiny, denied by fear the state of the responsible individual, they now
had an instrument of self-knowledge and mercy and they used it serious as children. "When they come to confession," wrote a pastor,
"they bring their sins, well studied, on a knotted string, indicating
the sins by the knots. . . ."

So, two simplicities met throughout most of the sixteenth and seventeenth centuries, until strife between the civil and religious authorities tore apart the hierarchical form of the Spanish society; and the Indians, over whom they strove, seeing the fierce weakness of which they were the disputed prize, revolted in 1680, destroyed much of the colony, drove its remainder downriver to the North Pass, and held their old lands for themselves for twelve years. They were unproductive years. The Indians were divided. Their ancestral ways persisted, yet were qualified by their Spanish teachings, which lingered; and in 1692 the Spaniards victoriously returned, led by the Captain-General de Vargas, who subdued the revolt, rebuilt Spanish towns, and made the same brave gestures as the first conquerors.

But now the great river country was known for what it was—barren, lacking gold, locked in distance, populated by peoples difficult to unite and lost in traditions which would seem forever resistant to complete reformation along Iberian lines. The crown government lost interest in its outlandish Rio Grande possession. A conquest became a mere holding action; and because a flag, and a cross, had been planted, a colony was maintained, unimaginably far away from its life-source, out of missionary resignation to vocation and royal habit. But the great world seemed farther and farther away, and at last, in the eighteenth century and much of the nineteenth, a local style of life took possession of the Spanish and Mexican people who remained. For duty or habitude—since each generation of human beings come to accept more readily what they know for themselves than what their elders remember and would preserve— the Spaniard's Mexican sons, and their New Mexican grandsons, made life along the great river of the Southwest in terms at last closer to the land than to the half-forgotten splendors of a once energetic foreign heritage.

3 · Hacienda & Village

i

Land &
House

The riverside groves were deep and cast a sweet chilling shade. In their silence, their dampness in the low ground, the composite sound of the river reached far along the cottonwood or poplar aisles. Silky flow could be heard, and little incidents of suck and seep, and the murmur of ducks talking, and the blurred clap of wings as a blue heron clambered slowly from mud bar to sky. Willow stands made little green rooms open to the air. Cutting through the boskies, the main ditch opened its mouth upstream at the riverbank to take in flow for irrigation. It was a ditch perhaps six feet broad, four feet deep. It had wooden gates and sluices. From its artery ran narrow shallow veins to the various fields. When the light was low and the earth was darkening, these little channels looked to hold quicksilver. In full noon, their water was seen to be heavy with mud, brown and sluggish.

But their work was visible in the green of the fields, which gave cool air to anyone who rode by them. Feed for animals grew there, and vegetables for the families who lived beyond the fields that separated them from the river. Orchards lay at the end of the field. Facing anywhere, the immediate land was flat. A few miles away mountains rose up, and against their hazy screens the slim poplars and broad cottonwoods of the foreground were dark. The clear deserts beyond the valley were cooked by the sun to give off an herby sweetness in the air, which travelled to the groves and fields and, mixing with their blue dampness and the rich muddy breath of the river, made an earthy smell that caused a pang of well-being and memory of place in those who now and then inhaled with sudden awareness.

The farms lay in narrow strips inland from the river. The earliest New Mexico grant under title was given in 1685. Where several clustered side by side, there were common enterprises. Cattle and sheep were grazed in the foothills rising away from the bottom lands, and tended for all by herders from not one farm but several. Corrals lay near to the house.

The house of a big hacienda was an image in earth of the family. Through generations it grew as the family grew. Its life faced inward. The outer walls were blind against the open country with its Indian dangers, and were entered by wide covered passageways as deep as a room, and barred with heavy wooden doors that were secured with massive iron locks. Within, the rooms all opened on a patio in which trees grew, that in time towered over the roofs. Where the clay hives of the classic Indian towns grew upward in terrace above terrace, the hacienda, built of the same materials, and using many of the pueblo's details in style and method, expanded along the ground in a single story. Beginning with one system of rooms about a square patio, the house, as new lives came, grew into another patio, and even another. The walls were often three feet thick, built of weighty adobe blocks and plastered with earth mixed with straw. Ceiling beams were peeled tree poles, and between them were laid peeled sapling sticks, often in a herringbone pattern. Windows facing the patio held sections of selenite or small panes of imported glass, and were shuttered with carved wooden panels, hung from iron or leather hinges or upon round wooden pegs fitted into carved wooden rings. The floors were of packed earth. Within the patios, an extension of the roof made a porch on all sides that was supported with wooden pillars and carved, scrolled corbels. In their plan—a succession of squares, either extended in line or grouped in checkerboard—the great earth houses might recall in their humble way the grille of the Escorial Palace.

In feudal containment, the river house threw its high clay wall around all the purposes and needs of its life. There was a great room, or *sala,* for grand occasions—dances, receptions, family gatherings. A family chapel sat at one corner of the oldest patio, and over its door might be a belfry with a bell from Mexico. Each parental bedroom was also a sitting room with its own fireplace. The kitchen was a long room where the family sat down to meals. Near it were long dark storerooms in one of which meat and game were hung. In another, dried fruits were stored, and piñones in bags, and grain of wheat and corn in jars. Beyond the walls of these rooms, and reached by a heavy rear gate, sparkled a little ditch, bringing a vein of water from the main ditch that drank of the river. Rooms for servants ran along the rear. A blacksmith shop with forge, anvil, and leather bellows and a tool house with carpentry supplies and hides stood side by side in a work patio, where pens for chickens and sheep, a stable for horses and a shed for milk cows closed the square. The soft lumber of the cottonwood, that yet weathered so well, turning a silvery gray and drying to hardness, was used for posts, rails, pegs, and joists.

The interior walls of the dwelling rooms and the inside patio walls were finished in a glowing white plaster of gesso, or gypsum, which occurred in deposits near the river, as at Cochiti. It was powdered and mixed with water, and applied by the family women with a soft pad of woolly sheepskin, in a craft that was common to the Moors of North Africa, the Spaniards of the homeland, and the Indians of the river pueblos. Around the base of the walls, rising two feet above the floor, a dado was painted with plaster made from the most colorful hue of the local earth—red or yellow or sienna—as a shield for the pure white walls against the dust of the floor. Where black earth could be found, it was mixed with fine sand and moisture until it could be spread on the floors in a smooth thin surface. When it dried hard, it was polished with the bare palm of the hand until it shone again.

In its essential form, the room was simple, and very close to the Indian's. The Indian at first lived on his floor. Later he made an earthen bench that hugged his wall, and if he sat, he had his wall to lean against. His very house was his furniture. The humble Spaniard made his earthen bench too, and in using it was tied to his wall. But the rich Spaniard moved away from the wall to the free center of the room, where he placed furniture, which was heavy, dark, and formal. Its character reflected his. If he sat in his chair, he must sit bolt upright, for the seat was narrow and shallow, its back straight, its arms high and hard, its legs tall. No matter how rich the materials that shaped it—carved wood, polychromed leather, Valencian velvet, Italian fringe and gold bullion lace, Peruvian serge—his repose was fixed in a discomfort that seemed proper to his decorum. His luxuries, even if he was rich, were spiritual, not material. Even the greatest of his kings had preferred to live and work in a bare stone room, taking little physical comfort in the midst of the magnificence that was his to command. In penance—an opinion that could be detected in many Spanish ways of life—in penance resided virtue. It was only suitable that even wealth brought its discomforts to be suffered in patience.

What grandeurs he allowed himself represented the Spanish colonist's pride more than his joy in luxury. There were beauties to be enjoyed in many of the objects accumulated in the river valley by a patriarchal family, and sentiments to be told over as heirlooms descended. Placed against the stark earthen walls of a valley house, imported furnishings and precious objects even at their richest never seemed out of place. Inlaid woods, gold leaf, velvets, crystal, pure silver, turned the master's rooms, which in form were like those of a pueblo, into the apartments of a Castilian palace. Profuse trade with the Indies brought European articles to New Spain, and some of these found their way to the northern kingdom, where they made references of nostalgia, pride, and respect for the past.

In the *sala* was a pair of Castilian *vargueños*—Spain's only invention in furniture—which were wooden chests honeycombed with little drawers and compartments, supported by high legs, and carved, inlaid with ivory and nacre, and studded with worked metals. There were tall straight chairs with leather seats, and stiff armchairs in crimson velvet rubbed pale at the edges. A long narrow table, so high that it could not be slouched over, recalling the style and discipline of the monastery, stood in the middle of the room. Along the unbroken whitewashed wall facing the patio windows across the room was a continuous bench made of wall-earth. It was covered with Indian-made blankets. Above it, for its whole length, fixed to the wall, was a strip of Dutch cotton cloth to protect from the whitewash the shoulders of those who leaned back as they sat. At one end of the room was a wide, deep fireplace. Its hearth was made of flagstones. Heavy iron fire tools stood by its maw. In its chimney face there might have been a design of Valencian tiles, showing birds, leaf and flower forms in dark red and white, or an animal drama, such as a wolf eating a rabbit. If the family had armorial bearings, these were displayed in Valencian blue and white tile. Near the fireplace, on the floor, sat a Mexican chest with heavy iron hinges, lock, and handles. Its panels were like little scenes in a theater, painted in brilliant colors, and illustrating stories of common knowledge. Many mirrors hung along the walls, some framed in gold leaf over carved wood, some in tortoise shell and ivory, some in little facets of mirror set in mosaic along the frame. The Mexico-Orient trade brought curious, gleaming fabrics from China, and for its rarity and strange richness of gold and silver thread, a strip of Chinese brocade was sometimes hung flat on the white wall. By daylight the room was cool and dim, for the patio windows were deep and low, and shaded outside by the overhang of the porch. The room was lighted at night by candles, held in iron candelabra, or others carved of wood, covered with gesso, and finished with gold leaf. The establishment was clean.

This was because there were enough servants and because the lady of the house was an energetic and demanding housekeeper. The bedroom that she shared with her husband revealed her duties and her preoccupations. The bed was big enough for two—thinly mattressed, covered with a richly embroidered spread done in native yarns by the mistress, who copied flowers off a Chinese shawl—and presided over at its head by a blue and gilt statue of Our Lady of Guadalupe. Clothes were kept in chests of leather studded with brass nails, or of carved unpainted wood. Indian rugs were on the hand-rubbed floor. There was a fireplace, and by the window stood a small worktable and a chair where the matriarch spent hours at her work. On the table was her mother-of-pearl needle case. Next to it was a Moorish box of tortoise shell, ivory,. and teakwood, which held her silver scissors, a little penknife, her spools of thread, her

gold thimble, and a magnifying glass in a silver-gilt handle. There
she embroidered altar cloths, bedspreads, tablecloths, linens, and
taught her daughters her skill. If they married, each must know, as
she had known, how to work on handkerchiefs with strands of her
own hair the name of her husband. They must be able to embroider
with beads. She kept little glass phials filled with beads of different
colors and with them made scenes, flowers, birds, and sentiments on
muslin strips. Vestments had to be embroidered and repaired. There
was a rage for poodles in eighteenth-century polite society, for the
King of Spain was a French Bourbon and the poodle was a French
dog. Ladies—in Mexico and New Mexico—sewed elaborate little
backgrounds into which tiny china poodles could be stitched, and
the whole framed and displayed in the *sala*. Callers admired these
objects and spoke of them as "very European"—always the highest
compliment a colonial could pay. A pair of silver daggers lay on the
bedroom table. On the deep window sill were a copper bowl and
pitcher, and by them stood a dark blue drinking glass ornamented
with golden roses and an inscription in gold that said "My Love."
In a corner was a long row of boots belonging to the master, a pair
for every task, as they showed, from walking in the river mud, to
riding spurred, to dancing in the *sala*. In the same corner leaned a
musket that was always loaded. On a wall of the bedroom hung a
likeness of Our Lady of Succor, embroidered on red velvet in
lifelike colors, her robe studded with baroque pearls. She was the
patroness of the river kingdom. It was impossible to pass her a
dozen times a day without each time in half-awareness wafting to
her a thought, a prayer, for protection for the house, its lives, and all
its possessions.

The kitchen was in many ways the richest room in the house. Its
graduated copper pots, hanging above the fireplace and its iron
oven, shone like treasure. On its wooden shelves gleamed rows of
dishes and glass. There was blue glass from Puebla—pitchers, mugs,
goblets. There were cups and tumblers and vases of glass, milk-
white and clear and colored, from La Granja de San Ildefonso in
the province of Toledo. There were deep cups and saucers of Tala-
vera pottery out of which to drink chocolate, and large breakfast
bowls of the same ware. Porcelain from China, Majolica from Mexico, jugs and bowls from the pueblos of the river stood on wooden
shelves or tiled ledges in the kitchen. Wood was used for utensils
too, long trough-shaped *bateas,* or bowls, in which clothes were
washed, or vegetables, or dishes. Large trays and bread plates were

fashioned out of cottonwood and, after use, were washed and set on edge to drain and dry. From much handling through many years, they were good to touch—smooth, softly polished, and loved through work. The kitchen furniture was not so grand as that in the *sala*. It was of plainly made, unfinished wood—long table, chairs, and benches. Against a wall stood several *trasteros*. These were tall cabinets with locked double doors whose upper panels were latticed, or pierced in designs, and inlaid with mosaic patterns of common straw that gleamed like gold. Through these openwork panels shone the highlights of the family silver. When the *trastero* doors were unlocked and swung open, the shelves revealed large silver platters, trays, and bowls standing on edge. There were piles of silver dinner plates, and rows of cups and saucers, mugs, pitchers, chocolate pots; knives, forks, and spoons. Some of it was made in Spain, and bore Spanish hallmarks; much of it in Mexico. All of it was heavy, almost pure in its silver content and, except for any blazons proudly belonging to the family, plain. Light struck from its surface as from water, with a faint suggestion of ripple that added richness of texture to weight of substance. Though massive, the silver pieces had grace, and though treasured, they bore the little pits and dents of daily use. To eat in the kitchen, off silver—in this were both the Spaniard's earthy simplicity and his pride.

His spirit he took across the main patio to the family chapel, entering through panelled doors that held the carved keys of Saint Peter and the Spanish Crown, side by side, the Two Majesties. The chapel was a small, plain room with an altar at the end. A crucifix of dark wood stood on the altar between candlesticks. The body of Christ was carved to show His agony, with drops of blood in relief and painted red, at brow, side, hands, and feet—symbol of a sacrifice never to be forgotten by the family, and lesson to sustain them in their own commonplace daily sufferings. The altar was clothed in a frontal of imported velvet or brocade; or if such was not to be had, in a *colcha* embroidery done at home, of dyed yarns, representing large flowers, leaves, and fruit. The family's favorite saints, in various representations, stood on pedestals or hung on the walls in paintings. To them, in mute appeal for aid in particular causes, were affixed little votive images called *milagros*. If a hand was injured, if an ear ached, if rheumatism crippled a leg; if a cow was sick; if sheep were threatened by mountain lions, little silver likenesses of these members or creatures were pinned to a saint in perpetual intercession for relief. A thoughtful household, obtaining these from Mexico, kept a supply on hand in a little velvet-covered casket and produced them as needed. The head of the household conducted family prayers in the chapel, and when the priest came, the altar was dressed with wild flowers and lighted with extra candles; a set of vestments kept for the purpose was produced; and all heard Mass. Those families who lived near towns went on Sunday to the town church. Albuquerque in the latter half of the eighteenth century was empty all week, but on Sunday was alive with the families who rode or drove from the river farms to attend services at Saint Philip of Neri's.

ii

Fashion

They wore their best for such an occasion. Indian servants kept their traditional dress, which showed little change since the Spanish colonization, except for woollen blankets which they had learned to make. Half-castes, and the poor soldiery serving time in New Mexico instead of in prison, and an occasional trail-driver, and the valley farmhands appeared in red, blue, or brown suits made of *jerga,* a coarse woollen serge woven in the province. Their hats were flat-brimmed like those of Cordova. The Spanish cloak was replaced by the Mexican serape, which in turn came from the Indian's shoulder blanket. The men's jackets were long-skirted and full-sleeved, and their trouser legs now reached to the foot, having dropped from the knee. All wore boots. A sash wrapped several times about the waist replaced a belt and held small weapons of blade or barrel. The wives of such humble men wore voluminous skirts of *jerga,* and shirts as elaborate as they could afford, over which were sleeveless little coats. On their heads and shoulders the women wore shawls, or rebozos, of bright solid colors, which they folded in a large triangle, and whose points they crossed at the throat to be thrown over the shoulders. The shawls were fringed, and the length of the fringe determined the worth of the article, and the wealth, the position, of its owner.

The leading families—those who called themselves *gentes de razón,* "those who use reason," "the educated ones," "the right people,"—had a handsome variety of dress to choose from, with many colors and precious materials. The men wore fine linen shirts and underclothes. Their suits were of velvet, or of thin soft leather, or French serge, heavy with gold or silver cording in elaborate traceries, and buttoned with gold or silver or diamond-paste buttons. A skirted coat, a short waistcoat, and long skintight trousers buttoned the whole length of the leg from waist to ankle made up such a suit. With it went small arms—dagger, pistol, short sword; a tightly woven serape large enough to cover the whole body when unfolded and slipped over the head by a slit in the center; and a hat, whether a tricorne edged with ostrich plumage, or a cordovan hat with a high crown banded in many rows of gold lace, either sometimes worn over a silk kerchief tied tightly over the head like a cap, and recalling the scarf worn under a steel helmet.

Women of the rich houses followed the fashion of Spain, which changed slowly, so that even if they were far away in time and distance from Madrid and the court, they were in the style in their tight bodices and long sleeves, their low necks, their pinched high waists and their spreading, shining skirts of heavy silk or satin, over which laces were cascaded and looped. They had a choice of rebozos, whether one of white lace, or one of China silk heavy with embroidered scarlet and yellow flowers and green leaves and blue shading and long red fringe, or one of silk that fell like water in plain solid colors, including black, or finally, one of black lace with its designs like the shadows of rose leaves. From their little ivory and velvet caskets they could choose their jewels—emerald and pearl and amethyst and gold earrings, bracelets, rings, and pins; and rose-cut diamonds from Ceylon set in clusters like bouquets; and a Paris-style lorgnette with mother-of-pearl and gold handles with which to follow the Missal and edify an Indian; and gold chains and flexible gold fish and pure gold tassels by the cunning goldsmiths of Germany. If such finery picked up its share of dust in the far valley, still it spoke formally of the proper way to live, wherever.

iii
*Family &
Work*

For in its own scale the family was as rigid and formal as the court of the King in respect to authority, reverence, and responsibility. So long as he lived the father was the lord, to be obeyed, respected, and loved. In turn he must provide the goods of life to those for whose lives he was responsible, and lead them wisely, and guide their work. The mother, in rich family or poor, was the lady of all, and worked harder than any at the endless household duties. Reverence was due to her, for she brought life and gave it to the world, and in doing so through the years received wisdom to which all would do well to listen. If her lord died before her, she until her death was the head of the family, and to the love and respect paid to her was now to be added obedience. Her ways were the right ways, no matter what the world tried to teach. She knew them without learning.

Often in the colonial family, if the father represented the earth's life and its work of seasons and its secrets of strength, the mother was the fire and the spirit, the divined imagination at the heart of things, which she seemed the older she lived to perceive the more brightly. Her sons and daughters dared to risk humor with her, though rarely with their father. The grandchildren and great-grand-children—for the families in their homemade sustenances were long-lived—stood in awe of their august forebears.

Relationships were stabilized, and each had its appropriate man-ner. Matrons of equal age and degree on meeting leaned their faces side by side and each kissed the air murmuring a politeness. Men, in greeting, formally folded each other in their arms, making two quick little slaps on the shoulder. Once a man declared himself *com-padre*—"co-father" or fellow godfather—with another man, he was bound in a friendship that had a sacred duty to remain unbroken. A community in which such fellowships were intershared by all the men was certain of its own harmony, for to break it was almost sac-rilegious, and could occur only through tragedy or passion.

When prayers in the chapel were finished for the day, all filed out past the senior member of the family who had led the prayers, and kissed his hand, genuflecting, in veneration of age. Arriving in a jolting, heavy carriage slung on leather straps, a great-aunt would come to stay with a rich family. She was received by the assembled relatives to whom she gave the most formal greeting. She stiffly put the tips of her small fingers, heavily jewelled, on the shoulders of each in turn. Her Indian maid followed her from the carriage, and men carried her shallow trunk of tanned rawhide that was stitched together in lozenges and squares, showing red flannel in between. The household soon learned her eccentric custom of crying out "Ave Maria" to anyone who took her notice. Who heard her was supposed to pause, cross his arms, and recite the whole prayer si-lently. She invited certain ones to join her in a compact of the Ave Maria. Hooking her right little finger in that of her friend, she led in reciting a charm:

> "How many hours has the day,
> Has Hail Mary whom we pray."

If she made a compact as *comadre,* or "co-mother," "sister god-mother," with another woman, they chanted together:

"Flower basket, scatter never
In this life and in the next,
We'll be *comadres* forever.

Tra-la-la and tra-la-loo
Whoever becomes *comadre*
Divides her heart in two."

To repudiate a shocking statement or action, the cross was invoked by putting the right thumb upright across the right forefinger held level, and saying *"Pongote la cruz"*—"I put the cross on you!"

Children, who wore miniatures of their parents' clothes, early echoed their parents' formality. They soon learned to stop crying over trifles. In their grave, dark, pearly faces with their large black eyes were reflected the animal repose, the spiritual certitude, and the mind's government that so generally marked the temperaments of their elders. These were qualities of order that could be shattered by passion or debauched by folly; but they survived, if not in the individual, then in the ideals of the conservative life he came from, in which the family, however large, remained tightly woven together; and in which a pride of inheritance gave rich and poor alike a dignity becoming to the heirs of Columbus and Cortés and Coronado and Oñate and Vargas, whose deeds and graces begot not only kingdoms but characters. In even his simplest acts the colonial Spaniard seemed to proclaim his proud heritage. For his beliefs and ways required a certain accompaniment of style; and in a remote land, poor in itself, style took effort to maintain. Behind the style of the big river households there was much work, for the men out of doors, for the women within.

While children played in the patio, under the prattling cottonwoods, and talked to their parrots, the mother had many tasks to oversee. For her embroidery and knitting, there was wool to be dyed. Favorite colors came in the Mexican trade—reds and blues from cochineal, indigo, and brazilwood. But these were scarce, and the old Indian dyes, used for centuries on sacred feathers and kachina masks, now colored the threads for embroidering bedspreads, altar cloths, upholstery, and clothing: yellow from rabbit brush, blue from larkspur, pink from the tag alder, blue-green from copper ore. Wool from brown and black sheep was used unchanged. With homespun yarns the women knitted stockings and wove brown and white rugs for the slippery floors. They made toilet soap from animal fats, adding melon seeds, rosemary, wild-rose leaves and bran starch, and grinding the whole mixture to paste, forming it in cakes, and setting them in the sun to dry. To make pomade for their hair, they mixed strained beef marrow, powdered rose leaves, and rosemary. If their skin was too swarthy, they bleached it with a paste prepared from wild raspberry juice mixed with powdered eggshells or ashes of elkhorns, soaked rice, and melon seeds. To hold curls in place, they used thick sugar-water. The women made candles, dipping a long cotton string into melted tallow or beeswax and hanging it up to cool. When it was cool, they dipped it again, and again, until the candle was as big as they liked. In the spring, they gathered up the blankets in the house, heaped them on a cart and drove them to the river to be washed. By the riverside a fire was built, water was heated in big copper kettles, and yucca root was beaten and thrown into a long wooden trough into which hot water was poured. The women, bare-armed and barefooted, knelt by the trough and flailed the water until they made suds. The blankets were then immersed, rubbed, and wrung until the country's unfading dye colors came clear again. At the river's edge, while mockingbirds, larks, and blackbirds swept above them with excitement, they rinsed the heavy cloths in the current, and then spread them in the meadow grass to dry.

If extra help was needed, women came from nearby families, but never to work for pay. Their men would have been offended to have money offered to their women. When the work was done, and the visitors returned home, they were willing to accept a little gift, of "whatever was handy." This had pride, remembering the pretensions of the starving hidalgos of long ago, and also good sense, if on another day the helpers needed help.

Food and drink took much work to produce. The women made spiced wine, simmered in an earthen pot for a day with spices and sugar, sealed with a ring of fresh dough. Sweet cookies were made with twenty-four egg yolks. On a heated metate stone, dense chocolate was made by grinding cocoa beans, stick cinnamon, pecans, and maple sugar—all imported—into a paste which was dried and cut into cakes. Cooked with thick whole milk, these made the black chocolate drink which was served at breakfast, and at four in the afternoon with cookies. The finest tortillas—large, thin, round corncakes—were made from blue corn meal. Three of these, layered with slices of pink onion and curls of yellow cheese and sprinkled with green lettuce and swimming in cooked red chili pepper sauce, made a favorite dish. When men butchered beeves or hogs in the work patio, the beef was cut in strips and dried in the sun, the pork was sliced and soaked in a juice of red chilis, sharp with garlic and salt. Pork fat was diced and fried in deep fat to make cracklings, which were used in place of bacon. A soupbone was used not once but many times, and was even passed from one poor family to another to boil with beans. Women harvested grapes, which they washed, drained in a basket, and hung in a storeroom from the beams to dry into raisins. In the fall, as the Pueblo people had done for centuries, the hacienda women cut up sweet pumpkins and melons, setting the pieces out on stakes to dry. Squashes and plums were dried on cloths spread over the flat roofs. When the cane was mature in the fall, it was time to make syrup, and all helped. Against an outdoor wall near the kitchen was a long oven made of earthen bricks. In its top were six round holes under which a fire was kept hot. The days were often cool and the evenings cold, and as the work was long, bonfires were kept burning to give warmth and light while men with wooden mauls pounded the fresh cane on fat logs, reducing it to a pulp. The pulp was put into a wide barrel, into which a round heavy press was fitted. To the press a long slender timber was attached so that it could rock free like a seesaw. Here now was boys' work, and two climbed on each end of the timber, and as they rode up and down in privileged delight, the press rose and fell, squeezing juice from the pulp which ran through a hole in the barrel's side into a wooden trough. Women took up the juice in dippers made of cut gourds, strained it into clay jars, and set these, six at a time, to boil on the oven until the juice was red and clear. In the bonfire-light after dusk all was animated, purposeful, and satisfactory, and when the first jar was ready, a sample of the syrup was passed about to be tasted by those who had helped to produce it.

The great families had Indian slaves. These were housed with the paid servants, and given lessons in catechism, and promised their freedom so soon as they might be, in the judgment of their owners, civilized enough to sustain it. They were allowed to marry, and their children were born free under the law. Female slaves were ladies' maids and kitchen helpers. Male slaves worked in the fields and among the animal herds. So few goods came by wagon train that the province had to sustain itself, and the raising of cattle and sheep, and the growing of food were the main concern of all. Crops, said a Franciscan survey, were "so limited that each inhabitant scarcely raises enough for himself." But by the middle of the eighteenth century there were millions of sheep grazing on the sparse slopes of the watershed. Between two hundred thousand and five hundred thousand sheep were driven every year to Mexico for sale. The grasses struggled for life in ordinary years and in dry years barely showed. The colonials looked at their hills and shook their heads. It was all very much like Spain, a condition of natural life that seemed impossible to govern. The tilted lands were growing more barren; the torrents—when it did rain—swept faster and cut deeper; the earth ran into the tributaries and into the river, piling up silt on the river floor; the river spilled over its old banks and made swamps on good farm land, and a man could only bow his head and invoke patience. Inherited practice had a firm hold upon him, at the expense of understanding the forces that his use of the land released in violence. Rain made grass, and he lifted up his eyes to look for rain. No other answer occurred to him. Animals had to eat. They had to stay on his own range or be stolen by roving Indians. He watched his sheep for signs of rain, for though they rarely gamboled, they would do so if rain were in the air. Before a rain, said the shepherds, a sheep would draw himself up and bleat and shake himself as though already wet. Before a rain, said the cowherders, a cow would throw her hind legs and bawl.

In May men rode out from the hacienda to help with lambing at the sheep camps. There were always goats with the herds, and when the men returned, they brought home kidskins of long, silky white hair. These were delivered to the mistress, who had them washed with soap and water. When they were dry, cooked sheep brains were rubbed into the hairless side. Set into the sun, the skins became soaked as the brains melted. Washed again, they were dried and worked by hand until they were soft as cloth and pure white. Some were dyed in brilliant colors and used as little hearthrugs in the bedrooms, to keep the feet warm while dressing and undressing by the fire.

All houses kept horses to ride, burros to carry packs, and mules to pull the massive wagons and carriages. Wheels were greased with a homemade lubricant of fat mixed with pine tar. When a family carriage went travelling, it was accompanied by armed outriders and postilions, not for style but for protection against waylaying Indians.

Where water power could be had from a ditch brought close to the house, a mill was set up in a room twelve feet square. The ditchwater turned a wooden wheel outside the walls, and beyond it fell booming into a pool, shaded by willows and huge hairy sunflowers, where the youths of the household bathed and swam. Inside the walls an axle from the wheel turned a massive wooden gear that revolved a pole fixed to a grinding stone. Hanging from the ceiling was a stiff bullhide hopper from which grain fell in a steady stream into the hole of the turning stone and was ground against a circular flat stone eighteen inches thick that was bound to the floor, and enclosed in a bin. The meal was taken from the bin, sacked, and sent to the house, where kitchenmaids spread it out on a large white cloth upon the floor. They sifted it through a swiss-cloth sieve that was made to rise and fall on a smooth pole held upright. One sifting prepared the flour for whole-wheat bread; a second, through a finer sieve, for pastries. This work began with a prayer, before the maids loosed their prattle. Later, setting the dough for bread, they murmured the name of the Holy Trinity, and marked the soft loaves with a cross, to insure a good baking.

After the harvest in the fall, and the threshing of beans, peas, and grains, orders were given by the master for a wagon to set out for the salines beyond the eastern mountains, where the household would obtain its year's supply of salt. As winter came on, outdoor work lessened, and wandering laborers were seen no more till spring. But others came. A tailor might stay for weeks, while he made suits for the family men. A shoemaker might appear with his boxes and tools to repair boots and make new ones with tough bullhide for the foot, and fine Cordovan leather for the tops. Now and then a startling creature or two would appear, dressed in wild stripes and shimmering and chiming with jewelry. These would be gypsies— Turks or Arabs—who came selling medals and rosaries, which they swore came from the Holy Land. Glaring strangely, they smiled over the secret which all knew they had, which was the power to put evil spells. Apprehensively they were made guests, their holy trash was purchased, and presently they moved on to the mingled relief and regret of the family, who saw so few visitors. An occasional government officer would appear from Viceroy's court in Mexico on his way to Santa Fe, and make himself at home. He was treated with respect, for Spaniards accepted authority. They might be skeptical and willing to change the authority under which they lived, but authority there must be. Even if the travelling official gave himself airs—which the farther he went from the capital seemed to grow grander—his hosts smiled. Many odd things came with the law, but the law was powerfully implanted in them from long ago, and its flourishes were in fact a pleasure instead of a nuisance. In any case, hospitality to the visitor was a sacred tradition, and every comfort, all exquisite courtesy were his no matter who he might be. And when off the dusty riverside trails there came a guest who brought with him more than his own simple claim as a man, who in fact was a legal and spiritual descendant of the Twelve Apostles, then the household outdid itself.

Three times during the eighteenth century the successive Bishops of Durango travelled from their cathedral city in New Spain to Santa Fe, the most outlandish town in their province. Each moved by heavy carriage, accompanied by baggage carts, a mounted guard, and various clergy. The Bishop made use of the hospitality of the great river houses. The chapel was thrown open, decorated, and lavishly lighted. His mitre, crozier, and cope were taken from their leather hampers; he was vested; he gave Benediction at the altar and, touring the premises, he blessed the house. Children were told off to be prepared for confirmation, which he would administer on his return from Santa Fe. The kitchen buzzed like a hive and steamed like a hot spring. The whole house sparkled and shone. It was like receiving royalty to have the Bishop and his train. Every last finery from the great cities to the south and over the seas was brought out, and every local grace was displayed with anxiety. The Lord Bishop was gratified, and weighed homage for its true value, which was the pleasure it brought the giver, not the receiver. When he entered his carriage again in his worn black with edges of purple, he looked only like a country priest, and when he drove off on his squealing wheels, he left whirling eddies of thought behind him. According to their temperaments, some members of the household, at this contact of the great world, were more content; others more dissatisfied, with the homely labors, loves, and beauties of family life in the valley.

In late November the yearly market caravan began to assemble, starting at the northernmost river towns, and coming down the valley to pick up wagons at each stop on its way to Mexico. The wagons were loaded with goods and covered with lashed wagon sheets. The cargoes included woollen blankets, dried meat, tanned buffalo and deer hides, strings of red and green chili. These articles would be sold or traded for products of Mexico, the Philippines, China, South America, and Europe. Silver and gold money found its way each year into the province when the train returned. But for the most part, transactions in New Mexico were completed in goods of the country, for almost no hard money circulated. A system of four kinds of pesos, dollars, came to custom among the people: silver dollars, which were very scarce, worth eight *reales,* "royals," or about an ounce of silver; "dollars of the future," worth six royals; "old" dollars, worth four royals; and "dollars of land," worth two royals. As all were called dollars, the Indians and simpler people accepted all as equal; but the traders always reckoned what they bought in "dollars of the land," or cheapest value, and what they sold in silver dollars, or highest value. It was a monetary system based on coinage but activated through barter. Blankets, hides, livestock changed hands instead of money.

iv
Mis-
chance

It was a picture of commerce somehow in harmony with the basic terms of production and survival in the valley estates. For in any day over the fields where the long, thick, low house sat in its boxes of light and shadow the thin distant cry of *"Indios!"* might be raised. The chapel bell would swing full circle until its clapper would now and then cleave to silence like a dry tongue in the mouth. All work was dropped. The men came running in a crouch from the fields. Children were angrily and dearly hauled up from their ditchside play. All streamed to the house, and once within the walls, they shut and barred the thick cottonwood gates. The men took to the roofs where they lay down by the waterspout openings with their muskets. The plumed line of dust that had started to make a circle beyond the fields and close in toward them now was drawing nearer and the nodding gallop of Apache horses could be seen and the naked sprawl of their riders. "At the expense of our blood, with arms in hand," said a householder, they were ready to defend their common life. The attackers might have both arrows and firearms. If they wounded or killed a fellow on the roof, the household swallowed its grief, though confronting death the women usually sought comfort in screams. Muskets fired from the roof. The crazy thieves took casualties. One might come close with a brand, hoping to fire the house. Another one or two might attack the rear gate or try to enter by the mill wheel. A man or a child from the house, who had not gained sanctuary with all others, might be found in the groves, dragged forth to view, and killed and killed, once in body, many times in idea, while the rooftops could only watch, and fire muskets, and rage. But the great house usually stood, though death and suffering had come in, and fields, if dry, might be burned, and ditches be broken and wanton flood result. The attack would be over as quickly as it had come. The swinging line of riders broke apart and their long dust plume died down. Each marauder streaked for the distant mountains by himself. Each made a column of dust that danced over the plain eastward like the little desert whirlwinds, the "sand devils," of hot afternoons. Long later, still watchful, the guards came off the roofs, and damage, wound, and death were reckoned, as mischances were reckoned under the weather, or any other large, hard, and inescapable condition of living.

There were more joyful occasions, and these they made for themselves in the river households. Religious feast days were celebrated with gaiety as well as devotion. In March there were prayers to San Isidro, patron of farmers, when the irrigation ditches were cleared of their golden winter stubble. If a ditch served several families, men from each came to do their share. The weeds were ignited. All day the ditches were watched to see that fire did not spread to the fields. Food was taken out to the watchers, and picnics for all the family sometimes followed. The ditch fires showed after dusk and were guarded all night. At home, the children, before going to bed, went to the heavy patio gates and looked through the cracks at the magic glow across the fields. On June twenty-fourth the water in the river and the ditches was declared holy, for this was the feast day of Saint John, who had baptized Jesus in the river Jordan. Early after sunup the women and girls went to the ditches or to the river and bathed. Good health would follow. When they returned, little children went and then youths and men. This order was observed out of decency, for they were people extremely modest and would not go to bathe in mingled sexes.

The great feast of Christmas was celebrated with food, song, prayer, theatre, and firelight. Special delicacies came out of the kitchen—fried tarts of mincemeat and piñon nuts, white corn tamales, sweet cakes. Little bands of young singers, called the Oremus Boys, went from house to house in the villages, or in a hacienda toured the living quarters, knocking at each door, before which they sang Christmas songs. When their song was done, they received freshly baked sweetmeats. The housetop was illuminated with dozens of lanterns burning candles. All day before Christmas special fires were laid of piñon sticks, in squares of four, and rising to eight or ten rows high. These were placed to outline the plan of a rambling house, or the road of a village, and even the profile of nearby hills. When darkness fell, they were lighted, and in their orderly distribu-

V

Feast

Days

tion, gallant columns of spark and smoke, and spirited crackle, they made a spectacle that delighted all. But they had more purpose than this. By the very signal of that firelight, the Holy Child born that night was to find His way to the homes of those who had made the fires. Boys ran among the bonfires, jumped over them, and dared rebuke. It came, in the form of the *Abuelo* (grandfather), or Bogeyman, who appeared once a year, always at Christmas, to threaten boys with punishment for badness. He carried a great whip which he cracked after them over the bonfires. He was a fright in tatters, with a false voice and a made-up face. They dreaded and dared him, laughingly. He chased them home where he made them kneel down and say their prayers. When he left, they burst out again into the sharp clear night where the aromatic piñon smoke smelled so sweet under a whole sky quivering with stars of Bethlehem.

It was not a season of personal gifts. The greater gift of the infant Jesus came to all in joyful renewal. In the great *sala,* by candlelight, after much whispered preparation, at one end of the room a company of family players appeared in costume to enact the tale of the Nativity, in many scenes, before the rest of the household and guests and neighbors. The shepherds told in verse of the star in the sky. The three kings appeared in finery with their gold, frankincense, and myrrh. At the door of an inn, someone knocked and sang, and all knew it was Saint Joseph.

> Where is there lodging
> For these wandering ones
> Who come so tired
> From long hard roads?

To this the landlord replied:

> Who knocks at the door
> In imprudent disturbance,
> Forgetting how late,
> And awakes all the house?

In the audience all knew what was coming but the littlest ones, and they learned and would never forget, as Saint Joseph sang:

> Sir, I beg of you
> In all your charity
> To give shelter to this Lady.

It was anguish to know the sufferings of that small and Holy Family when the landlord, reminding all of what mankind was capable, answered in his hardness:

My house awaits
Him who has money.
May God help him
Who has none.

So the scene shifted to a stable where, through a window, an ox and a mule put their heads, and where, attended by angels and visited by the three kings, the Child of the world was born again in the midst of homely music and passionate belief.

At midnight the patio was alight with fires and all moved to the chapel for services. Sometimes a priest from the town church was on hand, and held midnight Mass. At the elevation of the Host, the bell was rung, and with a hot coal a special salute was touched off from gunpowder poured on the blacksmith's anvil and covered by a big flagstone.

Other than fixed feast days, marriages were the highest occasions. There was no courtship. One day the father of a promising youth, accompanied by the boy's godfather or best friend, called upon the father of a suitable girl and presented a letter, or made a formal speech, proposing marriage between the two young people. No answer was expected immediately. Pleasantries were exchanged over cups of chocolate, and the callers withdrew. After a few weeks, the call was returned, with a refusal or an acceptance. If accepted, the bridegroom may have heard something earlier that told him of his happiness, for the house of the bride's family would be redecorated throughout for the wedding, and news of unusual activity in her household perhaps travelled. Neighboring families might be joined by the marriage, or families living far apart. Cousins in the second and third degree frequently married, for the great families took pride in keeping intact their pure Castilian blood, and to do so, where there were fewer Spanish than mixed strains, would marry within the clan. Once the date had been agreed upon, preparations went forward too in the groom's family, until at last they were ready to set out for the home of the bride. They went in their jarring carriage. In a wagon behind them came the groom's contributions to the wedding—all the food for the feast and cooks to prepare it; the leather trunks carrying the bride's wedding gown and her whole trousseau; and other gifts.

When they arrived, the groom's parents were given the freedom of the house, for they were to be in charge of the whole wedding fes-

vi

Wedding
Feasts

tivity. The godparents of both bride and groom were there too, and would serve as best man and matron of honor, and counsel the young couple until they were married. Marriage was a sacrament. The godparents had solemn duties in connection with such a great stage in life. The betrothal took place as soon as the wedding party was complete. All relatives gathered in the *sala,* where the families came together. The bride's father brought her forward and presented her to the groom's father saying, "Here is she whom you sought." The groom's father introduced her to all his own people, and then introduced the groom to all her family. It was possible that this was the first meeting of the betrothed. All then turned toward the bride's godfather, before whom the young couple knelt down on white cushions, while he solemnized the engagement by putting a rosary of corals or pearls—the two precious sea growths from the faraway Pacific—first over the groom's head and then over the bride's.

Now the trunks were brought in from the groom's wagon and presented to the bride. They were taken unopened to her bedroom, where a few privileged girls could see their contents with her. Happiness and importance filled the air now as the preparations for the wedding went rapidly ahead. It would follow the next day. The bride stood for her godmother to see if the wedding dress needed alteration, and tried on all the other clothes. The visiting cooks went to work, helped by the resident cooks. The mud ovens outdoors were heated up. The groom's comestibles were noticed, to determine if he was generous or stingy. Musicians arrived. Lanterns were put everywhere in the open. If the time of year permitted, the patio was decorated and used. Pine boughs were tied to the posts of the *portal* all around the court. Guests kept coming to stay. Kegs of wine, flagons of brandy from El Paso were set about. If the chapel was large enough for all, the wedding would take place there; but if it wasn't, an altar was set up in the patio or the *sala,* where the priest could administer the sacrament of holy matrimony. He would do this only with the provision that at the first opportunity the married couple must come to town, bringing their godparents, to hear a nuptial Mass and receive the blessing in church.

At last all was ready, and the engaged youth and maiden, who though under the same roof since their betrothal had kept away from each other, now met again before the altar in the evening, accompanied by their godparents. They were married in candlelight, with the hand-shaped earthen walls of their family about them, and a burden upon them of solemn commitment. Tensions broke when the vows were done. All gathered in the *sala* for the wedding feast. Now a river house had put forth another reach of growth and promise of the future, all in proper observance of ways that were as old as memory. In her white silk wedding dress the bride went on the arm of her husband in his rich silver-braided suit and his lace-ruffled shirt. Everyone came past to embrace them, and then the feast began. Roast chicken basted in spiced wine and stuffed with meat, piñons, and raisins; baked hams; ribs of beef; fresh bread of blue meal; cookies, cakes, sweets; beakers of chocolate and flasks of wine, bowls of hot chili; platters of tortillas, all stood upon extra tables draped to the floor with lace curtains. All feasted.

Then came music, and dark eyes fired up. The *sala* was cleared, while the musicians tuned up on two or three violins, a guitar, and a *guitarrón,* or bass guitar. Servants came to spread clean wheat straw on the earth floor to keep dust from rising, or stood by with jars of water from which to sprinkle the floor between dances. In the candlelight the faces of the women, heavily powdered with Mexican white lead, looked an ashen violet, in which their eyes were dark caves deeply harboring the ardent emotion of the occasion. The orchestra struck up. They danced quadrilles and minuets, whose figures drew all dancers into fleeting touch with each other. There were paired dances, like *la raspa,* with its heel thunderings and its laughing fast walk. There were marching dances, accompanied by spoken verses invented on the spot by someone who was famous as an improvisor. He would go to stand before a guest, bow, and without an instant's groping for what to say, recite an improvised ballad of eight-syllabled lines paying compliment to his subject whom he faced. He celebrated the beauty, charm, and talent of the bride, weaving in episodes of her childhood, alluding to her gallant ancestry, and promising her a dazzling future. The groom he saluted in another decima as a superb horseman and buffalo hunter, or trail-driver, or heir of an illustrious house. Sometimes he sang a riddle poem, and all tried to guess the answer.

While the dancing went on, the bride had an obligation to fulfill. Retiring from the floor in her wedding dress, she reappeared presently in another gown from her trousseau, and later in another, and another. Everyone was eager to see what she had been given. Politely and proudly she gratified them. They fingered her silks and examined the set of jewels given her by the groom—matching earrings, necklace, bracelets, combs, brooches, of gold inlaid with enamel, or seed pearls, rose diamonds, amethysts, or garnets.

Before midnight the bride retired not to reappear. Her maiden friends and her godmother went with her. The groom drank with the men in whose company he now belonged, while boys watched and nudged. The dancing continued, and humor went around. The groom's father, calling above the noise in the hot, hard-plastered room, urged everyone to keep right on enjoying themselves. Presently the groom managed to slip away. In the bridal chamber the ladies admitted him and left him with his bride. Across the patio the merriment continued. Voices were singing. Someone shouted a refrain. The violins jigged along in a remote monotonous sing, and the gulping throb of the *guitarrón* was like a pulse of mindless joy in the night.

So the river society renewed, celebrated, and blessed itself.

On the following day the groom took his bride home to his father's house, where new rooms would be added as their home, in which they would have privacy, even as they shared the communal life of the hacienda.

When the children were born of the marriage, they were baptized as soon as possible. There was no greater token of love than to dedicate them to God. If they died in infancy, grief was put aside for a sort of exalted rejoicing that in their christened innocence they had been gathered straightway to God in heaven. If they lived, they were cherished.

> Lullaby, little one,
> Lullaby, baby.
> For your cradle
> I give you my heart.

As they grew, like all children, they aped in their play what grown-ups did; but very early they were given tasks to do, and a little boy worked at a miniature share of his father's work, in field, corral, or shed; and a little girl learned at sewing table, or in kitchen. They were an observant part of all the family's large or small occasions. The largest of these was death.

vii
Mortality

There were sombre relish and conviviality in how death was received in the river kingdom. The Spaniard-Mexican had a black mind and a morbid tradition. Philip II lived in him for centuries. Death was the gateway to an eternal life, whether, by his own choice, in heaven or hell. Its symbols were always before him. They clattered in gaiety on All Souls' Day—toy skeletons, candy skulls, tiny trick coffins like a jack-in-the-box—and they presided over him daily in all the painted and bloody agonies of his household saints. He did not fear death more than most men, but more than most, he was an informed critic of the emotions of mortality, and at proper times summoned them forth for their own sake, gave them style, and so became their master.

When death from natural causes was seen to be coming, the family could only do its best to make the victim comfortable. There were no physicians anywhere on the river excepting the pueblo medicine doctors, and their concepts were too alien to Spanish life to be taken seriously. The parish priest was sent for if he was within reach. To die in sanctity was the most real of necessities. All prayers and observances were made. If the dying belonged to the sodality of Our Lady of Mount Carmel (who was the divine inspiration of Saint John of the Cross as theologian and poet), he knew that he might not die until once more he felt the earth. At his request a brick of clay was brought him to touch. Touching it, he believed his final struggles would be eased. His dear ones watched by his bed. When the last hour came, they sent for the *resador*, who always led prayers aloud at devotional services. He now had a duty to perform, and he came to join the watchers. He was an expert at knowing the exact moment of death. Relying on his wide experience and his natural gifts, he kept his gaze upon the dying face; and when he recognized the first veil of final mystery as it came, he cried loudly three times, as was his duty, the name of Jesus. At the moment of death, the soul took flight to its Savior's name. The best friend of the deceased or the oldest man present closed the eyes. Men dressed the corpse if it was that of a man; women if that of a woman, or a child.

And now that death was among them, the bereaved women screamed in grief. They did it as a form of artistry. They threw themselves from side to side and wailed formless words. This was expected of them, a mortal politeness that was understood and even judged. In obscure wisdom they set out to exhaust, to cure grief through its own excesses. Now and then in the midst of their working clamor, their interest might be seized by something beyond. They paused and gazed while their shrieks fell to whimpers. They were lost like staring children; and then, as always, life moved, their fixity was broken, and with a shake of the head they came back to their duty and redoubled their lamentations. Private loss became an experience to share in full measure with all who would partake of it. A woman shrieking and throwing herself required other women to hold her and give comfort. These in turn needed friends to relieve them at their enervating work. The whole society of women worked toward the seemliness of the event.

Men built the coffin of raw wood. The corpse was laid in it, and then with lighted candles at head and feet was placed on view in the *sala* for the wake, or *velorio*. All who could, attended to watch all night, while prayers were recited in unison, hymns of devotion to the patron saint were sung, and memories of the dead were exchanged. At midnight supper was served. The household was thronged and busy. Such an occasion was so much enjoyed that wakes were held even without death present. These were solemnized in honor of appropriate saints throughout the year. Men singing traditional laments in procession brought saintly statues from the church or the chapel, and communal meditations on death were observed as for a recent bereavement. A wake for a deceased person sometimes continued for two nights and was ended with burial. If the family lived near town, the coffin was borne to the parish church for a Requiem Mass, after which it was buried in the floor of the church while all present sang dolefully together. If the family lived far in the country, burial took place in the family chapel or in a cemetery upland from the river, out of reach of swampy soil. A fence of wooden pickets with ornamental tips stood around the family graveyard. A cairn of stones was put at the head of the grave to support a wooden cross. Late in the eighteenth century itinerant stone carvers sometimes appeared in the river settlements, and were hired to make a monument. One family, at Belén, had a carved stone mausoleum, built by sculptors who were brought from Italy. The funeral of a child was gay and impish, reflecting the happy fact that it died without sin. Dressed in white and decked with flowers and bright ribbons, the corpse was carried along in a procession that all but danced. The local musicians played furiously on their violins the tunes which everyone knew at their fandangos. The marchers chattered and laughed. Grief was out of place for one who had left the temptations of the world and already knew heavenly bliss.

For if life was a battle between good and evil, then the moment of decision came at the moment of death. Evil lived in the flesh, which would in the end lose the fight; but it also accompanied the spirit, and unless exorcised in piety before death promised eternal damnation. In the power of this conviction, Rio Grande Spaniards, like their most august forebears in Spain, strove to put down evil by punishing their own flesh. The flail of the Emperor Charles V, inherited and used by his son Philip II and willed in turn to his kingly heir, sounded in echo through the centuries amongst the villages and estates of the river kingdom. Their particular discipline in piety came alike to monarch and colonial from the thirteenth century, when self-flagellation in atonement was widespread amongst European religious orders and individuals, including the Third Order of Saint Francis. Searching for the river in the spring of 1598, Oñate's colony had paused in northern Mexico on Holy Thursday to seek redemption through pain, and "the night," wrote Captain Pérez de Villagrá later, "the night was one of prayer and penance for all. The soldiers, with cruel scourges, beat their backs unmercifully until the camp ran crimson with their blood. The humble Franciscan friars, barefoot and clothed in cruel thorny girdles, devoutly chanted their doleful hymns, praying forgiveness for their sins. . . . Don Juan, unknown to anyone except me, went to a secluded spot where he cruelly scourged himself, mingling bitter tears with the blood which flowed from his many wounds. . . ." By 1627, processions of flagellants in the Spanish river lands were mentioned as a matter of course, in official reports of the Father President. When Vargas took the crown back to Santa Fe, "The Third Order of Penitence"—not to be confused with the Third Order of Saint Francis—was established in the 1690s at Santa Fe and Santa Cruz, and legally recorded. In 1794 a cathedral document at Santa Fe named the same brotherhood, saying that it had "been in existence since the earliest years of the conquest." First administered under sacerdotal guidance, the brotherhood became more and more the responsibility of laymen, until in the latter half of the eighteenth century and throughout the nineteenth they alone conducted its ceremonies. For by then the Franciscans were rapidly losing their independent control of New Mexico's religious affairs, under pressure from the Bishops of Durango who worked, in the end successfully, to bring the river kingdom under their dominion. The Franciscan authorities were, as a consequence, withdrawing more and more of their friars from the vast province where few enough had ever been assigned.

Men of the Spanish villages and haciendas joined the fraternity to do bodily penance in atonement for their own sins and for the death of Jesus upon the cross. Calling themselves the Penitent Brothers, they were subdivided into two groups—the Brothers of Light, who administered the sodality, and the Brothers of Blood, who as the rank and file carried out its precepts. A village or a group of haciendas supported a *morada,* a chapter house of the Penitents. This was an earth chapel set away by itself. It had no windows, rarely a belfry, never more than one story, often only one room. It was as secret and as plain as a kiva. It was closed to all but initiates. Within was the bare furniture of piety—an altar, a wooden cross great enough for a man, lengths of chain, blood-spattered whips bearing thongs of leather studded with cactus thorns, locally made images of saints painted flat or carved and colored, and various representations of Christ, and a life-sized figure of death in a cart. Here the chapter met for business, in secrecy, and, as the calendar demanded, in pain spiritual or pain physical. The members discussed good works that they might perform, together or individually. Apart from the great houses, there was deep poverty in the valley of the haciendas, and much suffering, and if charity could be done, it must be. The brotherhood met for prayer, and thinking of the poor souls in purgatory, prayed for their delivery into heaven—an act, under their faith, of supreme charity.

A young man taken into the chapter was initiated through memorized ritual and ordeals of pain. He came after dark on an appointed night to the *morada,* remembering and awed at what he was told to do, that would soon sweep his humdrum life into new wonder, prestige, and expression of its deepest self. In the pathos of those who longed to conform, he lifted his hand and knocked upon the *morada's* door and said, "God's child knocks at this chapel door for His grace."

"Penance," replied a solemn voice from within, "penance is required by those who seek salvation."

"Saint Peter will open the gate," recited the novice, shivering at the analogy of heaven, "bathing me with the light in the name of Mary, with the seal of Jesus. I ask this brotherhood: Who gives this house light?"

"Jesus," answered the leader within.

"Who fills it with joy?"

"Mary."

"Who preserves it with faith?"

"Joseph."

The door was then opened to him. He was taken within and led to kneel and bend before a bench. His back was bared by the attendant Brothers of Light. He was exhorted in the duties of membership and secrecy. The *sangrador,* an officer empowered to draw the blood of the initiate, came to the kneeling youth and with a knife of obsidian cut three deep gashes the length of his back, and three more the width. Laying down his knife, the *sangrador* took up salt which he rubbed into the wounds and stepped back expectantly. The novice remembered what he must now say:

"For the love of God bestow upon me a reminder of the three meditations of the passion of our Lord."

Nodding in propriety, the *sangrador* marked the three meditations with three lashes of a rawhide whip on each side of the kneeling man's bare body.

"For the love of God," begged the novice, "bestow on me the reminder of the five wounds of Christ."

And when these were given with the whip, he asked for the bestowal of the Forty Days in the Wilderness, and the Seven Last Words of Christ, which were laid upon him. Then he was taken up and led aside, and his wounds were bathed for him, and he was by now lost in rapt endurance, and on his back were the welts of membership, as proofs of manhood, marks of prestige, and of faith.

When Lent approached, the Penitents made plans for its observance. In the whole Lenten canon of atonement they found the passionate theme of their own society, and led all others in public avowals of contrition and acts of penance. The tragedy of Christ's Passion was the central motive of their entire spiritual life, their art, and their acceptance of human estate. Through it they found the power to bear their own worldly sufferings and by it they were liberated from the burden of sin. Possessing so certainly a divine Champion, they attained a strong dignity that was their consolation no matter what their material or social estate in life. If they were for the most part poor people without education save that which came from their daily experience and from the lessons of the pastor, they yet knew in a philosophical achievement of a high order that man's nature, capable of evil as well as of good, needed to be redeemed for his inner peace. Such a conviction was a universal commonplace in the Spanish society of the river kingdom.

Each year at the beginning of Holy Week the Penitents began their most intense demonstrations of faith. They retired to the *morada,* and were not seen to emerge for four days, while women prepared and brought food to the door for them. With the stripping of the altars on Holy Thursday came the tenebrous thoughts that prepared all for Good Friday. Litanies and prayers were heard in the *morada.* Plain song, far removed from the glories of Old World compositions, modified by strange accidental dissonances, and accompanied by the thin wailing of a homemade flageolet, rose above the praying brotherhood. In the darkness of Good Friday eve they emerged from the chapter house. Chanting in procession, while their countrymen watched in kneeling rows or walked beside them holding torches of pitch, they whipped themselves with chains and flails until their backs ran red. Girls, called Veronicas, ran to wipe their faces with cloths. In the valley, the tributary canyons, of the northern river, such nights were cold. Returning to the *morada,* the processional members watched all night, at intervals renewing their flagellations, and crying out the psalm of the Miserere:

> Deliver me from blood, O God!
> Thou God of my salvation,
> And my tongue shall extol Thy Justice!

And on the following day, Good Friday, within the walls of the *morada* an ordeal of spiritual pain was enacted. From infancy the Spanish people were poignantly aware of the whole drama of Calvary, and in various ways strove to share in humanity's guilt for the death of Jesus, and to claim the redemption promised to them by that very death. The Penitents of the river in passionate earnest sought to identify themselves with the sacrifice of Christ, and to renew in themselves the blessings to be drawn from it. They elected one of their number to the awful role of the Savior. He was chosen for his goodness in life. Like any man, he knew fear when his life was in danger, and it was in danger now. Yet he was honored, and to face what was coming he was empowered by a sense of glory in his identity with Godhead. If the sweat stood out on his brow, his soul rose within him. He was ready when, within the blind walls of the *morada,* his brothers seized him roughly, as soldiers had seized Jesus, and brought him to judgment. While the reader of the brotherhood intoned the Passion of Christ from the gospels, the events he narrated were acted out by men who knew and deeply believed in what they were to do. Christ was questioned before the High Priest and he answered that he was the Son of God. The high priest cried, "He has blasphemed," and demanded of the populace what they desired, and they cried out for death, and struck at their brother in the *morada.* They took him a step or two elsewhere and faced him to Pilate, who washed his hands of him, and asked what was to be done with him, and they replied out of centuries and for all men, "Let Him be crucified!" The scene shifted in the narrow hall of the clay chapel, and was in the palace of the Procurator of Judea. There in mankind's reduction of all its victims to their animal being, the persecutors denuded the Christ and exposed him. They then put on him a royal scarlet robe, a crown of thorns made from wild-rose branches, gave him a rude sceptre, and paid him mocking honor, while the hearts of the brothers were moved at what they did—to jeer as a false king the one who was King of all creation. Their ire rose with the gospel. They took his sceptre from their brother and beat him with it. They spat at him. He stood for them, entranced. They stripped him again and put his own clothes on him.

Outside the *morada* all knew what was transpiring within. History recorded in the gospels told them, and local memory, and sounds that came on the cold night. The weather was often bitter in Holy Week on the river, and snow fell on the little foothills that rose from the valley, and the sparse bushes looked black in daylight. One of the hills near the settlement stood a little higher than others. A path led to its top. This was Calvary.

Late in the morning on Good Friday the Passion within the *morada* came into daylight. A procession was formed. The Penitents went barefoot in their black hoods and white trunks. A group of flagellants led the way. The Christ followed, bent under the man-sized cross which he carried from the *morada*. A little group of honored brothers pulled the *morada's* rough wooden cart in which sat a wooden skeleton with gaping jaws—the carved image of Death. It held a drawn bow with a real arrow. Spectators from the settlement knelt to watch, and if the cart jolted against one of them, this was counted a blessing. It was left to chance and the roughness of the cold ground whether Death's arrow would be jarred free from its stretched bowstring and fly away. The arrow, they said, once did so, and quivered into the flesh of a spectator, killing him. Death was everywhere. In fierce irony and challenge the people exposed themselves to its caprice, and ways of forgotten origin stirred in them out of the cultish death rituals of medieval Europe, as they now approached on the village Calvary the scene of the supreme death of their inheritance.

The mount was studded with rocks that pierced bare feet and with bushes that tore at bare bodies. Up a path worn by many generations that had walked the same hill for the same purpose the village Christ made his way, followed by all his neighbors. He fell three times and rose again to drag the cross to the appointed station at the top. The Veronicas wiped the faces of those who suffered in their imitations of Christ. The sound of whips on bleeding backs smote the air. To the cracked whistle of the flageolet, voices made their way in unison through the penitential psalms. With the marchers walked not only the history of Jesus Christ, but also the whole past of Israel, and Israel's whole past of Asiatic myth.

At the summit of the hill overlooking the lower river lands, the Christ was laid supine upon his cross, to which he was tied with bands of cotton cloth. His cross was raised against the white sky of the horizon. Those who watched saw a living bare body hanging upon the cruel tree and knew again what had been suffered for them in love at Golgotha. They fell to their knees at the instant of the crucifixion and, beating their breasts, cried out together, *"Peccado! Peccado!"*—"I have sinned! I have sinned!"—lost in the identity of the crucified. As the brother Christ hung on his cross wearing only black head-bag and white trunks, his body turned blue from the bindings that held him to it so tightly that his blood ceased to move in him. He was watched to detect the moment when he could endure no more and must die. When they saw it, his brothers lowered the cross and took him from it, bearing him away to the *morada* to restore him if possible.

With that moment the village Christ had enacted the giving up of the Ghost, and out of the Gospel of Saint Matthew the words came back to all who watched—how "the earth did quake, and the rocks rent, and the graves were opened: and many bodies of the saints arose," and how for three hours there was darkness. And so on Good Friday night the brothers gathered in the *morada* to imitate the anguish and darkness of all nature, in the service of the *Tinieblas*. Twelve candles were lighted upon the altar. The Brother Reader recited twelve psalms. At the conclusion of each, one candle was extinguished until there was total darkness. With that, sounds imitative of the world in anguish and upheaval broke out in terrifying volume. All roared and groaned, while chains clanked, and wooden rattles whirred, and sticks thumped on drums, and hammers struck metal. After minutes came sudden silence, and a single voice cried out, asking for a *sudario*—the cloth that covered the face of a corpse. This was an elevated idiom, meant to signify a prayer for a soul in purgatory. The prayer was recited by a leader, and all responded. The quaking uproar broke out again, and again a *sudario* was given, and for an hour in alternating clamor and prayer, the ceremony of darkness was observed, and at last the purifying terrors were over.

If the village Christ died, he was buried by his brotherhood in secrecy, and his shoes were put the next day on the doorstep of his
house to notify his family that he was dead. Grieved, they yet re-
joiced, for they believed that in his ritual sacrifice he had gained for
himself and them direct entry into heaven. His cross was left to
stand all year on the summit of his hill, and sometimes two others
were placed, one on each side of his, to recall the thieves who had
died on Calvary with the Son of Man. From a distance they looked
like twigs against the sky. Year round they had the power to prick
the thoughts of anyone who had sanctioned why they were there.

For the crosses were in fact a form of monumental art at its most
bare and artless. As such they stated starkly the whole purpose of
visual art in the lives of the river people. That purpose was horta-
tory, not ornamental or esthetic. Rather than primarily to delight
the eye, it was to compel goodness, which it did by means of images
of the cross, the Deity, and the saints, whose presence reminded the
people of sufferings on earth that led to glories in eternity. And in
their art—the art of the *santo,* or represented saint—the people revealed alike their longings and their own images, for the saints they
fashioned were self-portraits.

In their first century on the river, Spaniards had brought their
saints from Europe—large church paintings and carved images in the
styles of the High Renaissance. In them along with piety echoed the
civilized richness of court and cathedral, and through them shone
conventions of drawing, modelling, and painting that adored the
human body in its beauty, and strove to immortalize it with every
elegance. The exuberance of patronal society was raised in works of
art, even in religious themes, to a dazzling splendor, through superb techniques. Greek ideals of pagan beauty were revived to cele-
brate the persons and events of the Christian Church. Through imported works of art, European sophistication presided over the
worship of the river Spaniards and Indians in their rude adobe
churches—until the terror of 1680. And then in one overwhelming
gust of hatred, the Indians destroyed every vestige of the Spanish
spirit that could be burned, ripped, or uprooted, and the European
likenesses of Christ, the Holy Family, and the saints disappeared
from their places of reverence in the homes and churches of the
river. After their return to their impoverished kingdom, the colonists and the friars restored what they could of their property. But

the Crown had lost interest in spending money on New Mexico. The Franciscan order on its own could afford only the most meagre of supplies to keep the missions alive. The barest necessities of life were all that came north in the wagon trains. The river kingdom began to recede more and more into its northern remoteness with every year as the home government in Spain found itself increasingly absorbed and on the defensive in European affairs. Imperial Spain was slowly bled of its life flow, and almost all the goods of life along the river were now created locally. Among these were the very saints themselves.

For, one way or another, there had to be saints in every house, chapel, and mission, and if there were no saints from Europe, once again, the Franciscan friars—who, when necessary, could do anything—filled the need. They painted sacred pictures on buffalo skins. They remembered mannerisms of drawing and of coloring out of Europe, and their first efforts reflected these. On little tablets of wood they painted saints that could be hung up on a wall. Out of columns of cottonwood they carved statues, which they colored. The friars fiercely preserved the seemliness of religious places by founding a local school of saint makers. They taught what they knew about drawing, painting, and carving to those among their people who showed aptitude. As the eighteenth century passed, and the friars were gradually withdrawn, the work was left wholly with laymen. Born in the river world, they knew no direct European influence. A recognized profession of saint maker grew up, to create an original contribution of the Rio Grande to the art of the world.

It was an art that sought the universal divine, and expressed it through the humble daily likeness of the saint maker's own people. If this was the inevitable formula for the artist anywhere, then it was the qualifying locality, and the nature of style, that made the Rio Grande saints unique. The faces and postures of those saints were those that prevailed in the bosky farms of the river—little cramped gestures without grace and yet tense with spirit; poor thin faces with great eyes that had always looked on poverty and in the mystery of hardship had found an identity with the divine. If the actors in the penitential events of Holy Week were fixed suddenly in their stark attitudes, with their dark eyes, their angled arms, their gaunt bodies, black hair, pale olive skins, and brilliant lips, there, suddenly, would be seen the attitudes of the religious art of the Spanish Rio Grande. The *santos* at once gave and received a staring piety that exactly expressed the spirit of faith in all its vast, yet intimate, simplicity.

In time the saint maker became a familiar figure as he travelled up and down the river with his pack mule whose panniers contained a selection of saints to be sold at the rich houses or in the poor villages. He had tablets, or *retablos,* ranging in size from about four by six inches to about twelve by eighteen. He made these by first smoothing the wooden surface, then coating it with several washes of gypsum like that used on the walls of rooms. He ground his own pigments. Black came from charcoal; reds, browns and orange from iron ores; yellows from ochreous clay; blue and green, which faded, from the copper ores used by the Indians for their kachina painting. For his medium he used water and egg yolk, and, much later, oil. He drew the outline of his saint in black or dark brown, and then filled in the color. His tablet often had an ornamental painted border, and at the top, a lunette carved in shell-like flutings. He tied a rawhide thong through a little hole by which to hang the tablet on the wall.

In his pack there were wooden figures fashioned in the round that stood from a few inches to several feet tall. These he called bultos. He made them like dolls. The torso was of one piece, the arms and legs of others that were attached, sometimes by sockets, sometimes by strips of muslin pasted as hinges. He covered the face and body with his gypsum wash, and then painted the features and the flesh. Every saint had his attribute by which he was recognized— Michael with his sword and the scales of justice, Raphael and his fish, Peter and his keys, Veronica and her veil, John with his long cruciform staff and his lamb. The saint maker carved such attributes separately, and affixed them to the figure. He worked to make his creations as lifelike as possible. If his bodily proportions were inaccurate, and the modelling of face and hands and feet faulty, it was only because his skill was not equal to his intention. But the passion that begot his works had more power to express than his technical ignorance had to constrain. His failures in realism did not deny life to his works—the life that he breathed into them out of the depth of his feeling, the power of his faith, and his desire to please his customers. He was an artist for whose production there existed a lively demand throughout the society he was part of. This condition gave him dignity and fulfillment as man as well as artist. Fully integrated among his fellows, he gave in his work not only his own vision but theirs; and when he re-imagined their life in the presence of their reality, he became the means by which their society perpetuated its own image in art.

It was odd, but it was true, that though he had a set of severe conventions for painting faces, they never came out exactly alike, but had striking originality in characterization; and yet, however individual they might be, all his faces were unmistakably Spanish. He gave them deep porched eyes, heavily rimmed with black, and thick, arching black eyebrows, and coal-black hair. The women's faces he finished with a paint that made them look like matrons made up for fandangos, with the ash-violet complexions that came from their lead powder. To his portraits of Christ and other masculine saints, he gave beards, painted in shiny black. He often attached real hair to the heads of both male and female statues, and sometimes did not carve their clothing but made it out of cloth soaked in gypsum wash, arranged in folds when wet, and painted when stiffly dry.

Looking at the Mother of God bought from a saint maker, the owners could often see the living mother of their mud house in the valley. One statue showed her in sorrow, with a black rebozo, her brows lifted in pity above mica eyes, her full mouth trembling on the very taste of the grief that swelled in her round cheeks, with their touches of pink paint, and her full throat. Her dress was painted and so were its buttons, embroidery, and the rosary about her waist. Her hands were unduly large, and looked rough with work. Another divine-and-earthly mother had a calm, knowing gaze, above a great nose and a mouth shadowed with a wise smile, that seemed to rest upon daily concerns of husband, children, cooking pots, and domestic animals. A Saint Raphael holding his fish was a heavy-browed youth with huge eyes full of the joy of the fisherman who has taken his catch out of the river beyond his family fields. In the right hand of a Saint Joseph was his flowered staff that bore a cluster of yucca blossoms. In his other arm he held the infant Jesus, whose almond eyes and painted smile recalled the Mongol antiquity of the river Indians. The saint himself wore a look of grave, untutored wisdom in Indian fixity. In a crucifix were all the exhaustion, dryness, filthiness of caked wound and scab, the rivulets of painted blood, that countless people had seen on the village Christs of their own hill. His arms and legs were bound to the cross with miniature strips of cloth. In another carved Christ, with real hair hanging lank, the local face was focused in staring rapture upon universal mystery unseen but believed. In another Christ, recumbent in a wooden cage symbolic of the tomb, the carved and painted mouth with a row of revealed tiny teeth was fixed open upon a silent unending scream. The power in his face was like that in the open-mouthed masks of those clay figures buried with the dead in ancient Mexico. The Holy Trinity was represented by three bodies, joined, and three heads, as identical as the saint maker could make them, and the face of all was the square face of a handsome bearded farmer with roughly chiselled features, who in obedience and patience drew the term of his life out of the river earth. So in countless examples, stiff, angular, almost coerced into eloquence, the saints in tablet and statue spoke with passionate directness of the daily life whose daily need had called them forth in all their anguished divinity.

Though they had an awesome character, they had also an intimate personality. A favorite household saint was almost a member of the family, constantly included in the making of decisions, and consulted a dozen times a day in the comfort of half-thought and daydream. "What shall I do?" The *santo* would send the right answer. "May my harvest be good!" The *santo* would arrange it. "If the baby would only get well!" The *santo* must save it. "If I could only be loved!" The *santo*—if it was a legitimate love—might bless it. Living as such a personality, the *santo* was subject not only to reverence but on occasion to displeasure, when prayerful requests were not answered. Then the *santo* was turned with its face to the wall, or put away in a trunk, until the request was answered, or its purpose dwindled through passing time. Addresses to the saints now and then took on an Indian character. When storms came, an Indian cook in a Spanish house went out the door and, recalling the sacred use of corn meal in the pueblos, threw a handful of salt to the sky, making the shape of a cross, and praying:

> Saint Barbara, holy maid,
> Save us, Lady,
> In thunder and lightning afraid.

So in simplicity of spirit, and in direct productive life upon the land, with the most laborious of methods, the life of the hacienda valley took its way far from the great world. Out in the world, revolutions in psychology, and government, and science were creating new concepts of living. But Spain, the mother country, consciously closed herself to these; and barely a ripple of late eighteenth-century European movement reached the river kingdom. The machine was being discovered as a power in civilization. Technology was born.

ix
Provincials

Industry entered upon violent growth. But not in Spain, and not in the far valley of the Spanish river of North America. The Spanish had no gift for technology, generally speaking. Though the pure sciences were studied, their application was left to other nations. But even Spain's rich tradition of scholarly education did not reach to the river frontier. There were no schools for the haciendas, and no colleges. Even the Franciscan classes in the pueblo missions were disappearing in the last colonial century, as the teachers were withdrawn. Children of the river families learned what they could from their parents. This meant a sufficient skill at the jobs of working the land and saving the soul. But it brought little for the life of the mind. There was no printing press in New Mexico before the 1830s. The only books that came in the trade caravans went to the friars, and were of a professional religious nature, with perhaps a copy or two of the poems of Sister Juana Inés de la Cruz, Mexico's intellectual nun. An occasional youth was taught to read, write, and consider philosophy by a priest who guided him toward a vocation in the religious life and presently sent him to a seminary in Mexico. For the rest, only sons of the richest river families could hope for a formal education. Such young men were sent to Mexico City to college or to Spain. They were promising scholars. Baron von Humboldt in Mexico found "that the young men who have distinguished themselves by their rapid progress in the exact sciences came for a great part from the northernmost provinces of New Spain," where because of constant guard against wild Indians they had led "a singularly active life, which has to be spent mostly on horseback." When they came home, they might become leaders in local politics and enjoy the prestige of having seen the world. But the local horizons and ways of river prevailed over the sons as over the fathers. Now and then a proud daughter of a hacienda was taken south with the autumn wagons to be educated in a convent where she would learn the crafts of ladyship. In due course she would return to her family, ready to marry an eligible young man and maintain with him the combination of domestic grace and primitive husbandry that characterized life in the river estates.

For the rest, it was a life that had its arts. If these did not blaze and tremble with the peculiar acrid glory of Spain at her greatest, they yet glowed behind the sombre patience of the people like coals dying under ashes. If their spirit longed for poetry, it had to be content with the doggerel rhymes at dances, and in the place names of the land, like the name given to the mountains between Galisteo and the Rio Grande, which were called the Sierra de Dolores. In such a place name the Spaniards met the landscape of their souls. Their theatre was made of the artless plays enacted by amateurs at Christmas and in Holy Week with deep religious meaning. Their music sounded in the simple scratches of violins at parties, funerals, the wail of the flageolet in the Penitential passion, the singing of High Mass, the celebration of love and adventure in ballads. Their painting and sculpture showed in the saints made in the valley. Their architecture rose out of earth forms in the universal style of the adobe house and church. All expression in art was integrated in the occasions and forms of local living in the long valley. It was all unprofessional and traditional, and none of it was produced for its own sake, but always to serve primarily an intimate function of the society. As the ways of life were taken from the local earth, the texture of living more and more showed the face of local tradition with its Indian source. The river house, Indian dress, dyes, articles of trade, seasonal ceremonies like the opening of the ditches in spring, the drying of succulent foods, the kivalike form and secrecy of the *morada,* the bogeyman who benevolently scared children into goodness—such details stood for the gradual absorption of the Spaniards into the ancient environment where they came to conquer and remained to submit.

Did they see themselves in their long procession through the colonial centuries—thirsty for discovery, but often scornful of what they found; bearers of truths which all too often they bestowed with cruelty; lionhearted and greedy-minded; masters of great wildernesses that yet mastered them in the end?

Those who lived in the haciendas and villages of the river illustrated a last chapter of what it meant to be provincial in the Spanish empire. Through three centuries the colonials knew first how it was to move farther away from Spain; and then from Cuba, then from Mexico City, then from Culiacán; and from the big monasteries of New Biscay and Coahuila to the Rio Grande. Every stage brought reduced movement, less color, luxury, amenity, worldly importance in all things. In time, remote from their sources, the colonists lived on hearsay instead of communion. Folk artisanship replaced skilled professional craftsmanship. Barter substituted for money. Home-butchered animals instead of prepared commodities sustained life. Custom overshadowed law. It was a civilization falling asleep—remembering instead of creating, and then forgetting; and then learning the barest lessons of the new environment, until meagre local knowledge had to serve in place of the grandeurs of the source. As they were native lessons, so were they appropriate, but as their products in objects and ways were primitive, they were matters of marvel at what was produced not with so much skill, but with so little. A grand energy, a great civilization, having reached heights of expression in the arts of painting, poetry, architecture, faith, and arms, subsided across the world into the culture of the folk. Defeated by distance and time, the Rio Grande Spaniards finally lived as the Pueblo Indians lived—in a fixed, traditional present.

What they preserved were their distinction and grace of person and manner—all that was left of the Golden Age whose other attributes had once been so glorious, so powerful in two hemispheres.

And yet in their daily realities they found content. Escorials and armadas and missions over the seas were all very well, but now there was enough to do just to sustain life. All about them was a land whose forms of mountains, desert, and valley seemed to prefigure eternity. The brilliant sky called out life on the hacienda by day; and at night, with tasks done, and reviewed in prayer, and promised for the morrow, all seemed as it should be, with the sound of frogs and crickets, and the seep and suck of the river going forever by, and the cool breath of the fields, and the heavy sweet smell of the river mud, and the voluminous quiet of the cottonwood domes. The haciendas fell asleep under a blessing of nature.

X   A new energy, expressive of other ways of life, was already reaching westward toward the river.

New
Man &
New
Principles

BOOK FOUR

Anglo-American

Sons of Democracy

1·A Wild Strain: Mountain Men

The mountain system of the northern Rio Grande was a vast, secret world. Wandering Indians there made shrines of twig and feather and bone, and went their ways. Close to the high clouds that made their rivers, the inhuman peaks doubled the roar of thunder, or hissed with sheets of rain, or abided in massive silence. Below them lay every variation of park and meadow and lost lake; gashed canyon and rocky roomlike penetralia in the stupendous temples of the high wilderness. Along hidden watercourses and in little cupped lakes lived and worked the family of a small creature destined to be the first cause of great change in the human life of the river during the early nineteenth century. It was the beaver.

In still pool or mild current the beaver made his house of mud and twig. Its doorway was under water. The occupants dived to enter it and came up beyond into the dry shelter of their lodge which they had built of sticks and mud, where their food was stored and where they were safe from animal predators. The backwater before the den had to be three feet deep, and if this did not exist naturally, the beavers built dams to collect it. They chose a tree by the edge. Sitting upright, they chewed away bark in a belt, eating of it now and then from their paws. Down to bare wood, they gnawed away until the tree was ready to fall. Often it fell into water where it would make a stout beginning for a dam. Working in concert they brought from nearby woods bundles of stick and bush and starting out from the bank began to shore up their barrier. They dived to the bottom of the water and brought up loads of mud. This was plaster. With their broad tails they trowelled mud over the laid timbers, layer upon layer, always extending the reach of the dam until it touched the opposite limit of the course or cove where they worked. At times they paused to play, racing each other in the water, diving, and loudly slapping the water with their tails.

When house and dam were finished, it was time to lay up provisions within against winter when there would be no green sprouts of willow and cottonwood and fresh grass to eat in season. The beaver clan went foraging, often far inland from their water, in search of bark. The best bark was on the smaller branches high out of reach. The beavers brought down the tree, and then stripped the tender young bark off the branches laid low. They cut the bark into three-foot strips, pulled them to their water, and there floated them to the lodge. They made little signs to guide them as they went— mounds of twig and earth which they impregnated with castorum, a musk secreted by the animal itself, that attracted their sense of smell and reassuringly meant *beaver* and told them where the road lay. Once in the lodge and eating, they were neat and fastidious. They took out through the water doorway all the refuse of a meal and threw it into the current. Drifting away, it lodged down-current out of their way—bits of gnawed stick and knotty branch and hard root.

In the spring came the young. Leaving the mother during gestation, the male went travelling, often far away to other water, where he swam and frolicked, ate tender greens at the bank, and did not return home until the offspring were born. Then he took them in charge, trained them in work, and in the late summer led them out to forage before the sharp frosts and the thickening of their fur against the cold. Everywhere in the secret lakes and along the tributaries and in the quieter passages of the main river this lively cycle was continued by beavers in incalculable thousands, and wherever mountain and water met, evidences of it were scattered and lodged undisturbed—until the last Spanish and the first Mexican years of the Rio Grande, the first decades of the nineteenth century.

For by then the beaver's fur was in great demand for the making of men's hats. The hatters of London and Paris, New York, Boston, and Philadelphia consumed great cargoes of beaver pelt, and the fur trade moved westward out of St. Louis over the American continent to Astoria and the northern Rockies. While Stephen Austin was completing his organized arrangements with the new government of Mexico to bring new settlers from the east nearer to the lower Rio Grande, the river's upper reaches knew another sort of growing infiltration by men who, whether they came alone, or with a few companions, or many, still came without formal approval by the Mexican government, and with no resounding program of colonial loyalty or pious hope.

They came to take beaver in the mountain waters, in spring and autumn up north, or all through the winter in New Mexico if the season was mild. Many of them were French Canadians; the rest were from anywhere in the United States, though mostly from the frontier settlements. They outfitted themselves at St. Louis, and remembering what was commonly known out of earlier reports, like that of Lieutenant Zebulon M. Pike, crossed the plains and entered the mountains by the hundreds in the 1820s. Among their number were men who made the first trails beyond the prairies, that led overland so early as 1826, to the Pacific. Jedediah Smith, Charles Beaubien, the Roubidoux brothers, Céran St. Vrain, Bill Williams, and the youthful runaway Kit Carson, for whose return a reward of one cent was posted by the employer to whom he was apprenticed—such men went to the mountains after beaver skins to sell for a few dollars a pound, and all unwittingly showed the way across the continent.

The movement had already had its pioneer in James Purcell, the Kentuckian, who had been detained at Santa Fe in 1805 under the Spanish governor. Others entering New Mexico from the plains were arrested, to be marched down the Rio Grande to El Paso and the prisons of Chihuahua in 1812, after confiscation of their goods, and were not released until the freeing of Mexico in 1821. Another party of trappers were taken by the provincial Spanish government in 1817, jailed in irons for forty-eight days at Santa Fe, and were finally released after being stripped of thirty thousand dollars' worth of furs and supplies. Such actions by the government were meant to protect the trapping industry already worked on a small scale by the Mexicans of the valley. Regulations declared that only permanent residents might hunt beaver. They were required to buy a hunting license, their number in any party was carefully fixed and recorded, and so were the length of time to be spent in the hunt and the weapons to be used—traps, firearms, or snares. If the early American trappers could not buy official licenses, they soon found a way to get around the law. "The North Americans began to corrupt the New Mexicans," noted a Santa Fe lawyer, "by purchasing their licenses from them," and so risked arrest.

But still the trappers came, and against other hazards. The greatest of these were the roving Indians on the prairies and the eastern upsweeps of the Rocky Mountains. For an Indian hunter could read the menace that came with the white hunter; and he moved with every savagery to defend his hunting grounds. The trapper retaliated. He fought the Indian with Indian ways, and took scalps, and burned tepee villages, and abducted women, and pressed westward. He fought distance, hunger, and thirst, and if he was unwary enough to be bitten by a rattlesnake, he cauterized the wound by burning a thick pinch of gunpowder in it. Once in the mountains, he met his second greatest adversary in great numbers. This was the great grizzly bear, who was curious, fearless, and gifted with a swaying ursine intelligence. With lumbering speed the grizzlies could travel forty miles between dawn and dark through mountains. It was not unusual for trappers to kill five or six in a day, or to see fifty or sixty, and one hunter declared that one day he saw two hundred and twenty of them. The grizzly towered above a man. His forepaws were eight or nine inches wide, and his claws six inches long. He weighed from fifteen to eighteen hundred pounds. His embrace was certain death. So steadily did he smell and find the trappers that in a few decades by their guns his kind was made almost extinct.

The earthen village of Ranchos de Taos near the Rio Grande was the northern town nearest the beaver waters of the mountains, and there came the mountain men to organize their supplies for the trapping seasons. They found that some men of the Ranchos de Taos already, though to a limited degree, followed the trapper's life. Seeing how swarthy they were, the newcomers thought they must be of mixed Negro and Indian blood. It was astonishing how primitive were the ways of life in Taos—the farmers used only oxen in cultivating their fields, and a miserable plow made of a Y-shaped branch from a tree, with an iron head to its end that turned the earth. Hoes, axes, and other tools were all old-fashioned. There were no sawmills; no mechanical ingenuities to speed up work; and—what was oddest to the squinting and raring trappers from the East—the people seemed to have no desire for such means to change their slow, simple ways.

The mountain men encountered at Taos their first experience of the Mexican government. Taos was the seat of the northernmost government station of Mexico. As the trappers brought little to declare in goods for sale, they were evidently allowed to go about their preparations for departure into the mountains. They bought what flour and produce they could, and recruited an occasional Taoseño to join their parties, and made ready their equipment. In the far northern Rockies the trapping parties were often large, numbering from fifty to a hundred men. Most of these were camp personnel who maintained a base for the trappers and hunters who went forward into the wilderness. The "Frenchmen" from Canada sometimes kept Indian wives, and established in the mountains a semipermanent household with rude domestic amenities. Other parties were smaller and, instead of working for the great fur companies as contract employees, went their ways alone, as "free" trappers. Those who descended to the Rio Grande's northern reaches came more often than not in small units of a dozen, or three or four, or even a single man, who meant to take their furs and sell them to the highest bidder at the season's end. But all the trappers shared aspects of costume, equipment, and even character, many of which grew from the tradition of the forest frontiersman of the late eighteenth century.

The mountain man was almost Indian-colored from exposure to the weather. His hair hung upon his shoulders. He was bearded. Next to his skin he wore a red flannel loincloth. His outer clothes were of buckskin, fringed at all the seams. The jacket sometimes reached to the knee over tight, wrinkled leggings. His feet were covered by moccasins made of deer or buffalo leather. Around his waist was a leather belt into which he thrust his flintlock pistols, his knife for skinning or scalping, and his shingling hatchet. Over one shoulder hung his bullet pouch, and over the other his powder horn. To their baldrics were attached his bullet mould, ball screw, wiper, and an awl for working leather. When he moved, he shimmered with fringe and rang and clanked with accoutrements of metal and wood. The most important of these were his traps, of which he carried five or six, and his firearm with its slender separate crutch of hardwood. It was always a rifle—never a shotgun, which he scorned as an easy fowling piece. Made in the gun works of the brothers Jacob and Samuel Hawken, of St. Louis, the rifle had two locks for which he kept about him a hundred flints, twenty-five pounds of powder, and several pounds of lead. The barrel, thirty-six inches long, was made by hand of soft iron. The recoil of its blast shocked into a hardwood stock beautifully turned and slender. Peering vividly out from under his low-crowned hat of rough wool, he was an American original, as hard as the hardest thing that could happen to him.

Alone, or with a companion or a small party, he packed his supplies on two horses and, riding a third, left Taos for the mountains in the autumn. He was wary of roaming Indians, dangerous animals—and other trapper parties. For nobody could stake a claim on hunting country, and every trapper party competed against every other. He did his best to keep his movement and direction secret, to throw others off the trail, and find the wildest country where he would be most free from rivalry. Following the groins of the foothills, the mountain men came among high slopes and rocky screens. If two worked as a pair, they sought for a concealed place where they could make camp and tether their horses, near beaver water. There they built a shelter, and if their goal was a mountain lake, or a slow passage of stream, they set to work hacking out a cottonwood canoe. In natural forest paths they looked for the little musky mounds that marked beaver trails. They searched currents for the drift of gnawed beaver sticks. Every such sign took them closer to their prey. When they were sure they had found its little world, at evening under the pure suspended light of mountain skies they silently coasted along the shores of quiet water to set their traps.

They laid each trap two or three inches underwater on the slope of the shore, and, a little removed, they fixed a pole in deep mud and chained the trap to it. They stripped a twig of its bark and dipped one end into a supply of castorum, the beaver's own secretion that would be his bait. They fastened the twig between the open jaws of the trap leaving the musky end four inches above water. The beaver in the night-time was drawn to it by scent. He raised his muzzle to inhale, his hind quarters went lower in the water, and the trap seized him. He threw himself into deeper water; but the trap held him, and the pole held the trap, and presently he sank to drown. In the high, still daybreak, the trappers coasted by their traps again in the canoe, and took up their catch.

Working a rocky stream from the bank, the trappers lodged the trap and its chained pole in the current, where the beaver found the scent. In his struggles he might drag the trap and pole to the shore, where his burden became entangled in "thickets of brook willows," and held him till found. Sometimes he struggled to deeper midstream water, where the pole floated as a marker; and then the trappers, putting off their buckskins that, if saturated, would dry slowly and then be hard as wood, went naked and shivering into the cold mountain stream to swim for their take. And some parties rafted down the whole length of the river in New Mexico, all the way to El Paso. Their method astonished the New Mexicans, to whom it seemed suspect because it was new. Was it proper to use a new kind of trap, and float noiselessly to a beaver site taking their catch by surprise, and spend the night in midstream with the raft moored to trees on each bank to be out of the reach of wild animals? And at the end of the journey, to sell the timbers of the raft for a good price at El Paso where wood was so scarce, take up the catch and vanish overland eastward without reporting to the government? The New Mexicans frowned at such ingenuity, energy, and novelty.

When in the mountains they had exhausted a beaver site, the trappers moved on to another. With their traps over their shoulders they forded streams amidst floating ice; or with their traps hanging down their backs, they scaled and descended the hard ridges between watercourses where the harder the country the better the chance that no others had come there before them. The trap weighed about five pounds, and its chain was about five feet long. A full-grown beaver weighed between thirty and forty pounds. The catch was an awkward burden to carry back to camp for skinning. Removing the pelt from the animal, the trappers stretched it on a frame of sprung willow withes to dry. The flesh they cooked by hanging it before a fire from a thong. The carcass turned by its own weight, roasting evenly. The broad, flat tail they liked best of all. They cut it off, skinned it, toasted it at the end of a stick, and ate it with relish, as a relief from the usual hunter's diet of deer, elk, antelope, bear, lynx, or buffalo meat, or buffalo marrowbones, or buffalo blood drunk spurting and warm from the throat of a newly killed specimen.

All through the winter-fast months the mountain men worked, obedient to animal laws, and themselves almost animal in their isolation, freedom, and harmony with the wilderness. Their peltries were cached and piles grew, in the end to be baled with rawhide thongs. A trapper took in a good season about four hundred pounds of beaver skins. Sometimes his cache was invaded and destroyed by prowling animals, or stolen by mountain Indians; and then his months of hardship went for nothing. But if he kept his pile, he was ready to come out of the boxed mountains whose cool winds brushing all day over high-tilted meadows carried the scent of wild flowers down the open slopes where he descended with his haul. At five dollars a pound it would bring him two thousand dollars in the market.

But once again in Taos, he might then meet trouble with the Mexican authorities. Now that he had his cargo, they showed an interest in him. If he was unlucky, they questioned him, examined his bales, and, invoking regulations that nobody mentioned when he started out months before, confiscated his whole catch. If he resisted, he was taken to Santa Fe and jailed, with official talk about the

Mexican decree of 1824 that prohibited trapping by foreigners in Mexican territory. Since there were no public warehouses, hunters could only store their catches in towns by making deals with local citizens for storage space on private premises. If a Mexican citizen gave protection to a foreign trapper, he was in danger from his own government. At Peña Blanca on the Rio Grande in 1827 one Luís María Cabeza de Baca hid in his house the "contraband" of beaver skins left there for safe keeping by a trapper named Young. From Santa Fe a corporal and eight soldiers of the presidial company came to seize it. Cabeza de Vaca resisted them, firing upon them in protection of his home. The soldiers returned the fire and killed him. The official report of the affair stated that "the deceased died while defending a violation of the . . . rights of the Nation," and asked exoneration for the corporal and his squad.

But local officials might be bribed, and a license trumped up, and the catch restored to the trapper. In any case, after his mountain months, he was ready to burst his bonds of solitude, and he did so with raw delight. All the general passion and violence that his mountain work required him to suppress while moving lithe and crafty after watchful creatures he now broke free in the clay village where he returned among men and women. He had a frosty look of filth over him. His hair was knotted and his beard was a catch-all for the refuse of months. His clothes reeked like his body. His mouth was dry with one kind of thirst and his flesh on fire with another. If the one tavern in the town was full, he went to a house and asked for a corner of the packed mud floor where he could throw his gear, and was granted it. The family knew what he came to seek with his comrades. The women took kettles out of doors and built fires around them to heat water. When it was hot they brought it in, and found him waiting in his crusted skin sitting in a wooden tub. The women poured the water over him. He thrashed. He was as hairy as an animal and as unmindedly lustful. The water hit him and he gave the recognized cry of the mountain man— "Wagh!"—a grunt, a warning, and a boast. Bathing as violently as he did all other acts, he began again to know forgotten satisfactions. As he emerged with wet light running on his skin, white everywhere but on face and hands whose weather would not wash off, he was a new man.

The whiskey of Taos—they called it "lightning"—now warmed him within. He drank until he had fire under his scowl. The women did what they could to improve his clothes. He rattled his money and they made him a supper that burned him inside with chilis and spices. Early in the evening he stamped his way to the tavern in the plaza where a fandango was about to start. All benches and tables were pushed back against the walls of the large room. Tin lanterns pierced with little nail holes in a design hung from the raw beams of the ceiling. Two fiddlers, a guitarist, and a flutist began to make up the music together. They played popular ballads—the same ones that at slower tempos also served for accompaniments to the Mass and to processions. As the crowd grew, the room was hazed with blue cigarette smoke from the mouths of men and women alike. The women were powdered till their faces looked pale lavender. They clustered together at one side of the room. From the other the men came and took them somewhat as cocks took hens—a dusty pounce met by a bridling glare, and then an impassive harmony between the sexes suggesting absent-minded enjoyment. Lacking milled lumber the floor was a hard and polished cake of earth. The couples moved with expressionless faces—all but the mountain man. In his face there glared a starved animation. His heels made muffled thunder on the ground. The Mexican dances were set pieces, with evolutions and patterns. He did not heed them. He threw himself in baleful joy through whatever movements occurred to him, "Wagh!" The lightning jug went around. The music scratched and squealed. The windows of the tavern hall were like lanterns in the pure darkness below Taos Mountain. When the fandango was over, all went home. The mountain man took a woman from the ball to her house. At rut like a big, fanged mountain cat— "Wa-a-a-g-h!" he spent the night with her to nobody's surprise or censure; and, as one such man said, he had no reason afterward to bring "charges of severity" against her.

Presently he travelled to a trading post on the prairies, or to St. Louis, to sell his catch. In the frontier cities of the United States he was a prodigal spender, uneasy in their relatively ordered society, loose as it was compared to life in older and more easterly places. When the season again rolled around, he was off again to his lost lakes and rivers where obscurely content he felt most like the self he imagined until it came true.

For over three decades the trapping trade flourished. At its height the annual shipment of beaver skins from Abiquiu on the Chama and Taos on the Rio Grande was worth two hundred thousand dollars. But in the 1830s the market for beaver began to break, for the China trade out of England and New England was growing, and

the clipper ships were bringing silk in great quantities to the manu-
facturing cities of the world. Fashion changed. Silk was offered for
hats instead of fur; and the change brought the decline and finally
the almost virtual abolishment of the Rocky Mountain fur trade.
The trapper was cast adrift to find new work. He could abide it
only in the land of his hardy prowess, and there he found it,
whether he joined the overland commercial caravans as a wagon
hand, or the American Army's later surveying expeditions as a
guide, or amazingly settled on river land as a farmer. He knew the
craft of the wilderness and he made its first trails for the westering
white man. Some of the earliest venturers in the Mexico trade were
trappers; and as the trade continued to grow and establish its bases
ever farther west, the trappers met it with their wares; and what
had been a memorized path became a visible road; and along it
moved another of the unofficial invasions of the Mexican Rio
Grande that could only end by changing nations. The first sustained
effort toward that end was made by the individual trapper. His
greatest power to achieve it lay in his individualism. Where the
Mexican was hedged by governmental authority, the trapper made
his own. Where the Mexican was formal, he was wild. Where the
one was indolent, the other was consumed by a fanatical driving impulse. The invasion, unorganized as it was, commercial in purpose,
wild and free in its individuals, seemed to express some secret personal motive beyond the material. The trappers forecast a new, a
wild, strain of human society to come to the northern river.

2·*The Mexico Trade*

"We are caraing on a smart Trade with St. tefee from the boons
lick country," wrote a Missouri merchant as early as 1824. For three
centuries the flow of colonial life had moved by the compass needle
north and south, from Mexico to the river and back again—captains
and friars and householders; convicts paroled as colonists; an occasional bishop in his large, upholstered wagon; merchant trains with
their Indian drivers; military inspectors of the Spanish Crown visiting frontier garrisons of forty men and four hundred horses and

twenty firearms; journeyman artisans and now and then a student
travelling between wilderness and a Spanish university: all in their
slow glisten and wonderful persistence travelled north and south.

And then, with the nineteenth century, in a swing of the needle,
the compass began to show life flowing toward the river along a
new axis, from east to west, in a new measure of knowledge, and at
a quickened pace. New paths were imagined. One much speculated
upon in 1825 was the Red River, in spite of the immense "Raft" of
tangled timber that hung over its course like a low thick canopy for
almost a hundred miles, so that the river ran unseen as if in a sub-
terranean current. But its upper end pointed generally toward Santa
Fe, though its source fell short of there by a hundred and fifty
miles, and the talk was that if the Raft could be cleared away, as
men were now planning to clear it, then "Steam boats will be able
to assend within a day or two's Journey from Sta Fee," and "if this
is done the whole current of the Intercourse with New Mexico will
be by way of Red River and the whole valley of it will Soon be settled. and the time may come when more cotton may go out of Red
River than now goes out of the mississippi. . . ." For many reasons
the Red River undertaking never materialized. For one thing, the
clearing of the Great Raft was too difficult to do. For another, the
upper reaches of the Red River could not float steamboats except
perhaps in storm water. And finally, the Mexico trade already in
progress overland to Chihuahua by way of the prairies and Santa Fe
grew so fast that the Santa Fe trail quickly became the established
route.

It had been Spain's firm policy to exclude all trade from the
United States except through the severely controlled port of Vera-
cruz. There came North American goods by sea, and, if any reached
the Rio Grande and Santa Fe, went northward by the old cottonwood carts from Mexico. By the time it arrived, merchandise cost
the New Mexicans dearly. One common item—calico and even
"bleached and brown domestic goods"—sold for two or three dollars
a yard.

But with the independence of Mexico in 1821, the restrictions
were, if somewhat capriciously, relaxed. The trappers of the mountains showed the way to the Rio Grande overland. Both Anglo-
Americans and Mexicans wondered whether trails might turn into
roads; and in 1824, a group of citizens from Mexican Santa Fe
crossed the plains to invite trade from the Mississippi valley. Stephen Austin's brother wrote to him about it: "A Deputation from

Santa Fe arrived a few weeks ago at the council Bluffs—the object of their visit was to ascertain the most eligable Situation for a road to be cut from Santa Fe—to that place—and also to enter into some arrangement to Secure traders (to and from the Province of New Mexico)—from attacks of the indians—and to appoint agents for the purpose of facilitating an intercourse and commerce to the United States—."

By then the Mexico trade was a reality. In 1821 William Becknell had taken out to the plains "a company of men destined to the westward for the purpose of trading for Horses and Mules, and catching wild animals of every description," as his announcement stated in the *Missouri Intelligencer*. His intention was to trade with Indians; but on the prairies he met a wandering group of Santa Feans who persuaded the Missourians "to accompany them to the new emporium [Santa Fe], where, notwithstanding the trifling amount of merchandise they were possessed of, they realized a very handsome profit. . . ." The expedition was equipped only with pack animals, and so were those few that went out again in the following year. In May of 1824 Becknell introduced an important innovation on the trail to Santa Fe. When taking out another merchandise train, he hauled his goods in wagons for the first time. The wagons were a success, for "no where else on the American continent," observed a trader, "can be found a route of 800 miles in extent more easily traversed by wagons than the one between Independence and Santa Fe."

The volume of traffic grew faster than the Mexicans had expected. Ready to measure by their own experience of the single, dawdling, annual train of the Rio Grande valley, and their own unhurried natures, they were hardly prepared to see so many caravans, and so many traders, and so much merchandise rolling past their vaguely defined boundaries. It was alarming. So much business could only mean so much power eventually in the hands of the Anglo-American visitors. Mexico went no further with deputations to the States to establish roads and propose commerce. But it was too late. The gates had been opened, and the flood had started, and would increase.

The first trade road led to Taos, where the trappers had gone. It was the port of entry for New Mexico, where papers were examined. The customs house was at Santa Fe, and there the serious business of taxation, and sometimes of confiscation, was done. As the trade grew, if Mexico could not exclude it, she could at least bear upon it every tedium and elaboration of government control that a Spanish heritage could suggest. Months before setting out, the trader had to have his entire bill of merchandise made out and translated into Spanish. This was copied in duplicate, and sent by traveller, or by mail if possible, to the point of destination, whether Santa Fe or Chihuahua, or any point between them. Once entered, the invoice could not be altered in any way, and any error in further copying it, even to a slip of the pen, was enough to subject the cargo to confiscation when it later arrived. The invoice was stamped, and a copy was returned to the trader with a *"guiá,"* or routing. The *guiá* was permitted to name three points of destination for the shipment, which thereafter could go nowhere else. There was a time limit on the validity of the *guiá.* If its return to the trader were delayed by the officials, or by uncertainty of mails, the trader was sure to be late in his travel, for he could not start without this clearance in hand. And if he was late in arriving, then he was taxed double the duty levied on his goods.

But at last, if he had his papers, the trader could depart. The wagon train commander carried a document issued by the Superintendent of Indian Affairs at St. Louis, showing the names of all men in the trading party, and granting them permission "to pass into and through the Indian country, &c . . . to the province of Mexico." The trail to Santa Fe soon found an easier way than going by Taos and down the black rocky canyon of the river west of the Sangre de Cristo mountains. It took a diagonal on entering New Mexico and came around the southern prow of the mountains and, passing through San Miguel del Vado, entered Santa Fe from the southeast. If the question was raised why the wagon trains, whose cargo was destined chiefly for Chihuahua, did not go directly there instead of so far out of the way as Santa Fe, a trader gave the answer: "I answer, that we dreaded a journey across the southern prairies on account of the reputed aridity of the country in that direction, and I had no great desire to venture directly into a southern port in the present state of uncertainty as to the conditions of entry." El Paso * and Presidio del Norte were ports of entry on the Rio Grande below New Mexico, but received little direct traffic from the states.

Every summer saw the traders come in sight through the blue-green hills southeast of Santa Fe. The long wagon trains gritted and creaked their way into the plaza, and the traders inhaled on the cool

* Present-day Juárez.

air the poignant scent of the piñon smoke that always hovered over the old royal city. An arrival was a great event. The Santa Feans came flocking to see the newcomers, who stared back at them, while both thought they had never seen such outlandish creatures. In the trading company there were many diverse men whom the taverns, gambling rooms, and certain Mexican women prepared to entertain —city merchants, frontiersmen, wandering tinkers, farmers, hunters, wagoners. They often represented many nationalities, and in one train there were men of "seven distinct nations, each speaking his own native tongue," and a trader noted a voluble Frenchman who was given to "curious gesticulations," and "two phlegmatic wanderers from Germany," and two Polish exiles of a "calm eccentricity," and various Indians including a Creek and a Chickasaw, and "sundry loquacious Mexicans," and Americans who "were mostly backwoodsmen, who could handle the rifle better than the whip, but who nevertheless officiated as wagoners." Santa Fe had never seen the like.

They wore anything and everything. The merchant was the most elegant, in his dark, fustian long coat with its many pockets in which he could carry so much, his light trousers, and his round hat. The backwoodsman wore a shirt of linsey that was made of mixed wool and flax, or a fringed leather jacket. The farmer's coat of twilled cotton cloth was already known as blue jean. The wagoner's vest had flannel sleeves. The party bristled with arms until they gave a "very brigand-like appearance." The hunter had his long rifle, and derided the "scatter-gun," as he called the double-barrelled fowling piece carried by Americans who back home went shooting for sport. But the scatter-gun had its serious uses, for on the prairies among enemy Indians "a charge of buckshot in night attacks (which are most common) will of course be more like to do execution than a single rifle-ball fired at random. . . ." Almost everyone carried pistols and knives. Now and then a large, rich train brought along artillery: "We had two swivels mounted upon one pair of wheels . . . one of these was a long brass piece made to order, with a calibre of but an inch and a quarter, yet of sufficient metal to throw a leaden ball . . . a mile with surprising accuracy. The other was iron, and a little larger."

The freight wagons of the train were long, heavy, and narrow, with wheels higher at the rear than at the front, and double hoods of Osnabrück linen stretched over arched bows. From a little distance and seen from the end, such a wagon seemed to be wearing a great sunbonnet. The most popular wagons were made in Pennsylvania, first at Conestoga, later at Pittsburgh. Each could carry a load of about five thousand pounds. To pull it took three span of oxen, horses, or mules. Each of these wore a collar of bells. The cargo was remarkably various, containing textiles of all sorts, from calico to velvet; clothes for men and women, including ribbons, handkerchiefs, hats, suspender buttons, rhinestones, and kid gloves; building materials, cutlery, glassware, tools, baskets, furniture, paper, ink, and paints; foods and spices of every kind and medicines and tobacco and almanacs and champagne and candles and colored lithographs and—a popular item—jew's harps.

The wagons crowded into the plaza like fishing boats in a small harbor after a long hazard at sea. The journey had taken ten weeks from Old Franklin in Howard County on the Missouri River. The eastern terminus moved westward for decades, to Independence, and then Westport, and then Westport Landing which became Kansas City. The road was an extension of the long westward walk of Daniel Boone, that had ended near Boone's Lick with his life. In the fourth year of the trade Congress authorized the President of the United States to "cause a road to be marked out from the western frontier of Missouri to the confines of New Mexico," and the government treated with Plains Indians for the right to cross to Santa Fe, paying the Osage and Kansa tribes eight hundred dollars each. Early encounters with Indians were peaceful; but it was not long until traders, regarding the Indians as inferior creatures, abused them; and Indians replied with all their ancient skill in savage warfare. Trading trains could not have protection by United States troops west of the Arkansas River because of treaty conditions. A trader of the 1830s thought that "such an extensive unhabitable waste as the great prairies are, ought certainly to be under maritime regulations," and considering the principal destinations of the trains, he recommended that "some internal arrangements should be made between the United States and Texas (a republic) or Mexico, whereby the armies of either might indiscriminately range upon this desert, as ships of war upon the ocean. . . ."

Traders often thought of the sea in their great prairie crossings. The vast open land looked like the sea, and the sky over it rimmed the world at the horizons without obstruction. "Seas of grass," they said, and "prairie schooner," and "prairie ocean." They found the journey, like a sea voyage, a giver of health, and many a frontier doctor sent a sickling on a prairie "enterprise" and saw him come alive of it. It was an affirmative experience. The voyagers believed in their work, which few others had performed; they had a sense of their worth and need; and they knew health of body and spirit. One said, "The insatiable appetite acquired by travellers is almost incredible, and the quantity of coffee drank is even more so. . . ." Each man did full justice to the rations he was required to bring— fifty pounds each of bacon and flour, twenty pounds of sugar, ten pounds of coffee, and salt, beans, and crackers—and to the game he brought down with his rifle or scatter-gun on the way. His job was hard, and the bonneted wagons rarely made more than eleven to fifteen miles a day. He came through Indian alarms and terrifying storms and prairie fires. If he and the wind moved in the same direction, a prairie fire ahead of him was no great trouble, for "fire burns so slowly back against the wind even through tall grass, wagons can be driven through it with safety." But if the wind came driving the fire from ahead, "it would often (particularly in tall grass) set both wagon and team in flames." Under a favoring wind a train once passed safely through a fire; but at night the wind changed, and the fire caught up with the wagons the next day.

At the end of the first lap of the journey, as night came down over Santa Fe, it was time to let go. The public rooms of Santa Fe were crowded early in the evening, and private ones later. Monte games—one trader of severe tastes called them "pandemoniums"— raged, and a fandango was called, and Taos whiskey and El Paso brandy flowed, and music, yells and ebullient salvos from firearms broke the mountain-clasped night. Tomorrow would come the ordeal of the customs house, with its rattle of papers, long official silences that chilled the hearts of the traders, and the glitter of greed in the eyes of the motley Mexican soldiers who watched the checking of the cargoes. The process might take several days; but once the papers were declared in order, and the duties paid, it would be time to tear the traders away from the rude joys of Santa Fe, and take the train down the river to El Paso, and beyond, to the city of Chihuahua.

They took the old road on the east bank all the way. After the empty plains the narrow valley with its many little villages of earth, its separate estate farms, seemed like civilization; and so it was, though odd to Yankee eyes. Yet the valley in the second quarter of the nineteenth century was so much terrorized by Apaches and even occasional Comanches that the traders could not hope to strike out on their own, however plain the road and frequent the settlements.

If they staged few battles against riding Indians, it was because the trains made a great show of force and circumstance that discouraged attack.

The wagons creaked their way down the escarpment of La Bajada off Santa Fe plain, and along the valley road, soon passing in and out of cottonwood shade, a river grace. The bridge at San Felipe had long since been washed away by storm water, and all the way on the river until near to the mouth fifteen hundred miles away there was not a single ferry. This troubled few who wanted to cross, for during three quarters of the year, the river could be forded wherever there was an easy bank. Troubles mostly came otherwise, and took official form; for in any town where there was a squad of soldiery and an *alcalde* who saw his duty as an extension of his personality, the long toiling train was apt to be halted by authority of the Mexican nation, and the whole customs inspection repeated, while the train commanders held their breaths, and wagoners bathed in the sweet-scented muddy river, and animals grazed, and summertime slipped away. It was no use to look for back roads that bypassed the little garrisons; for any train discovered off the main highway was, however orderly its papers, subject to immediate and entire confiscation.

But at last they moved on again, and saw how one little river town after another, only a few miles apart—Peralta, Valencia, Tomé, Adelino—seemed isolated from one another, with local differences in building style, costume and church furnishings. None of the river towns below Santa Fe had an inn or public house. Stopping for the night, the traders parked their train on the outskirts of a village, near water, and under trees, and built their fires and put down their blankets on the ground. The townspeople came to look at them as they pastured their animals and cooked their supper, and heard them talk, and sing, and recite to amuse one another, and watched them dance to fiddles and clapped hands under upward fire light on green leaves, and perhaps saw them take a man and bare his back and tie him to a tree to give him lashes with a bullwhip; and if they asked why this was done, they were told that the man was a bad debtor who was being made to pay off what he owed at a dollar a lash. In the morning, with bellow and bray and holler, the rankle of harness bells, and the grind of axles and the complaint of wagon wood, the train moved on into the deserts above Socorro and below. There were no towns in that stretch, but many camping sites that had been used for generations by riverside travellers—Pascual,

El Contadero, Alemán, Robledo, San Diego, Fray Cristóbal—before entering the Dead Man's March.* Such places had no permanent habitation or structure; but filled and emptied as travel went by.

The Mexican postrider carried the mail between Chihuahua and Santa Fe over this route, though since the raiding Indians had become active, he could not keep his schedule of two trips a month. Most writers sent their letters by private hands, to avoid loss, and also to keep them from being opened, and their business aired, in the post offices of Albuquerque and Santa Fe—the only ones in New Mexico. The postrider carried the leather post bag. It was locked. But because there was a shortage of keys on deposit at the post offices, he also carried the only key. His life was dangerous, and making a living was hard, and it came to him that a little extra silver would be his if he gave to inquisitive persons the privilege of ransacking the mail in his charge. One day in the Dead Man's March a Missouri trader saw a New Mexican ride up to the postrider who was passing by on his service. They conversed briefly, coming to an agreement; and then the postman unlocked his pouch and dumped its contents on the ground. His client searched the mail, and for the privilege handed him "the moderate price of one dollar."

Pressing on through the Dead Man's March as fast as they could, for water was still scarce, and their emergency casks were emptied all too soon, the traders returned to the riverside again and came upon one after another settlement that "had formerly been the seat of opulence and prosperity," but which had "long since been abandoned in consequence of the marauding incursions of the Apaches." Nearing El Paso, if the river was high at the ford six miles above town, they faced a hard job. Nowhere was there a sign of a bridge —the old one had gone in flood. The traders now had to unload the cargo and take the wagons apart and, using a thirty-foot dugout "canoe" that was at hand, float the wagon parts one by one across the river, and assemble them again on the opposite bank. The cargo followed. Sometimes they met quicksand at the ford, and then had to work fast to "drag mules out by the ears," and "to carry out the loading package by package," and "to haul out the wagon piece by piece—wheel by wheel."

Once across the river, the train rolled on, and in about three miles came to a dam of stone and brush that diverted the waters to the El

* The *Jornada del Muerto,* an arid stretch separated from the river by a mountain range.

Paso settlements for irrigation. Three miles farther loomed the tower of Guadalupe, at one corner of the plaza. Again the customs inspection delayed progress. The inspector was exacting and disagreeable. While he did his duty, the traders who could be spared from the ordeal wandered about the district, and ate local grapes "of the most exquisite flavor," and drank "Pass wine" and "Pass whiskey," and saw how the town hardly extended beyond the plaza, though as they resumed their march into Mexico, they realized that the settlements continued for ten or twelve miles down the river in a "series of plantations," with cornfields, orchards, and vineyards under cultivation. At their end, the road left the river, and the train headed due south for the city of Chihuahua, and the southern terminus of the long journey from Missouri.

In an early year the Mexico trade did a business of about fifteen thousand dollars. Twenty years later, the total annual value of cargoes was nearly a million dollars, and a single enterprise brought back one hundred and fifty thousand dollars. Traders were paid by the Mexicans in gold and silver for their merchandise—gold dust from a placer mine near Santa Fe, silver bullion from the mines of Chihuahua. Silver was moulded into ingots weighing between fifty and eighty pounds each, and worth fifteen hundred dollars. Rich men in Chihuahua stacked silver bars in their cellars, where a Missourian saw such cords that looked like "a winter's supply of firewood." If the payment was made in specie, the traders poured their coins into newly made sacks of green rawhide, which as it dried stiff and hard compressed the money in a tight bale.

If all went well for a train, the traders could dispose of their wares in Chihuahua and return to Santa Fe in time to leave for Missouri in the autumn. But if beset by accidents, too many official delays, slow markets, or a wet summer that kept the rivers at flood, they might have to spend nearly a year on the round trip, staying the winter in Santa Fe; for once winter was on the mountains and on the plains, the men could not venture homeward. Pasturage was poor as autumn advanced, and the open road that was so passable in summertime was in winter a terrible passage exposed to the drive of blizzards. The traders hurried their business and their return to Santa Fe up the river. In addition to their bales and bars and buckskin sacks of silver and gold, they brought Mexican cargoes to sell at home—buffalo rugs, furs, wool, coarse blankets of Mexican and Indian make; and they drove herds of Mexican mules and asses. The eastbound wagonloads were kept light, with no more than two thousand pounds of goods in each, to ease the pull on animals who would feed poorly on the autumnal forage, and to make fast marches possible as the days became short and cold and promised trouble in a prairie winter. The westward drive to Santa Fe in early summer had taken seventy days. The return trip, with light wagons and increased knowledge, took forty. With every summer the number of trains increased, and with every trip, the traders, fixed upon their own concerns and aware of no larger purpose, advanced the process that would in time make foreigners of the Mexicans in their own long valley of the Rio Grande.

3·Collective Prophecy

i
Frontier
Attitudes

General Taylor's army on the north bank of the Rio Grande in March, 1846, for the war with Mexico, represented the third of the three great peoples who came to the river. The massed American soldiers, taken together, were prophets of a time to come. The collective prophecy they carried was not plain to all its carriers, but it stirred in them like their own seed, and sow it they must. Its nature could be read from fragments out of the ancestries of idea, issue, motive, and way of life that had created them in a society new to the world—a society formed around a central passion: the freedom and equality of democratic man. A taste of this—the American theme—had already come near to the river with the Texan settlers in the south, and the trappers and traders in the north; but now once again change, coming with a final sovereignty, was about to make its way along the whole river with an energy and a complexity unknown in the earlier societies of the Indian, the Spaniard, and the Mexican.

Until 1846 it was the frontier people from the United States who had made new life in the Far West. In that year the whole nation began to take part, through the national army, in the life of the West, which was tied to all the United States by longing, and letters, and hope. But what had made the frontiersmen had also made their successors; and out of the past of the seventy-year-old nation, and of the impulses—some of them as old as the great ages of Mediterranean life—that had created it, marched the Americans, who with all their regional differences showed common traits and beliefs that seemed to the rest of the world like the marks of a new order of associated men. In America, ideally, a man was an individual not merely to himself, but to all his fellows, under restraints and aids agreed upon by all, in the interest of each.

The settlement of eastern North America was not an expression of the parent state, like the colonial acts of Spain in Mexico, first done eighty-eight years before the founding of Virginia. It came as a movement of various individuals and minorities out of England, the Netherlands, the German States, and France, who even under crown charters and with various motives—religious, commercial, and adventurous—soon revealed if they did not first proclaim that their essential desire was for self-government, under a system of social equality. When this desire came plain in the various scattered colonies of the eastern seaboard, even with their differing localisms, it seemed to draw them together to reinforce one another in their essential drive for realized individualism for their people. For whatever reason, they had all come to feel in the old world that they had reached the limits of their hopes for growth, freedom, and self-expression. To attain these they proved themselves willing to take great risks and undertake great labors. They were plants turning toward the light and space of a new Eden. Cotton Mather said "the whole earth is the Lord's garden—why should men not tend its empty places?" The idea of liberty separated the early settlers from other people in European societies. Were there two kinds of men—those who feared liberty, and those who held it above earthly authority?

They who left "all the pleasant accommodations of their native country" to pass over "a terrible *ocean,* into a more terrible *desart"* in search of freedom under God brought an energy that was more powerful than any already established in the New World. The Indian society had always been arrested in an anonymous communal arrangement by the absence of the idea of the individual. The Spanish society was built on an inertia which allowed the high cultivation of the individual, yet denied it any expression that was not in harmony with the prevailing official position of the state. Now imagining new experience until it occurred, the American settlers brought a frame of life in which the individual was not only permitted but obliged to create himself socially. The forces that obliged him so were the unexampled frontier environment, the swift emergence of a self-made culture, the extension of democratic doctrine, and the joyful sanction of anyone who grew to his own individualism, comely or rude. A poetry of action was inherent in all such obligational forces; and it both contained and exposed a mighty volume of spiritual strength.

That strength was great enough to bring the colonies together to make a new nation, and to survive the terrible hazards of the struggle to design a government for all citizens that would not destroy the essential freedom of each. That this was achieved, and swiftly, as the lives of nations were reckoned, was a matter of fame. European observers came among the Americans, to live their life, and record what they examined, and return with a book manuscript to Europe.

"The happy and the powerful," remarked one, thinking about the occasion of the colonies, "do not go into exile, and there are no surer guarantees of equality among men than poverty and misfortune." And another, seeing in his mind's eye the migration over the ocean, reflected of the Americans that "everything has tended to regenerate them: new laws, a new mode of living, a new social system. Here they are become men. In Europe they were so many useless plants, wanting vegetative mold and refreshing showers. They withered; and were mowed down by want, hunger, and war. . . . The American is a new man, who acts upon new principles. . . ."

When before had a new land and a new idea of man been brought together in their newness? Even the vast soil of America in its primeval bounty and beauty and untouchedness seemed ordained —"in this state it is offered to man," observed Tocqueville; man who was "not barbarous, ignorant and isolated, as he was in the early ages, but already in possession of the most important secrets of nature, united to his fellow men, and instructed by the experience of fifty centuries. . . ." He saw that in older migrations—say, at the fall of Rome—peoples scattering for new places carried with them destruction and death; while in America, each settler brought "the elements of prosperity and life." They knew full well the nature, and the might, of their achievement. They paid reverence to one of its humblest symbols, and moved Tocqueville as they did so. It was Plymouth Rock. "Here," he said, "is a stone which the feet of a few poor fugitives pressed for an instant, and this stone becomes famous; it is treasured by a great nation, a fragment is prized as a relic. But what," he asked, remembering Europe and its symbols, "what has become of the doorsteps of a thousand palaces? Who troubles himself about them?"

It was not to build palaces or make vast conquests that the Americans went to work on their new lands. Tocqueville saw that all they then wanted to do was to add a few yards of land to a farm, put out an orchard, build a room or two—and always to make life easier. He marvelled at how hard they worked to gain such ends— what "feverish ardor" and "avidity" they spent to improve their material circumstances. Indeed, there was a danger in their zeal, their "vague dread . . . lest they should not have chosen the shortest path" that might lead to their own welfare: for such a pursuit might "at last shut out the rest of the world," and even come between "itself and heaven." This was a meditation for a philospher; it did not deter later emigrants from Europe.

For in swelling numbers they came to the American Atlantic coast, and established themselves for hire, so freeing countless American-born citizens for their plunge into the interior of the continent. This "double migration was incessant," wrote Tocqueville. "It begins in the middle of Europe, it crosses the Atlantic Ocean, and it advances over the solitudes of the New World. Millions of men are marching at once toward the same horizon; their language, religion, manners, differ; their object is the same. Fortune has been promised to them somewhere in the West, and to the West they go to find it. . . ."

For in the early nineteenth century the American West was already the world's marvel. With the Louisiana Purchase in 1803, Jefferson had committed the nation to a continental reach. But more, in his whole concept of democracy he had opened political frontiers in the thoughts of men that only the West, in its sheer space, could contain. "In early youth," said a pioneer toward the end of his days, "we removed to and settled in a country universally known over the continent as the 'Great West'. . . . Towns, steamboats, post offices and children were named 'Far West' in honor of that wonderful country. . . ." It was there for the taking. After 1820 land was to be bought from the government for $1.25 an acre. In most American families, as well as in the newer arrivals from overseas, the memory was still keen of how the Old World society was based on great landlords and their holdings. Space was narrow in Europe. Hierarchies and classes constricted men in fixed places into which they had been born. Who could simply go forth anywhere in Europe and take land to make a new life for himself out of it? And even if land were available, how little of it was there at best, compared to what lay between the Alleghenies and the Rockies, and beyond. . . .

In their constant search for better, easier ways of life, the Americans as they moved on westward repudiated one past after another —that of Europe, that of the Atlantic coast, that of their first inland settlements. A Frenchman at the end of the eighteenth century saw this as "complete proof of the American indifference to love and friendship and of failure to form attachments to anything. . . ." The American abandoned, "without reluctance, the place where he first drew breath, the church in which he first perceived the idea of a supreme being, the tombs of his ancestors, the friends of his infancy, the companions of his youth, and all the pleasures of his society"— all for land, new land. If this was a desire deep in the individual, it must reappear as an element in the national character; and it was seen by some as a driving force behind the march of General Taylor's army to the river. Abraham Lincoln, who opposed the Mexican War, supported his point with a joke about an Illinois farmer who said, "I ain't greedy about land. I only want what jines mine." That farmer's self-pardoning greed suggested the temperament of some of the earliest settlers to cross the Alleghenies, who struck Tocqueville as "only an agglomeration of adventurers and speculators . . . we are amazed at the persons [there] invested with authority," and he asked how from such settlers could a proper life be made to grow.

But such pioneers were not for long alone on the frontier. Others —all kinds—kept coming; and among the adventurers who pushed out beyond the settlements were various Europeans of high degree who appeared to view the West as a great park where they might hunt, and explore, and record marvels new to the inquiring and cultivated intelligence. There were German princes with grand suites and striped canvas pavilions and personal physicians; British sportsmen elaborately armed and staffed with frontier scouts; and hired artists who sketched and painted for their noble patrons the Indians, the game, and the landscapes of the prairies and the Rocky Mountains. They took away with them after their grand tours a body of information to be published or exhibited abroad; while the settlers remained to enact the freedom they had designed for themselves.

As each succeeding frontier was settled, it was resolved into the form of a state government; and its most significant act was to give form to the convictions of liberty for which it had been populated.

The new states spread their energy and influence not only westward, but eastward; for their new constitutions popularly adopted universal manhood suffrage, and under their example the old Atlantic states were required by their people to set aside religious and property qualifications for the vote and in their turn to adopt universal manhood suffrage also. The same impulse that thrust individual Americans westward returned a fuller democracy to the states they had left behind them.

But if liberty was not a new idea in mankind, then it was new to equate it with comparative solitude. The Americans brought distance with them as a virtue, dragging it along to separate them from their fellows, in an endless appetite for freedom. In Louisiana, Audubon came upon the wilderness cabin of a Connecticut family. When he asked why they had moved to such a "wild and solitary spot," the husband replied, "The people are growing too numerous now to thrive in New England." The very nation was founded on the concept of the integrity and self-sufficiency of the individual. The frontier attitude was perhaps a caricature of this—its lines all too black, its features too coarse, its sentiments rising in balloons of comment too fiercely rude, and its shading too rough in its crosshatching; but, like many a wood-engraved political cartoon of the period, it was true in its essential quality. Freedom meant not only independence of spirit and belief; it meant also a chance to dominate the material environment. This was new in North America, where before the environment had dominated the Indian and the Spaniard.

Passing over the eastern mountains, taking the rivers if they flowed west or southwest, and coming to the forest frontier, the settlers took down trees if necessary to let their road go on. Almost at once organized communication followed them. The mail travelled by small cart, in a green darkness by day, and by night through firelight cast all about by torches of pine cut and held by the driver. Every so often the cart reached a hut in the woods. This was the post office. There, a bundle of letters was thrown off, the cart galloped on and, when they could, the forest settlers came from their hidden cabins to leaf through the folded, sealed papers for their mail. The cart now and then carried a passenger. One of them marvelled at signs of how fast and how soon settlers had deserted their recent clearings and cabins as they moved westward to look once more for a better life. And soon, too, the woods took back what they had lost to the clearings. The post traveller would come upon a little opening of light through the green density and there see a chimney in the woods, standing alone above its blackened hearth; or the remains of a cabin whose logs were sprouting anew, while vines and flowers hung like veils from the corner uprights, making a bower. The only sounds to be heard in the high green aisles were dove song and woodpecker drillings. The traveller asked himself if ruins, then, were already there; and like many who came after him, he tried to recreate in his mind the character of the men to whom the woods had allowed passage, only to spring up behind them as they went.

The Americans were

> Those that look carelessly in the faces
> of Presidents and governors, as to say,
> *Who are you?*,
> Those of earth-born passion, simple,
> never constrain'd, never obedient,
>
> Those of inland America,

sang Walt Whitman. The people, he said, were "ungrammatical, untidy, and their sins gaunt and ill-bred," and yet they had "measureless wealth of latent power and capacity, their vast artistic contrasts of lights and shades, with . . . entire reliability in emergencies, and a certain breadth of historic grandeur, of peace or war . . . the peaceablest and most good-natured race in the world, and the most personally independent and intelligent. . . . Grand, common stock! to me the accomplish'd and convincing growth, prophetic of the future; proof undeniable to sharpest sense, of perfect beauty, tenderness and pluck. . . ."

From the first, the frontiersman saw himself as a new breed of cat, and behaved accordingly, in cutting himself off from the past. Whenever he saw that he was regarded as rude and coarse, he at once acted more coarsely and rudely. He jeered at any of his fellows who echoed the manners and tastes of the East, or of England. His patriotism was deep and true, but he pounded Eastern or foreign visitors into exhaustion with his defiant assertions of it. Yankee Doodle was a figure in a piercing little song, but he was more. He was a reality who made actual appearances among frontier crowds, when some fellow felt like dressing up in striped trousers, a blue tail coat and a tall beaver hat, to remind himself and all others of what an American looked like. He was regarded without surprise or question. Any man had a sanction for oddity. Audubon saw a

man in New Orleans on the levee wearing a flop-brimmed hat, a
bright green coat, wide yellow nankeen pants, a pink vest, and a
frilled shirt. In his shirt was a bunch of magnolias from which the
head of a live baby alligator swung to and fro. He carried a loud
silk umbrella with one hand, and with the other a cage of brightly
feathered birds. Stalking grandly, he was singing, "My love is but a
lassie yet" in a Scottish dialect; but when he talked, his speech was
native American. He was a one-man drama, and his right to create
a spectacle was granted. He was exaggerating his individualism, and
his observers let him be in his dreamlike commitment that was
haunted by his passion—arising from buried discontents dimly understood by all—to be distinguished among his kind, in any way he
desired.

In certain ways, the American not only created a new kind of society; he also began to look like a new kind of man. His inner likeness gave him a new and characteristic outer bearing, and his physical experience in overcoming a virgin land brought to him and his
sons rugged health and taller, broader, harder bodies. Drawing con-
tributors from many Old World nationalities, the American race in
a few generations through common experience, spirit, and belief,
shaped them into a general type that even with its myriad variations
yet stood forth as a recognizable ideal figure for Western democratic
man. This American was tall and rangy, and he walked with a long
stride, pressing his legs against the unknown distance and future in
a steady gait that gave a breathing swing to his upper body. Beyond
physical dimensions and details, it was his quality of movement that
gave him his most characteristic appearance; for movement expressed nature and will. His nature was to be free, strong and original; his will was to succeed in these aims, against obstacles of tradition and wilderness country; and all that he had in mind and met
in nature helped to make his aspect new among mankind.

Going West, he clothed himself in few garments, all designed for
work. As such, they not only covered but revealed his body, ignor-
ing style and ornament for the simpler value of leaving him free in
the gestures of labor. If he worked in open prairies or on wide rivers,
his hat was wide-brimmed to shade him from the sun. If he worked
in mountains or woods, he had a fur cap for warmth, and for kin-
ship with the animals he hunted and loved in their defeat. Now and
then he wore a felt hat wetted and dried in the shape of the tricorne
of the Revolution. His shirt was loose, cut to hang over his shoulders front and back, with sleeves seamed to the rest between shoul-

der and elbow, and tightened around the wrist with a lace or a button. His trousers were tight from waist to knee, and made either to hang over or fit inside his boots with their thick soles and squared toes. For jacket he often wore a cloth or hide vest, and for coat on occasions of leisure a long-skirted affair with pockets inside the tails. The materials were mostly homespun, and were often left undyed. When colored, they showed the colors of berries or spices— frosty blue, dark cranberry red, sassafrass yellow, cinnamon or nut brown, leaf green. The trapper or scout in buckskin was deer-colored and from a little distance in a wood, if he held still, was hardly to be mistaken for anything but another deer. The farther he went from settled life the more he tended to resemble a creature of the wilds, until an occasional one could only be spoken of in animal terms, like the man who was observed "mounted on a mountain mustang, his face, what little of it could be seen besides hair, looking very much like a small piece of buffalo meat, and with hair standing out like porcupine quills. . . ."

Embracing the farthest wilderness, the first settlers struck an occasional cultivated observer as men who reverted to savagery. Crèvecoeur said they had "an instinctive fondness for the reckless savage life, alternately indolent and laborious, full and fasting, occupied in hunting, fishing, feasting, intriguing, amours, interdicted by no laws, or difficult morals, or any restraints, but the invisible ones of Indian habit and opinion." Again, "these men appear to be no better than carnivorous animals, of a superior rank, living on the flesh of wild animals when they can catch them, and when they are not able, subsisting on grain." And again, "remote from the power of example and the check of shame, many families exhibit the most hideous part of our society. They are a kind of forlorn hope, preceding by ten or twelve years, the most respectable" who "come after them. In that space, prosperity will polish some, vice and law will drive off the rest, who, uniting with others like themselves, will recede still farther, making room for more industrious people, who will finish their improvements. . . ."

What showed in a later light was the prophetic persistence of image of a new life which led the forerunners to enact their own folklore as they thought of it amidst surroundings for which there was no previous pattern. The real binder of the new society was a willingness on the part of all to endure poverty for the sake of independence—"Poverty & Independence," as Audubon wrote in his journal for 1820, ". . . the only friends that will travel together through the world." The nation had begun as "a people of cultivators, scattered over an immense territory," as Crèvecoeur saw. But among the Western settlers every level of social position was represented, and every degree of development in cultural aspect and expression, from the wildcat primitive to the classical scholar, the tinker to the craftsman, the lawless scout to the maker of communities of calm and organic order, the man who governed his fellows by a spirit of fire to the one who led them by rational science. Together they might seem to glisten and seethe inseparable as sands in light, but in their ways and manners, they could be remembered as separate grains each shining sharply for itself.

As the individual felt equal to the vast wilderness, so he was able to get on with the job of turning a continent into a neighborhood. Despite the fifty centuries of social cultivation behind him, the instant he had to be ready to practice wilderness craft he was ready. An ancient atavism of man against animal sprang close in time and memory; and a fabled breed of hunters was the result across the Appalachians. As marksmanship was their craft, it became their art and their entertainment, even their inducement to waste what sustained them. General William Henry Harrison, writing to the Secretary of War and Marine from Fort Saint Vincent, Indiana, in 1801, said, "One white hunter will destroy more game than five of the common Indians, the latter generally contenting himself with a sufficiency for present subsistence, while the other, eager for game, hunts for the skin of the animal alone." The hunters, tenacious, wasteful, wilful, were men who would kill one bounty of nature to obtain another, and in taking the wilderness with violence would not be stayed by moderation or thought of the future's needs. Merely to take a treed racoon, they would chop down the tree, at night, by a woods pool or bayou, with torches guttering and dogs dancing.

Compared to others, they were a nation of sharpshooters. Their skill was what won Texas and plains battles against riding Indians. To prove their skill men held contests to show their wonderful handling of the long rifle. Audubon saw them at it. The rifleman first cleaned his barrel. He then took a ball from his leather pouch, cupped it in the palm of his hand, and from his slung horn poured just enough powder to cover the ball. He poured the powder into the tube, set the ball in after it, and wadded it with a patch of six-hundred-thread linen, and rammed it all home with a hickory rod. He then faced the target. Sometimes this was a nail, driven two-thirds into a board forty paces away. In one of three shots, he was able to finish driving the nail. He could trim the wick of a lighted candle at fifty paces without putting it out. At a hundred yards he could cut off a turkey's head. At comparable distances, he could hit the eye of an enemy. He could bark a squirrel, as Audubon saw Daniel Boone do it. The hunter aimed at a branch just where a squirrel sat, and hit the bark. The concussion killed the squirrel and sent him spinning in the air, to fall to the ground with his fur and flesh undamaged. The report of the long rifle made a crack like a whip. Men who could shoot like that, and who otherwise knew how to use themselves against the wilds, made a close community.

They gave later comers a hard time until able to prove themselves in the same terms. This habit sometimes showed itself in a comic hostility that masked a process of shrewd appraisal and suspended judgment until the newcomer could earn acceptance in the occupations and diversions of the initiated. Such hazing sometimes went to the limits of test and danger. Dimly it wanted to prove that a stranger could take care of himself or if need be do his part for the common safety in situations of peril. But further, the attitude was so exaggerated, so preposterously more than itself, that it suggested some obscure but grinding necessity to enlarge and insist upon all the masculine attributes that were taken for granted by most men in most other environments. It seemed as though a predominantly male society like that of the frontier was obliged to accentuate its maleness to make an outsize virtue of it, and so preserve in eternal boyhood the secrets and discoveries of essential virility that in the boy's first awareness of them assumed such proud, obsessive, and exciting value. In many of its social expression the early frontier West resembled a vast boys' club whose members dealt with puzzling perils and uncertainties by shouting them down with incantations of prowess.

Wildcats? Such a man could lick his weight in wildcats, and so stated with truculence and often. He would cry that he was a black snake, the longest, slickest, wisest of all. He was a weasel, clever enough to steal whatever he wanted. He was a raccoon, a tornado, an earth-screamer, a river at flood, a gamecock; he used a pine tree for a toothpick and he drank a lake if he was thirsty; he was cocked on a hair trigger and it was sure death merely to look at him in a certain way. He would as soon fight as eat; and—he sighed like a gale and belched like a geyser—he just loved to eat. He would take anybody on with a gun, or a knife, or bare hands with thumbs to gouge out eyes, and all for the pleasure of it, both received and

given. If anyone thought he was just fooling, let him take up the ultimate challenge, and consent to fight him naked, straddling a
bench or a log and strapped to it within a few inches of each other,
and armed with a knife each; and see who finally fell over cut and
bleeding, and who still sat there able to spit when the onlookers
came forward to untie the both of them, one live and one dead. It
was a challenge that was actually given and taken when doubt or
boredom reached desperation.

Aggressive humility was another frontier attitude, perhaps less to
be trusted than open truculence. It suggested envy, and private
schemes to take what was wanted. Many frontiersmen could man-
age their faces with an actor's control. This was a technique of
shrewdness, to wipe off any expression from which another could
read intention or attitude. It was the poker face, and it could conceal either a teeming mind or one absolutely empty and at a loss. If
a man felt ignorant, he did well to conceal his feeling; and in any
case, who knew everything? If men believed in equality, then what
one man didn't know was just as good as what another didn't
know. Out of tact, knowledge was often as carefully concealed as ignorance. It appeared that the ideas of the democratic citizen either
dealt exactly with small matters, or vaguely with large ones, with no
thoughts in between.

But if there were few learned men in the new society, there were
few ignorant. The American cared "more to know a great deal
quickly than anything well," Tocqueville said, and further noted
that "the habit of inattention must be considered the greatest defect
of the democratic character." The citizen's mind was always busy
with his own concerns—chiefly those of business, his own situation,
the assertion in thought of his own plans. These were his diversion
as well as his livelihood; and they left little room for the charms of
useless but delightful ideas. Like all generations, those of the early
republic went in for rages and fads of belief that seemed to en-
lighten the people even while giving them a thin authority in obscure affairs, which they could display with elegance. Among the
most gratifying of these were phrenology and its offshoots, which
seemed to provide a penetrating key to human capacities. It was a
period accomplishment to know with finality the secrets of personality by a glance and a touch upon the skull; and it was a popular
pleasure to say, as if it meant something, that Fauvel-Gouraud's system of Phreno-Mnemotechny operated "through the intellectual and
not the mechanical action of the mind."

Gravely accepted at the time, such imported fantasy seemed to give tone to the society. But there were more local notions of fantasy that really caught something of its likeness. David Crockett passed from life into legend before his death, and was quoted in a body of literature written down long after its invention. One time, out hunting when the sun rose he lighted his pipe from it, shouldered his bear, walked home, "introducin' people to the fresh daylight with a piece of sunrise in my pocket." The expression held something of the blitheness, the sweet fresh primality, the sense of outset as at dawn, of the early nation. Confidence dwelled in such a large view, and reflected the trust with which Americans moved alone through solitudes. When they met one another, they fell into easy, immediate fellowship, a habit they would never lose. Despite natural dangers, Audubon said, ". . . So little risk do travellers run in the United States that no one ever dreams of any to be encountered on the road."

—Though one night putting up at a forest cabin where he was allowed to enter and scrape a cake out of the ashes to eat for his supper, and make a bed of skins from a heap in the corner, he was seen to possess a handsome gold watch. Later in the night he heard his hostess, "an infernal hag," plotting with her drunken sons to murder him and steal the watch. He was saved by the arrival of other travellers and had the satisfaction of seeing the murderous family executed, their goods given to a wounded young Indian who also had taken refuge under the same roof, and their cabin burned. Justice so swift proved how rare was such a crime against a traveller's faith; and how trustworthy was the ordinary forest home.

*ii

Woman
& Home*

It was woman who gave home its grace and amenity, with whatever materials were at hand. Her courage was as great and her work as hard as her husband's. Her satisfactions were all tacit. Unlike the European who flattered women but did not treat them as his equal, the American almost never complimented his wife, but showed her in other ways how fully he valued and counted upon her partnership in a wilderness venture. If as a figure she was idealized in countless impersonal episodes of frontier lore, she was, like the men, also projected in the grotesque vein. Mike Fink, the river boatman who was translated into myth, had an incredible daughter. She was so huge she tamed a full-grown bear; and all at once she could chew with one side of her mouth, whistle with the other, and scream with the middle. Grandeurs and amenities abandoned with the East merged with the talents and symbols of the West in a description of another frontier maiden, whose bonnet was a hornet's nest. Her gown was a whole bear's hide, with the tail for a train. She could drink from a creek without a cup, shoot a wild goose flying, wade the Mississippi without getting wet, outscream a catamount, and jump over her own shadow. She had good, strong horse sense, knew a woodchuck from a skunk, and could dance down any fellow. . . . Such monstrous views of woman were in a perverse way a proof of her equality with men whose experience she wholly shared in the job of making the new life. After the troubles of migration, it was she who gave heart to the cabin home.

"A pleasing uniformity of decent competence," said Crèvecoeur, "appears throughout our habitations. The meanest of our log houses is a dry and comfortable habitation." It was put together of trees felled by axe to make a clearing. The stumps were burned away in a long chore that boys could do. Seedlings showed in the rubble, and were cut down or allowed to grow, depending on where they sprang. Larger trees with heavy foliage were circled through the bark to kill their shade and let light through upon patches of corn sowed between them.

The house was about thirty feet long, fifteen feet wide, and fifteen feet high. It was all one room, and it had a single window hung with a muslin curtain. At one end rose the chimney made of stones hauled from a creek nearby or dug out of the ground. The hearth was of packed clay. The fireplace was wide and high, to hold an immense fire, that not only heated but lighted the whole room. Over the hearth hung a long rifle on iron hooks, and above it, for decoration, perhaps a deer- or bearskin, and a clutch of eagle or hawk feathers. On the wall to the right of the chimney was tacked an engraved map of the United States on Pennsylvania laid paper. From its eastern parts where it showed dense hatching of towns, roads, waterways, and mountains in lines of black ink, the map faded toward the Mississippi until beyond the river westward it showed little but the names of Indian tribes bitten into spaces of white paper, with a straggle of the Rocky Mountains like a spine of tiny pine cones, and a tentative broken curve for the empty Pacific coast. Near the map hung a single plank shelf on which rested the family's books—a Bible, the first six books of Milton, a volume of Shakespeare, an almanac. Along the wall instead of closets stood wooden chests. In the center of the room was a long table built in the clearing. Its legs still held bark. On the table was a teapot of English china, a handful of silver spoons by Revere or Hurd of Boston, some teacups, and a little pile of old newspapers. Such a dwelling as Tocqueville saw it was "a little world, an ark of civilization amid an ocean of foliage. . . ."

Here was enclosed all the life of the family, for parents, children and dogs; here ate and slept the traveller in the common firelight under the protecting rooftree made by the father; and here presided the mother. She was in many cases a woman of gentle cultivation who had left the home of prosperous parents to risk with her husband the trials of the Great West, bringing with her as best she could all the graces she had learned. Her life was hard. She bore children frequently and in countless cases without any aid but that of her husband. Her day began with sunup and until her daughters were old enough, she did its womanly tasks alone. She aged fast. Her appearance was inclined to be "at once sad but resolute." If she seemed exhausted, yet it was with pride that her life should be so insatiably used by her man, her children, and her place on earth; and when travellers came, she and her husband gave what they had of shelter, food, and floor. This was done as a duty, impassively, with no pretense that uninvited guests were in every case occasions of joy.

Like an Indian woman, the mother cooked out of doors except on the coldest winter days, when she set her kettles and skillets in the great indoor fireplace. She lighted her fire with flint and steel, or punk and tinder, until about 1829, when something else came along that was described with amazement. A tall red-haired young man— he turned out to be Alexander William Doniphan who would appear on the New Mexico Rio Grande in 1846—"took from his pocket the like of which I had never before seen . . . rubbed it on the sole of his boot and lo! there was combustion fire." The phosphorus-tipped friction match quickly sprang into wide use. On a spit the mother cooked all sorts of game brought in by her husband and her sons. When they went on a bee hunt, they came home with plenty of wild honey. In deep kettles she made a variety of stews, seasoned with herbs for which the woods were combed. Out of corn and wheat flour ground at home she baked bread and cakes. From wild berries and fruits she made sweets. In time she would be able to gather produce from her own orchards, after her little trees began to bear. Out of the woods she took her medicines, from which she mixed a general remedy called bitters. To a draught of whiskey she added sarsaparilla roots, dock roots, black snakeroot, the bark of

dogwood and of wild cherry, and a few beads of black pine gum.
This was fed to grownups and children alike when indicated.

When she wasn't cooking, she was working toward cloth at her spinning wheel or loom; or making new garments; or mending old ones. It was said on the frontier that the first thing a young man did was to get him a wife so's to have her make him some clothes. When she wasn't sewing, she was teaching the children their ABC's, and how to read, and how to cipher, and who the Lord Jesus was, and where their grandparents were, and what America was, and how a living was made. She had very little money and needed no more, for her husband obtained goods by trade; and what money they had was enough to pay the government, "as there were no unreasonable taxes." The mother told her young ones of what was dangerous in the surrounding country—wolves, snakes, big cats, bears. She made it plain that not all Indians were to be feared, for many went by on camping and hunting trips, and though queer and with outlandish notions, and a shock to see with all the cranky nakedness they showed, many of them were almost friends. She spoke of other kinds, of whom all had heard, who came with brand and scream and arrow and stolen rifle, to kill all who lived in a cabin like hers. Thinking of it, she raised her head, and put her hand under her children's chins and made them raise theirs, and said that fear was no excuse not to stay where you wanted to stay, if you did no harm there, and bore your share of work. There were days when she even found time to surprise the children with a cornhusk doll, dressed and painted, or a rag doll that she had made for the girls; for the boys, perhaps a little horse made of twigs and a spool, or a toy bear stuffed with pine needles, or a beanbag, or a buckskin ball worked and worked until its seams met just right to create the sphere.

She kept her girls by her till late; the boys she lost early. The boys had hardly a cubhood. They went from boy to man; for as soon as their bodies were lengthening and filling to meet physical toil, they were ready to do a man's work; and were granted leave to do it. None could read the prickling thoughts of a youth or guess where they would turn him. The father watched his sons come to independence; and he saw this with pride, as an extension of the national ideal of equality and democratic opportunity. If the son wanted to stay at home to work, he was welcome; he was equally at liberty to do what many did at fourteen or fifteen—make a bundle of what he owned, take a rifle from the family's armory, and with a sweet bloom of ignorance on his confident face, go out on his own to a still farther West than the one he grew up in. He went with trading trains, or trapping parties, or with exploring expeditions of the Army, or joined a wild and dissolute crew of rivermen; and what he learned he measured by the gaunt, strong image of life to which he was born in the forest clearing, where in little he saw the community of work that in the large held America together. Everyone worked, and no job for man or woman was high or low, but all were respectable if honest. No one was embarrassed to work for pay. The President himself was paid.

iii
Commun-
ity
Expression

As neighborhoods took form, and the habits of a family were united with those of others, a sense of community governed all; and after the time when every day required ceaseless work, the neighbors at last were able to keep the Sabbath. They came together for worship in a clearing, or presently built a meeting house where they could be enclosed with the spirit of holiness that, they felt, arose more powerfully from all than from each. Going to church they carried in hand their shoes and stockings to keep them clean and only when near the meetinghouse did they sit down on a log and put them on to enter into worship presently. Democracy spoke through a frontier hymn of 1800:

> Come hungry, come thirsty, come ragged, come bare,
> Come filthy, come lousy, come just as you are. . . .

And when they were gathered, it was one of their number who emerged to speak for them. There was always one who could "preach a pretty fair backwoods hardshell sermon." His expression was geared not to vaults and ambulatories and transepts but to groves and clearings and roughhewn rafters. Emotion—raw, contagious—was what they came to release, in the name of God. When the spirit was on them, they worshipped somewhat in the vein of the frontier fantasy that gave them identity with wildcat, tornado, ring-tailed roarer, and earth-screamer.

For daily close to violent peril and the large acts of birth, life, and death with no specialized skills to meet them, when they gathered to deal with human destiny under God, their prayer took violent forms in the forest revival meetings of 1800 and after. The wildcat was licked over and over in testimonials given in meeting against Satan. The earth-screamer rose and jabbered sounds that, if they

were words, belonged to an unknown tongue; but their message of
guilt and release was understood by all. Shouting people fell to the
ground in convulsions of humility and brief lost-mindedness. They
writhed, jerked, crawled and trembled, while their tears streamed
into the dust, and those who watched and heard felt strange longings begin to shake within themselves, and soon they too were lost
to the hard world and were thrown down by a power greater than
each—the power of all together. Crying of David's dance before the
Ark of the Covenant, one would suddenly leap into the air, crack
his heels as for a hoedown, and start to jig like a man on a river
boat. Born of the intention to worship, there took form among them
the essential acts of theatre, dance, and concert—every satisfaction,
however rude, of the desire to find through formal emotion a delivery from the limitations of the flesh, in its connotations of hardship,
suffering, and sin. So led by one of their number they gave themselves up to each other in the name of the Lamb; and purged by
spectacular emotion in which all took part, returned to their ordinary selves with sighs of renewed innocence and strength.

It was a mood, then, proper to other Sabbath pastimes, against the
misted blue distances beyond woods, and river hills, and creekside
meadows; the lyric, gold-washed afternoons of the frontier landscapes. A man would bring a horse to the meeting; and for hours
the horse was judged by a ring of critics who squinted at his general conformation, felt his withers, counted his teeth, stroked his
coat. Another, prosperous, donated a beef or a turkey as a prize for
the best marksman; and the long rifles cracked like whips in a
shooting contest. Others—men and women alike—fished at the edge
of a stream with thoughts upside down in clear water. Others sat
and "visited," feeling the past week in bone and flesh, and letting
their weight rest till tomorrow. Someone sang—"The Soldier's
Tear," "Long, Long Ago"—

> Now that you've come, all my griefs are removed,
> Let me forget that so long you have roved,
> Let me believe that you love as you loved
> > Long, long ago,
> > Long ago.

From the long-ago, drifts of the national heritage glowed and faded
in memory, hearsay, and gossip—how General Washington used to
hold a levee at Philadelphia in his black velvet court dress, wearing
a beautiful little sword and an expression of calm elevation, while

Lady Washington watched him to see whom to speak to; how a man who, when lightning struck a tree, was reminded that as a boy-sailor on the U.S.S. *Constellation* he saw the foremast of the French frigate *Insurgente* crack and fall; how another who had sailed with Decatur never forgot the burning of the *Philadelphia* before Tripoli; how a woman watched Madam Madison carry a picture and a parrot out of the White House when the British came to burn the capital; how Daniel Boone tried out his coffin—there was a picture of him doing it—before he died; how you could ride from Lockport to Albany on the Erie Canal so smoothly; how the remarkable new hotels of New York, five stories tall, had parlors for ladies, and music in the dining rooms; how the word "Slavery" had best not be mentioned till you knew which side you were talking to; how the public still took passage on river steamboats even though so many burst their boilers and sank on fire; and the railroads—how you got cinders in your eyes not only from riding on them, but just from standing in your own field and watching them go by; how printing presses, if you could believe what you heard, would all be run by steam in the end; and why didn't Daniel Webster go the whole hog and go to England to live, where the whiskey was better, and he would feel at home if he loved them so; and if Santy Anno did what they said he did in Texas, why did they let him go; and if so many men had seen the famous white mustang wild on the prairies, how come nobody ever took and caught him; and how the women in Santa Fe, every one of them, young or old, pretty or plain, smoked what they called seegaritos and blew the smoke in the faces of men at dances; and—sooner or later the talk all got around to it—who ought to be thrown out of office, and why, and who was going to be elected. . . .

For, as to politics, every American was an expert. He knew this was true, for he *was* the government. To make him so, his forebears had fought and died; and to keep him so, he would fight and die himself. He saw himself as the people at large, and the people as embodied in himself. He, the voter, projected into the people, was the source and object of everything. The people, observed Tocqueville, reigned in the world of the United States politics as the Deity did in the universe. If, as Crèvecoeur thought, the American was a new man who acted upon new principles, "he must therefore entertain new ideas and form new opinions." Politics was the supreme topic for American conversation; and its object was liberty. "In this country," wryly declared the French Bourbon royalist Montlezun, "where the word liberty is never omitted in conversation, there is the greatest tyranny of opinion; that is, of political opinion, for that is the only kind that seems important." What this royalist authoritarian failed to note was the immensely important fact that the opinion was not that of a single controlling individual, but of a majority of individuals who controlled. An art of collective living was at birth; and as it would govern the destinies of all, so it took the energies of all, at the expense of other values that in older societies were exquisitely developed as ornaments of life—the fine arts, the abstract pleasures of philosophy, all the tones of aristocratic systems that had for so long hidden matter under manner.

For man himself was the proper heart of the matter of life; and when the Americans rediscovered the fact, and the world heard them talk about it, they were listened to with a sense of recognition. Tocqueville observed that "the political debates of a democratic people, however small it may be, have a degree of breadth that often renders them attractive to mankind. All men are interested by them because they treat of *man,* who is everywhere the same." America seemed to stand not only for equality of opportunity; but to be also the land of mankind's second chance. To the degree that the Americans were interested in each other, the world was interested in them.

And indeed, Americans took a lively, sometimes a prying interest in one another's affairs. It seemed to one student of the new democracy that "if an American were condemned to confine his activity to his own affairs, he would be robbed of one half of his existence; he would feel an immense void in . . . life, and his wretchedness would be unbearable." What saved all was again the general consent to the will of the majority; and the majority on occasion not only made the laws, but even reserved the right to break them. For once law was established, if it appeared to bear too closely upon the rights of the individual, he was free to enlist others with him in an effort to change it to resist the power of central authority, and to remake, over and over again, the image of the nation in the likeness of his view of life. The citizen's training began early—schoolchildren made up rules for their own games and clamored for their observance among themselves. In any contingency developing in public—a traffic upset, a quarrel, a complaint against a merchant or innkeeper—the onlookers formed themselves into a deliberative body, and resolved upon what to do. Committees met to decide upon all manner of things—even to the drinking of alcoholic beverages. In the early nineteenth century temperance societies with over two hundred and seventy thousand members carried a stern influence. Their cheerless sway in Pennsylvania alone in one year reduced the consumption of alcohol by five hundred thousand gallons.

iv

Language

Such effect could arise only from an inexhaustible outpouring of speech. The Americans were talkative. With opinions sharply ready, they spoke their pieces freely. To rise and be heard was not only essential to their system of life; it was almost the only social joy they knew. In the absence of well-established theatrical life, and opera companies, and museums, the debating societies of the Americans had to serve as substitutes. They were popular. In their meeting rooms citizens rehearsed the postures and appeals that must serve them if they ever went to Congress; and the habits of debate became so satisfying that even in intimate conversation the member was likely to forget that he was talking to an individual and to fall into the larger airs of one who swayed a meeting, and if his style rose with his opinion, so that he became heated, he swept the air with his arm, and, carried away by his own sound, he addressed his lone listener as "Gentlemen. . . ." For oratory could always sweep him away, his own most of all. Newly the possessor of the parliamentary arts, he sometimes lost himself in them to the point of forensic nonsense. But more important to the habit of democracy than the nonsense of manner was the right of all citizens to be heard.

"Eloquence is, in fact, after gold, their highest ideal," said Father Grassi, an Italian Jesuit who gazed at the Americans during his five years as president of Georgetown College from 1810 to 1815. He went on to say that New World orators paid less mind to the inner values of a speech—originality and beauty of thought, weight of ideas, force of argument and logical development—than they did to its manner. They knew their success with a public waiting to be edified rested upon other details—florid metaphor, elegant words, grand periods. The American speaker confessed that he was impatient of "a vulgar and sterile state of facts." What the people wanted must be offered. "A people who have fresh and lively feelings will always relish oratory." The oratory of the West was "free, lofty, agitating, grand, impassioned. . . ." It was a people's art; and like a people's art, it had a curious double spirit. It both derided and imitated the richness of more aristocratic or better-educated models. It was aware of the idiom of a donnish class, an élite in whom all elevated expression was reposed by older societies; and rejected it in the name of a whole population who shared equally the joys and powers of making utterances that could sound splendiferous, whatever on earth they might mean. Much frontier oratory in its inflation took to kidding on the level. The inflation was perfectly conscious and was often meant to be comic—and yet at the same time, it hoped to intoxicate with its reminders of large acts, projected fantasies of patriotism, and a new historical spirit. For metaphor it drew freely on the marvels of the unfolding continent—the might of Niagara, the sweep of the prairies, the noble rise of the Rockies, the blaze of Western starlight, the arc of heaven that embraced America from coast to coast, and endlessly the scowling American eagle who dwelt on pinnacles and crags, and soared in freedom above the restraints of earth. Like all the arts of the people, frontier oratory expressed desire and character. Its inflations and exaggerations were brandished in reply to the vastness of the West, the bulk of mountains, where man was so little. If there was vulgarity in its expression, there was also pathos; for what showed plain was the violent dancing of a spirit that must assert or be lost.

As the country—its land, political purpose, and united energy—was new, so must its most common means of expression—language itself—be new. For the old forms of English the people laid down new rules and made up new words. Inventing his character, and adopting wilderness ways with which he had to achieve physical victory, the American needed new means with which to express himself. By 1815 he had a new dialect that was a distinct tangent of the mother tongue. Much of its vocabulary was consciously fantastic; and any man was privileged to coin vivid, homely, and extravagant locutions, and might even become a virtuoso of the process. The frontier talked the raw materials of a new literature. Politics, work, and daily character in shrewd masquerade stimulated the most vigorous flow of new speech expressions. Those that had a real spark of aptness, a truth in their color, passed into current use. Stump speakers flung them back at their creators; they were picked up by newspapers; and in time passed into general acceptance as correct. It was a language that sought understanding at the level of least education. It reflected a general suspiciousness of studied correctness, and in the beginning it even disdained formal recognition of different social levels. "Our dictionary," noted Crèvecoeur before the nineteenth century, "is short in words of dignity and names of honor." But it was not long until the frontier granted titles to anyone whose

calling or whose knack of impersonation seemed to demand them—
Judge, General, Colonel, Doctor, Reverend. . . .

Tocqueville found American speech full of abstract terms which
enlarged and obscured the thoughts they were intended to convey,
and he concluded that democratic nations preferred obscurity to labor—the labor of speaking and writing correctly and clearly. His observation again caught something of the essential character of people
working out a great experiment in equality. Make it *sound* grand,
they seemed to say, and you *are* grand. Keep it loose, and you are
not committed. Generalize, and you are delivered from the concrete,
which in terms of your own life may be hard and graceless. Roar,
and inconvenient truth or painful accuracy may be stilled. To the
untutored ear, the accents of education sounded fancy. So, without
education, adopt the fanciness, and you will sound educated. Upon
such a trait much comic character was based—the itinerant preacher,
the courtly Negro, the windy swindler, the congressman as a master of polysyllabic ambiguity.

American humor rested less on inherent wit or sharp observation
of human failings than on rough drolleries full of exaggeration and
strange usage for its own sake. The speech became noisy and profuse. It imitated sounds of sucking and smacking and cracking and
slicing and chopping and sawing and thumping and poking and
digging and clapping and exclaiming and hushing. It stuck in extra
syllables for elegance and comic surprise. It liked to repeat in the
same word the sound of dental consonants that gave a jerky, droll
effect. It made comedy out of mouth-widening vowel sounds and
speech-yodels whose effect depended upon a swallowed *l*—the gob-
ble of the North American turkey. It was at times almost abstract
sound. Its character stripped of known words and their meaning,
and left only with sound, might still suggest the meaning intended,
along with the hard, simple, and at times lyrically beautiful life
from which it came.

To throw fits into someone was to cornuck him. To mean huge
was to say monstropolous. A total abstainer from alcohol abstained
teetotaciously. An angelical character was angeliferous. Someone
who wanted to flee skedaddled, which meant that he absquatulated.
Something complete was bodaciously so. To defeat or overcome was
to ramsquaddle and to obliterate was to obflisticate. A strong man
was a screamer, and an important one a ripstaver. If a fellow took
off his clothes, he shucked himself; and a woman suffering from a
certain nervous disorder had the peedoodles. If there was a kettle of

meat and vegetable stew for supper, it was known as burgoo. To
cheat someone, or to deceive with false love, was to honeyfogle. . . .
It took only a few such words salted through an otherwise conventional passage of speech or writing to change its character into something entirely new in effect. The effect was that of imaginative en-
largement of experience. Even place names reflected the tendency.
Audubon on the Mississippi recorded in 1820 that "many places on
this River are rendered More terrible in Idea by their Extraordinary
Names than real difficulties—." And if the native speech could evoke
pictures of rough, hilarious, or absurd experience, it could also summon forward much of the accidental beauty that pervaded the memories of the westering people. Again it was Audubon who noted a
lovely usage that summoned up a picture of countless frontier en-
campments: firelight, he said, "is named in some parts of the country, *forest light.* . . ."

In both the grotesque and the lyric lay predictions of the national
literature that was to come.

V

Arts &
Utility

With the open secret of the whopping lie the frontier made its
own first conscious literature. Competitions of tall tales were held in
which the people tried to create their own myths. Boasts of prowess,
marvels of animal origin or reincarnation, farces of anthropomorphism, fabulous reversals of the natural order, minglings of Indian,
Gaelic, and huntsman's lore—these were typical raw materials for
the made-up stories with which improvisers in camp hoped to entertain and stun one another. As they dealt highhandedly with the
mysteries of nature, they were in great contrast to the mythologies
of all Indians, who stood in awe before the elements; and as they
celebrated the rebellious triumphs or howling humiliations of a man
alone in the fantastic world, they were opposed in spirit to the deco-
rousness of the Spanish character. So long as there were new sights
to behold, new endurances to encounter, the frontier's own literature
held the character of a mythology. But it was not long—a matter of
a generation—before experience seen in those terms from the inside
became the subject of a commercial literature that saw the West
from the outside, and found for it a huge national audience. In the
end, the commercial literature came back to the frontier, and there
the living subjects of its formularistic romances read with credulity
and love what it told about the West, very little of which was real
or true.

The novels of Fenimore Cooper grafted the frontier forest upon the conventions of European romanticism, and soon a flood of imitations of Cooper's popular creations poured forth from the steam printing presses of the East, and were known as "steam literature." If these were full of wild inaccuracy, they met the desire of whole populations at home and abroad to participate in the early nineteenth century's only new physical adventure.

But truer meanings of the American adventure were gathering to be heard, and would proclaim through Emerson the American mind that must convert the world, and through Whitman the American body that must father upon it a new breed. The Yankee philosopher spoke for the freedom of the individual intellect and its responsibility in a democracy. The crowd-roaming poet, revealing the true polarities of the feminine and the masculine in himself, passionately celebrated the body of the recumbent land and the body of the democratic man who possessed it. In the central ideas of these two interpreters of the new nation lay seeds that would grow throughout all significant American literature after them; for they were mystically sensitive to the essential quality in the early national experience, and like prophets, spoke it forth to the future, over the heads of the people, as it were, to their common heirs.

Meanwhile, the people, close to what they had known on the frontier, gratified in countless ways the memorial impulse, creating the "old-timer." At a settlers' meeting in Missouri someone read a metrical catalog of early families, written in a tradition if not in a meter that recalled Michael Drayton and the Battle of Agincourt, with the names of common heroes standing forth to kindle the minds of those who had helped to win a wilderness, a century, a nation:

> Sam Lucas, Boggs and Swearingen,
> The Nolands and the Fristoes, then,
> The Greggs, with Owens two;
> The Davises and the Flournoys,
> The Kings and Staytons and McCoys,
> And Dailey with his twenty boys—
> All these and more we knew. . . .

In such a purpose, however humbly, literature came to the service of the people.

It was a service required of all the arts in early America. "Nothing," declared Dr. Franklin, "nothing is good or beautiful but in the measure that it is useful: yet all things have a utility under particular circumstances. Thus poetry, painting, music (and the stage of their embodiment) are all necessary and proper gratifications of a refined state of society but"—and here was suggested an admonitory glance from aside his small curlicue spectacles—"but objectionable at an earlier period, since their cultivation would make a taste for their enjoyment precede its means." But Franklin was looking east, not west, and thinking of opera houses, theatres, and museums in the cities of Europe. He saw that utility must be a determining value for the arts of a forming democracy; but having little of the creative temperament, he forgot that the arts would never wait for ideal conditions or a refinement of society to bring them forth. Even as the frontier took its westward course they came forth because it was in their nature never to be denied; and as they appeared in the context of democracy they spoke both to the people and for them.

By river and by road troupes of theatre players followed the settlers. Floating along waterways actors rehearsed in costume on deck, to the astonishment of people working in riverside fields or travelling along towpaths. In their costume hampers were stuffed the wrinkled habiliments of their repertoire the blacks of Hamlet, the stripes of Yankee Doodle, the crowns and swords and ermine and velvet for Richard III, plumes for Pizarro. When they came to towns, they played in halls, meetinghouses, later in theatres; and the actors eddied in and out of the public life offstage in grand strangeness, ample of manner, of swelling speech, and garbed in bright colors that would not bear close inspection after hard travel and measly pay. Every frontier American was a hot critic, for he knew something himself about making a character and the art of dissembling. The roving theatre brought with it the magic of a heightened life, and in its freedom of movement and fancy, probed into the longings of its audiences, revealing to them the hidden discontents and shortfallings of the selves that glowed in their desires and that were never so disturbing as when they watched the enactment of a heroic play, however ragged its character, or poor its scenes. Many a playgoer, facile with the emotions of revival and tall tale, fell into confusion watching the actors, and forgetting what was imaginary and what was real, had to be restrained by neighbors from intervening in the acted drama. In the face of such familiar transports the actors were patient; for it was, every time, the greatest tribute they could

vi
Light
in the
Clearing

receive; and for what it signified they stoutly and willingly fought like other pioneers the dangers of frontier travel—Indian attacks upon their little troupe, an occasional robber, uneasy threats by backwoodsmen who resented the appearance of actors with their silky airs, their humbling literacy, their swagger and color, their way with women. . . .

But towns were far between, and the theatre company was ready to play wherever anyone would attend. A cluster of cabins on a riverside, a clearing in a forest—anywhere. In such places the play was given out of doors, with no curtain, and for scenery, only what the woods provided. A space between thickets served as stage, with real trees for "wings" from behind which the actors could enter. Scene and location and date were affirmed, in Elizabethan style, in the spoken text. Tallow candles held in potatoes made footlights, unless the settlement was too poor to spare these, when the lights were made out of old linen rag wicks burning in pans of fat. If not even these were to be had, then the play was given in the dark, and imaginary life rode forth on the voices of actors unseen but speaking with doubled intensity to pierce their listeners who sat on benches facing them, or on the ground. But perhaps the moon was out, and then, silvered in common magic, the forest, the animated figures striving with one another, the spectators, were united in a creation of spirit as powerful as it was mysterious, and as poignant as it was fugitive; a little point of light shining one night in the deep continental darkness.

The wandering players had their specialties, turns of song, recitation or dance which they gave between the acts of a play, or put together in a whole program as a minstrel show. Their plays were expedient versions of those popular in established Eastern theatres, and sometimes included a vehicle for a famous star, like Junius Brutus Booth, who found on the frontier a certain fulfillment of his mystical and libertarian nature. Some of the plays were of American origin, and many of these were written around a central stock character. They were Yankee plays—*Jonathan Postfree,* or *The Honest Yankee* (1807); *The Saw-Mill,* or, *A Yankee Trick* (1829); *Solon Shingle, The People's Lawyer* (1839). A recurring figure in plays improvised within a strict convention was the rube who for four acts served as the dupe of clever, rich, educated and cruel men, such as lawyers, bankers, and land speculators; and who in act five turned upon them with blinking innocence that got the best of them every time. The hick in the city presented variations of this democratic passion in which the central figure—in his carrot-red wig, his blacked-out teeth, his baggy pants into which he kept looking with a squirm to see if what he lost was to be found in there, only to be embarrassed to discover the audience watching him in the act—raised the people by impersonating someone laughably lower than their lowest specimen. There were plays on episodes of early American history—*The Arab Chief and the Pirate of the East* (1834), which recalled naval adventures in the Barbary wars; dramas in which Washington appeared; and adaptations of Cooper's novels.

But the most popular native theme was the Indian. In the theatres of the East, and in the very clearings and at woods-edges where the people had killed and known killings by Indians, Indian plays were acted in such profusion that in time it was said that they had become "perfect *nuisances.*" They presented the tragedy of the Indian, and recalled promises made by white men and broken. In their explorations, and perhaps expiations, of the betrayals of human relations and rights, they accepted the Indian as a human being, with none of the legalistic debate as to his nature that had for so long occupied the colonial Spaniard. The Indian of the early American theatre was an ideal figure of natural man, echoing Rousseau's concept of the savage. In *Metamora,* or, *The Last of the Wampanoags,* written by John Augustus Stone in 1829, and played for decades by Edwin Forrest, the Indian hero ended the play with an apostrophe to the white soldiers who have killed him: " My curses on you, white men! May the Great Spirit curse you when he speaks in his war voice from the clouds! Murderers! . . . May your graves and the graves of your children be in the path the red man shall trace! And may the wolf and the panther howl over your fleshless bones, fit banquet for the destroyers! Spirits of the grave, I come! But the curse of Metamora stays with the white man! I die. . . . [Falls and dies."] With this play, and in nearly forty others on Indian themes, the audiences who made them so popular seemed to make gestures of poetic redress, and to bring into the light a sense of guilt toward the Indian who had suffered the destruction of his liberty and the loss of his land. Audubon's view of the Indian in 1820 found its echoes in the theatre of the people for many decades: "Whenever I meet *Indians* I feel the greatness of our Creator in all its Splendor, for there I see the Man Naked from his Hand and yet free from Acquired Sorrow . . ." By what they responded to and thus made profitable the people shaped their own democratic image in the creative arts of America. The theatre seemed to make one further gesture in self-portraiture, for even as they continued to take the continent from the Indians, the people used the theatre as a medium of confession.

vii

Sons of Harmony

In their music, too, they found community, whether in joining together for religious, political, social, or working occasions. American music was essentially an art of performance rather than of invention. The Puritans brought their hymns with them; and as North American life became more polite than pious, grand musical societies with serious purpose were founded in the cities to produce works of Haydn, Bach, Pleyel, Mozart, Handel, Purcell, Dr. Thomas Arne, and Sir Henry Bishop. The Revolution, with its achievement of freedom through martial valor, was followed by a new popularity of music. Francis Hopkinson of Philadelphia came forward as the first sophisticated native composer, composing songs that echoed the manner of Dr. Arne, and reflected the simple sweetness of morning light. His works for harpsichord were given in proper concerts, and a company came to present French opera in New York and Philadelphia, and soon there were attempts to shape dialogue-and-ballad operas on native subjects.

In a more popular vein the fife became the rage. Its shrillness and panic vivacity suggested the state of the national feeling. With little stinging scales it challenged the conservatism of the past, forcing an animated vision of a future as brisk and insistent as its own voice. The fife presided at the head of parades and at rallies. If the fifer went travelling, his instrument provided a walking skirl to keep him company and announce him when he arrived at inns, fairs, or parties, where, being asked, he would play solo airs and tweedling songs.

William Billings in the late eighteenth century brought a new formal excitement into the prevailing church music of Puritan psalms sung in unison. In primitive imitation of the high contrapuntal style he arranged them in harmonies for part singing. His tunes made an immediate appeal and on being published in engraved sheets sold widely. They were, he declared, "twenty times as powerful as the old slow tunes," and calling them "fuges," he described their new character in terms of contest between the parts, "each part striving for mastery and victory, the audience entertained and delighted, their minds surpassingly agitated and extremely fluctuated, sometimes declaring for one part, and sometimes for another"—for all the world like partisans in democratic politics. "Now the solemn bass demands their attention, now the manly tenor; now the lofty counter, now the volatile treble. Now here, now there; now here again—O ecstatic!" he cried to his creations, quite carried away by the sense of movement in his art, "Rush on, you sons of harmony!"

As music went west with the frontier settlers it lost the opportunity for formal performance offered by the cities. In the mountains and forests, it took the form of traditional songs from the British highlands and, through the Negro, from the west coast of Africa. The frontier made up few new songs, for the settlers were already past the phase of civilization in which primitive people originated a folk music. Appalachian and savannah and prairie song were all modifications of old expressions long before developed over the Atlantic in the British Isles and Africa, and were often corruptions of these. But they were augmented by accidental beauties of tonal expression that Western life produced in its work. On the crystal rivers when a flatboat or keelboat came to a bend, a boatman sounded a warning on a horn, playing a vagrant tune that drifted on the water and was lost in the trees—

> O, Boatman! wind that horn again
> For never did the listening air
> Upon its lambent bosom bear
> So wild, so soft, so sweet a strain!

In the golden mists of river perspective it made a signal of wonder, nostalgia, and the stir of going over America, much as the sound of the railroad whistles would do in later times. Steamboats put the boatman's horn to rest, for with them came steam screams, a new sound in the nation's work that must in time find expression in its music. And so too, the ringing of anvils, the chinking of harness, the locust song of the power saw. . . .

If music in early America drew all its substance from the Old World, and made little if any gift to the creation of new music, then the rhythms of work and simple social occasion led to a style of instrumentation and accompaniment that made do with materials caught up out of common life. Rough, witty, percussive, the style, listened to fastidiously, might have seemed almost antimusical; yet in the primitive sense it performed an essentially musical task—to make rhythm and beat with many percussive means, and assign melody to a single line for violin, flageolet, voice or group of voices.

Western music devoted itself to a lively function—the levitation of the body. To hear it was to see physical gesture—cakewalk, dance figure, the waggles of convivial drollery. There was little contemplative or serious role for music. But in its simple repetitive drive lay translations of work beats, the blows of mauls and axes and hammers which in a group of working men always fell into accidental syncopation, and these, even more than Negro rhythms, may have prefigured the jazz idiom of a century after. Of all percussion instruments, hands were the easiest to use. The gesture again prefigured the form, and evoked the scene with the rhythm of handclaps, either on the beat or off, with single clap or double to the beat —people in a ring, or in line, or in a square, dappled by sunlight through shade out of doors, or shown by the bloom of lanterns indoors, when intense conviviality erased distance and void and wilderness, with choral shrillings and the threeked echo of handclaps in the eaves; in high musical terms a performance rude and graceless, but worthy of respect as a means to let the people stand forth in their hunger for exchange and delivery of spirit. For popular music (like all other popular arts) held little abstract artistic value, but was wonderfully eloquent in describing its makers and users.

Percussion effects to express the simple rhythms that dominated frontier music came from anywhere and everywhere. George Caleb Bingham drew a young riverman sitting on a sawhorse and holding a skillet in one hand while he stroked and struck it with the knuckles of the other, to accompany the sound of a fiddle played by another man sitting on a keg. Negro musicians brought their drumheaded banjos into the people's music, and also taught countless boys how to hold polished pork-rib bones between their knuckles and shake, rattle, and roll them with brilliant effect. The jew's-harp, though capable of giving an illusion of different pitches, made a humming monotone whose only variations were percussive. Drumsticks like knuckles performed on any surface. Flute, flageolet, and violin sang melody—if they survived egocentric drives encountered on the frontier: Audubon hearing "a great uproar" one night in his guest room went to find Rafinesque, the naturalist, "running about the room naked, holding the handle of my favorite violin, the body of which he had battered to pieces against the walls in attempting to kill the bats"—of a rare species—"which had entered by the open window." The violin, a Cremona, was demolished. But Audubon still had his flageolet, and when he travelled, staying overnight with strangers, he repaid their hospitality with "a few airs" before taking his leave in the morning.

Popular songs heard in theatres brought together verse and music in strong declamation that swept the audience into joining the refrain, as in a piece that kindled every patriot with its narrative of Jackson's victory over the British in Louisiana:

But Jackson he was wide awake, and wasn't scar'd at trifles
For well he knew what aim we take with our Kentucky rifles;
So he led us down to Cypress Swamp, the ground was low and mucky;
There stood John Bull in martial pomp: *but here was old Kentucky....*

The actor, dressed in buckskins, threw down his fur cap and took aim with his property rifle, and the audience, with handclaps, footstamps and roaring voices, crashed out the chorus between stanzas:

> Oh, Kentucky!
> The hunters of Kentucky!
> Oh, Kentucky!
> The hunters of Kentucky!

Such a song, in both its subject and its clean, hard style, would have the power to evoke its singers and stompers long afterward.

Group song was a popular pleasure, and the singers developed their own kind of literacy through a simplified system of musical notation. It was a system that employed notes of distinctive shape repeated for the several intervals of the scale—some square, others triangular, others oval, so that they looked like little scatterings of buckwheat heads on the staff lines. From this resemblance the system, which originated in Lancashire, was called "Buckwheat Notation," at first in derision, later in simple acceptance, as its use spread fast among singers who found conventional musical notation difficult for sight reading. With the turn of the eighteenth century, when religious revival meetings swept the West, shape-note singing became a general accomplishment that was never to be lost among untrained but fervent folk singers of America. Songbooks sold widely, and westering travellers took along copies of such as *The Western Lyre,* issued at Cincinnati in 1831, and *The Missouri Harmony,* at St. Louis in 1837. Even blank music books went with the emigrants, who when they heard new songs wrote down text and tune in buckwheat notation to share them with new friends when their journey allowed. In the hoot and glee of their mingled voices the early travellers celebrated the community of their hopes, the

power of their faith, and an eternal trial at rising above sin. If
what they sang was not transcendent as music, it served a purpose
in harmony with what they were, taking the voice of each, and for
a little while making them all one, in rude recollection of the
equality and democracy they strove to create together with their
lives.

viii
Knacks &
Crafts

A frontiersman "boasted that with only hickory withes and a
jack-knife he could make a very good wagon."

In such a statement lay the seed of all the arts and crafts—the
"practical arts" as they were called—in early America. Dr. Franklin's concern for the marriage of beauty and utility was uncon-
sciously answered by the men and women who in successive settlements were obliged by scarcity of rich materials to equip and
ornament their daily tasks with objects of their own making. It was
natural that the indigenous arts in a democracy were first of all functional. If the conditions of their lives denied to the settlers access to
the fine arts, there was also in the crotchety plainness of the people
a hint that the fine arts were suspect. Puritan bleakness was partly
responsible for such a view. But another and overriding sense had
effect too. This was a democratic suspicion that the fine arts had always been identified with aristocratic patronage. Palaces crammed
with splendors, artists appointed to court, prestige and expense attached to the work of master-artists—such airs of luxury seemed
highfalutin, and to partake of them called for a whole world of experience, education, and allusion in which the democrat could only
feel at a disadvantage. In their gnarled self-respect the people must
earn their own evolvement of the arts. If at first they must be content with making a beautifully finished rake handle that felt good
to the grasp, or a plain little chair that looked polite as it sat empty
and felt good as it was occupied, or a wooden decoy duck carved
and painted to fool a game bird in early daylight and otherwise to
ornament a shelf with its sleek green, brown, gray, black, and white
reminders of sport and sustenance, then what they fashioned so
honestly had the authority of answering honest needs.

In the pattern of ordinary social development the settlers would
have climbed through primitive generations or centuries toward a
flowering of refined art based on their utilitarian creations. But
there were two reasons why such a sequence was not necessary.
First, the settlers were not socially primitive people, but civilized

people taking new land with a new social idea; and second, to their new idea of man and to new land in which to realize it there was soon added a third newness that swept the first two along at an amazing rate of historical development. This was the discovery and spreading use of technological methods—many new means of making corporate life closer, and individual life easier, so that united to his fellows the individual was to be relatively free from toil. The frontiering and geographical completion of the American continent took place during the first years of a world revolution in technology. The effect of this coincidence upon the people's expression in the arts was to drive home more deeply than ever the love of usefulness over beauty—if it came to a choice. The handicraft of the settler would soon exert itself in designing for machine crafts. Machine crafts would make possible through duplication of copies a wide-spread use of what before had been limited to an original and its user, who was so often its maker. The spirit of the copy said, My value is in serving as many people as possible, to help in their lives. Has this work not its own beauty? The spirit of the original said, I am unique, and my beauty lies in my rarity, for the touch of my creator is on me everywhere. What matter that I serve only one?

But there the matter came to a point. For the democratic impulse sought to bring the goods and beauties of life to as many people as possible, in contrast to the aristocratic impulse that granted patronage to art forms for an élite. If traditional fine-art forms were the highest expression of creative spirit in civilization, then the Americans seemed to have forgotten the fact; and to have busied themselves with an expression of creative spirit for which the raw material was mankind itself, in a powerful belief that the arts of living together must come first. Their masterpiece of creative spirit was the forging of human liberty and equality in a coherent society. In the process they illustrated the difference between the practical arts and the fine or inutile arts, considered as historical records.

Through articles made for use, the practical arts left an uncritical likeness of the society that produced them. On the other hand, the fine, or inutile, arts always made a conscious criticism or interpretation of the life from which they grew. This was one of their chief intentions. The record they left was formal, and while it suggested the taste of the times, it suggested even more sharply the personality of the designer. The position and character of the arts in America seemed to equate utility with the anonymous people, and formal beauty with the individual creator in the fine arts. And as it was the body of the people together who made the conditions of life, it was their popular expression in the arts and crafts that achieved originality, style, and freshness; while to the scattered few "fine" artists was left the task of treating American subject matter in techniques and visions imitative of European models. The universal American tinker became a maker of machines for work, the whittler became a sculptor of workaday signs, artisan and artist were one; and their genius for the practical became a national characteristic that would lead to a standard of material life new to the world.

In their conviction of purpose there could also be delight in how they worked; and in countless objects made for use they celebrated their own gaunt graces, and left a record of how, in their spirits, fancy and patience and good sense could meet.

Where color was used, they used it exuberantly, on wood, metal or in fabrics. On the other hand, form was frugal, as the gestures of labor were frugal, with the inference of meeting a purpose with not too little, or too much, but just enough energy. The Conestoga wagon illustrated both idioms of color and form. Shaped like a great open coffer, and slung on wheels to go away, it was just a plain receptacle; but with its bright blue sides, vermilion wheels and dazzling creamy hood of Osnabrück linen, it recalled the painting palette of the Pennsylvania Germans, who made flowers in such frank colors, and stars, fruit, doves, parrots, on their boxes, furniture, and certificates of occasion.

Wood was the commonest American material. The continent had a seemingly inexhaustible supply. The frontier American craftsman used it for most houses he built; and for most of the objects that went into a house or served business. He made all manner of chests, none exactly alike, but all sharing a common plainness. If he made a tall clock case, it was severely plain. His benches, beautifully surfaced, remained as close as possible to their original parts of plank and branch. Such severity suggested not only that the maker was a plain man, for religious or other reasons unsympathetic toward rich ornament; but also that he was in a hurry, with many another task awaiting him. But when he came to make machines of wood, his pace of work must have been measured and easy; for what resulted sometimes were such masterpieces of functional design that their beauty would satisfy long later any interest in abstract art. Such machines were a Shaker spinning wheel, with its large delicate wheel suspended above a base remarkably light on slender legs; and a fork for pitching barley and straw that extended four wooden tines in repeated tapering curves in a gesture of work that combined exquisite efficiency with elegance. Something of the same beauty brought thoughtlessly to life out of a grave concern for a good feel and a perfect usefulness could be seen in the wooden stocks made to support the cast metal parts of American firearms. Their tactile appeal, combined out of finish and shape, was so great that no man could see a good one without wanting to run his hand over it, even if he wasn't thinking directly about how a white morning came over whitening water where game must rise with the day.

Wooden crafts and painting came together in various needs for painted sculpture, and for outdoor commercial signs. Ships built in the Eastern yards were given carved figureheads that were portraits of real men or women, great figures out of the young national history, or idealized allegorical creations. In their proud realism, these were often heroic in scale, and carved with wonderful, wavelike freedom of scrolling design. They were brightly painted and heightened with gold leaf, and when installed under the bowsprit leaning over the bosom of the waters, they made visible the personality with which men have always endowed ships. At the stern, there was often opportunity to create carving and gilding, where the ship's name and home port were shown. In such long horizontal panels a peculiarly American style of decoration, using letters and ornaments, treated space with the balance and grace of the printer's art.

Other figures of popular sculpture were life-sized wooden Indians or Turks or Negroes to stand before tobacco stores in bright paint and arresting stare. It took twelve days to make such a figure—six for the carving at a foot a day, and six for the finishing. To produce hanging signs for inns, shops, barbers, the craftsman again allied woodworking to painting, and often called again on the serene severities of typography to govern the spacing of his symbols and letters. Many such signs were beautifully contrived and when they called to the customer, did so calmly, offering, at inns, the one word, "Entertainment," and displaying, for shops, carved likenesses of wares in bas-relief.

Painting was allied to metal crafts in the production of such articles as tin utensils, canisters, pots, trays, and boxes; andirons and bootjacks and hitching posts that represented human or animal figures; and various toys. The metal craftsman made weather vanes in every kind of symbol. The conventional cock was joined by new designs, with certain ones recurring to reflect the interests of the public—a fish, a whale, a grasshopper, a trotting horse, a horse in extended racing stride, a cow, a frigate in full sail, a locomotive and tender. These were painted or treated entirely with gold leaf or left in the black silhouette of wrought iron. Lanterns and candlesticks and trivets; locks, hinges and latches; firemarks in iron with designs that again recalled typography—all had simple grace and the occasional appealing falter whereby the hand of the originator could be detected. It was in duplicated objects of cast metal that the impersonality of the coming steam power era was suggested—rifle barrels, spread eagles for flagpole and cornice finials, plain iron kettles with their three little legs cast on the pouchlike belly.

In weaving, embroidering, rugmaking, quilting, women contributed to the idiom of American crafts. The richly colored floral and vinelike designs of crewel embroidery derived from Jacobean England were succeeded by plainer patterns in hard homespun cloth. Weaving tablecloths and bedspreads and coverlets, the housewife developed simple geometries that repeated variations based on squares and triangles, frequently in colors of blue and white. Her most personal style appeared in quilting. Here was an exercise in thrift, for she used patches of cloth saved from every which source; and in ingenuity, for her hope was to achieve symmetrical patterns out of scraps that came along with no rhyme or reason; and in patience, for a quilt was big, to fit on a man-and-wife bed, and to make only one six-inch-square patch of the ten dozen or so needed would call for thousands of stitches. But she persisted, and produced an original work whose simplicity and modesty told much about her life and the joys of her labors throughout many hours made up of a few minutes here, a few there, when in repose she was not idle.

ix
First Interpreters

Little—almost none—of the formal art of painting told as much about American life as such workaday crafts. Before the 1840s only two painters—Edward Hicks and James John Audubon—brought together matter and manner in styles that yielded out of imagination and experience true images of the new America. Hicks was a native artist whose painting arose from two other prepossessions— religion and his trade as a coach builder. He was a Quaker preacher, and the austere tenets of his church gave simplicity to his vision, and educated him in terms of Biblical literalism. His working trade called for decorative painting on the panels of carriages, and for it he learned to grind his own color, and to make his own brushes. Moving from Pennsylvania to New York, and on to Maryland, and

Ohio, he worked as house painter, sign painter, and carriagemaker,
rising in Quaker meeting wherever he might be. Something in his
spirit told him that painting pictures was ungodly, yet something
else told him more strongly that it was a delight and in the end a
necessity. He tried to compose his warring spirits by devoting his
paints to religious themes. His pictures took well with the public,
and in time even the Quakers encouraged him in his art, provided
he pursued it "within the bounds of innocence." Self-trained, his talent developed until in his most famous subject matter he gave forth
in composed enchantment his vision of life. It described the human
and animal worlds as he would see them, and it identified the act of
colonization in North America with the ultimate equality of creatures promised by the prophet Isaiah:

> The wolf also shall dwell with the lamb, and the leopard
> shall lie down with the kid; and the calf and the
> young lion and the fatling together; and a little
> child shall lead them. And the cow and the bear
> shall feed; their young ones shall lie down together;
> and the lion shall eat straw like the ox. And the
> sucking child shall play on the hole of the asp, and
> the weaned child shall put his hand on the cockatrice'
> den. They shall not hurt nor destroy in all my holy
> mountain; for the earth shall be full of the knowledge
> of the Lord, as the waters cover the sea.

The Reverend Mr. Hicks painted a picture of that vision. If he had
painted it only once, it would perhaps not have furnished sufficient
evidence for his general emotion. But he painted it over thirty times,
and its idyllic democracy stood for what he felt in his nation, believed of his God, and desired of his fellow creatures. His treatment of Isaiah's vision was perfectly literal. There were the animals, clustered together in peace—he called his subject "The Peacea-
ble Kingdom"—and yes, there a little child led them, and other little
children set their hands over the serpents' pits; and upon the animal
faces lingered bewitched expressions that seemed to veil yet reveal
human thoughts. In the middle distance was an allegorical group
representing William Penn making his treaty with the Indians, and
on a lovely bay beyond lay a ship with pearly sails. "Come," said the
painting, "let all manner of men, as well as all manner of animals,
dwell together in peace." Let this occur, it implied further, in our
great land of North America, with its waters, mountains, and endless depths of forest. With one huge oak set against dense shadowy

foliage Hicks suggested inexhaustible America; and in the prim, sweet compliance of his animals and Indians and colonists with the spirit of peace and equality he captured the desire that had conceived America. Everything in the work was "within the bounds of innocence"—the concept, the drawing, the design, the color scheme; nothing in it owed a debt to European conventions of art.

The reverend carriagemaker illustrated in his career how in America's early arts they best saw and captured America who sought her humbly, through crafts and other acts of work.

A number of beautifully gifted artists before Hicks painted American portraits and historical subjects, but by the spirit of their training and technique, they remained colonials. Copley was the American Reynolds, Stuart the American Romney, Sully the American Lawrence, and so on. However rich and copious their productions, they could not suggest the new America so well as the work of another artist who, when he went to work, had no conscious plan to catch a likeness of America. But that was what he caught, in the general passion of his first purpose, which was scientific. That he was not a native American made no difference to his capture of the American essence in his work. Beginning with Asiatic migrations after the ice age, America was always peopled by foreigners. What mattered was how he saw a new land in its new lights:

"Imagine," wrote a French critic who saw a first showing of his work in 1827 at Edinburgh, "imagine a landscape wholly American, trees, flowers, grass, even the tints of the sky and the waters, quickened with a life that is real, peculiar, trans-Atlantic. On twigs, branches, bits of shore, copied by the brush with the strictest fidelity, sport the feathered races of the New World, in the size of life, each in its particular attitude, its individuality and peculiarities. Their plumages"—and it was of course Audubon's birds of which he wrote—"sparkle with nature's own tints; you see them in motion or at rest . . . singing, running, asleep, just awakened, beating the air, skimming the waves, or rending one another in their battles. It is a real and palpable vision of the New World, with its atmosphere, its imposing vegetation, and its tribes which know not the yoke of man. The sun shines athwart the clearing in the woods; the swan floats suspended between a cloudless sky and a glittering wave; strange and majestic figures keep pace with the sun; . . . and this realization of an entire hemisphere, this picture of a nature so lusty and strong, is due to the brush of a single man; such an unheard-of-triumph of patience and genuis!"

If the French critic did not know America, it was likely that he

knew Europe; and the important thing in his impression of Audubon's world was that it was strange and new, in its golden stands of
light, its vast river prospects, its blue perspectives stepping away into
woods and mountains; all incidental to the bird or animal so stu-
diously arrested in the foreground—incidental, but again, as though
early America had to be seen obliquely lest she vanish, standing
forth in the truth. Over his shoulder, so to speak, and beyond his
scientific purpose, Audubon saw the land and fixed it forever in its
spacious morning sense.

There were other painters who combined scientific interests with
the arts, like little Leonardos. The Peales of Philadelphia operated a
museum of curiosities that included scientific specimens. Samuel
F. B. Morse along with his telegraph and Robert Fulton with his
improved steamboat were literate painters in conventional styles.
The American forerunner in any craft of life seemed required to
possess various knacks, if he would be self-sufficient, and also serve
his countrymen with all the talents needed to throw together a new
culture.

X
The
American
Art

"It is not," wrote John Adams to his wife Abigail from Paris in
1780, "it is not indeed the fine arts which our country requires; the
useful, the mechanic arts are those which we have occasion for in a
young country." Wandering about Paris, he could have filled vol-
umes with descriptions of temples and palaces, paintings, sculptures,
tapestry, porcelain, and so on, if he only had the time. But this, he
said, he could not do without neglecting his duty. And what was
his duty? "The science of government is my duty to study, more
than all other sciences." And as for the arts—". . . the arts of legisla-
tion and administration and negotiation ought to take the place of,
indeed, to exclude, in a manner, all other arts. I must study politics
and war, that my sons may have liberty to study mathematics and
geography, natural history and naval architecture, navigation, commerce, and agriculture, in order to give their children a right to
study painting, poetry, music, architecture, statuary, tapestry and
porcelain. Adieu."

In 1817 he still had qualms about the general subject. "Is it possible to enlist the 'fine arts,'" he asked, "on the side of truth, of virtue, of piety, or even of honor? From the dawn of history they have
been prostituted to the service of superstition and despotism." He
even graded the arts in the order of their perfidy. "History and epic
poetry are worse than architecture, sculpture, and painting, because

they are more lasting deceptions." But though he felt that the sciences and arts, for all their failings, had "vastly and immensely ameliorated the condition of man, and even improved his morals," there seemed actually little to be done about disciplining them. "It is in vain to think of restraining the fine arts," he concluded. "Luxury will follow riches and the fine arts will come with luxury in spite of all that wisdom can do. . . ."

John Adams did not see how widely characteristic of the American people was Dr. Franklin's notion that beauty depended wholly upon utility. If what the people made for usefulness had beauty, it lay in abstract qualities that recalled the gestures of human purpose and use. Every act of building and equipping America for work was admittedly a worthwhile social achievement. But was it any the less an aesthetic achievement to create the very subject of America at work than to comment upon the subject afterward in the formal processes of art? This was the question that America asked of the traditional arts, and would continue to ask in creating all forms of technological design. To make the society itself flower and sprout color and fulfill purpose—this was the American art, and its medium was the liberty of the individual citizen, at least in the ideal.

In the immense neighborhoods of the frontier the settlers came together from their scatterings in field and forest to help each other at tasks too great for a single family. And when they gathered, they made entertainment out of their work, at husking bees, flax-scutching bees, house-raising bees. Whiskey flowed, and great meals were cooked out of doors in pits of embers, and not only many hands, but shared ideas of how to do it, made light work. Holding strong desires for freedom from all bondages, including that of primitive labor, the Americans became virtuosos of convenience in living. What they discovered about the conquest of manual labor they were able to share by the same means that would in the end make them neighbors in common knowledge over the whole continent—instruments of communication such as those that came into being and use at the very time of the westward movements of the first half of the nineteenth century—the steamboat, the electric telegraph, developments in printing methods, the steam locomotive. An American song gave a sense of exhilaration that came with the railroads:

> Singing through the forest,
> Rattling over the ridges,
> Shooting under arches,
> Running over bridges. . . .

The job of westward settlement revealed a national genius for "make-do." The boundaries of material development seemed to be pushed back in a new dimension of ingenuity; and the nation felt the brisk joy of working all technical limitations to their utmost limit. Common sense was put to work with uncommon energy; and Dr. Franklin's imported rationalism, the seed of technology, appeared to become an American trait. In its spirit of inquiry, it faced the Americans not only to the west, but also to the morrow. If the Indians in their dateless time had been bound by the present, and the Spaniards by the past in their collective memory, then the Americans had a passion for the future. The future was the American theme. To make a better life today, yes, they strove; but there would be tomorrow a still better one, right there on earth; and to achieve this, as surely it would be achieved, every citizen believed he had his chance, in his own way. Because enough people believed so, they created a nation of the many, governed by all, for the benefit of each in his own terms of life, liberty, and the pursuit of happiness so long as these did not undo the voted will of the majority.

This creation was the inheritance of the Anglo-Americans who penetrated and finally owned the continental United States. In the Southwest, as elsewhere, they bore living evidence of the national character. If it was a complex character, yet through all the common expressions of its owners—their vision of human possibilities, their energy and materialism, their politics and oratory and language, their dominant religion and mythology, their music and theatre and crafts, their absorption in the affairs of work and business—shone a single faith. It was faith in democracy. They had seen it work, on frontier after frontier, even to the last one.

4 · The Last Frontiersman

Ever since the eighteenth century the raising and tending of large herds of beef cattle had been practiced on the Texas Rio Grande's wide, flat borderlands. All descended from animals brought to Mexico in the sixteenth century by Spaniards, there were several types of cattle on the river plains, of which the most distinctive had tremendously long horns doubled up and backward for half their length; heavy thin heads; tall legs, and narrow, powerful flanks. They were haired in various colors, with white patches. By the hundred thousand, wild cattle roved at large over the uninhabited land on both sides of the border, and constituted its prevailing form of wealth. As such they were always prizes for Indians, Mexicans, and Americans, who in an unbroken tradition of border violence raided the herds— preferably those already gathered into ownership by other men— and drove away thousands of animals to sell on the hoof, or to kill for their hides which were baled and sold to traders, while the carcasses were left to carrion, and the bones to workers who gathered them up and hauled them for sale as fertilizer to Texas farming towns.

Even in the face of such hazard a few cattle traders drove herds east to New Orleans, north to Missouri, and west even as far as California, before the Civil War. But the trade was unorganized, and the principal markets, New Orleans and Mobile, were supplied by cattle steamers that sailed out of the Texas Gulf ports. The longhorn cattle they carried were called "coasters" or "sea lions." The coastwise cattle trade was limited by a monopoly held on Gulf shipping by the Morgan Line. "To anyone outside of the ship company," wrote an early cattle trader, "an enormous rate of freight was exacted, practically debarring the ordinary shipper." And when the Civil War took levies of man power from the cattle business, the trade was further constricted. In consequence of such conditions, "for a quarter of a century or more," the trader remarked, "the herds of Texas continued to increase much faster than the mature surplus was marketed. In fact, no market accessible existed sufficiently to consume this surplus, and of course the stock [became] less valuable in proportion as it became plentiful." But shortly after the Civil War the cattle trade was revived, and by the 'seventies, the herds of Texas owners were the largest in the United States. Of these, some of the largest belonged to great companies operating where the nation's range cattle industry had its origin—along the Rio Grande between the Pecos and the Gulf of Mexico.

It was the *brasada,* the brush country, stretching from the Nueces to the Rio Grande. It was profuse in growths—but almost all were thorned. It was either swept with gray dust borne on blistering winds, or beaten by deluges that hissed as they first struck the hot ground, or raked by blizzards that came whistling out of the north. In its interlocking thickets that enclosed small clearings where grew curly mesquite grass, cattle could graze by thousands and hardly be seen by horsemen who sought them. There cicadas sang of the heat, and sharp-haired peccaries rooted among the thorns, and blue quail ran amidst the wiry shadows, and rattlesnakes sought the cool and sometimes were drummed to death by wild turkey gobblers at whose destroying wings they struck and struck with no effect on nerveless quill and feather. It was a land of hard secrets, the best kept of which was the location of water. Its few rivers ran in abruptly cut trenches walled with pink or yellow or slate-blue limestone, and could not be seen except from their very brinks. In every direction the wilderness looked the same. There were no distant mountains to be seen. The land swelled away toward the white sky in slow rolls and shimmered in the heat that blended the ashen color of the ground with the olive greens of the brush until across the distance there seemed to hang a veil of dusty lilac.

It was astonishing how much human activity there was in a land so hostile to man's needs. It was the scene of habitual Indian travels, and of the military campaigns of the Mexicans and Texans in their wars, and of the United States Army in its Rio Grande movements, and of travelling traders, missioners, and criminals. In its thickets there was even an occasional small ranch, locked in isolation by sun, distance, and the poverty of its occupants, who possessed even few wishes. And it became the scene of organized work in the cattle business. Animals born and grown there were taken in herds to the milder prairies above the Nueces, and across the rest of Texas and Oklahoma to beef markets in the north. ". . . The cow boys, as the common laborers are termed," said a cattleman who saw the industry develop, "go in squads of four or five scouting over the entire range, camping wherever night overtakes them, catching with the lasso upon the prairies every young animal found whose mother bears their employer's brand." It was "legal and a universal practice to capture any unmarked and unbranded animal upon the range and mark and brand the same in their employer's brand, no matter to whom the animal may really belong, so be it is over one year old and unbranded. . . ."

The cow boy was the last of the clearly original types of Western American to draw his general tradition and character from the kind of land he worked in, and the kind of work he did. His forerunners were the trapper of the mountains and the trader of the plains. Of the three, he left the fullest legacy of romance and to see him as he first was, it would be necessary in a later century to clear a way back to him through a dense folk literature of the printed page, the moving-picture film, and the TV tube, which in using all his symbols would almost never touch the reality that supported them.

His work was monotonous in hardship and loneliness, and occasionally it was shot through with excitement that rose from danger. The country where he worked was in its dimensions and character his enemy; and yet it was also in an intimate way almost a completion of his nature, that revelled in vast vacant privacies, and fixed its vision on the distance as though to avoid any social responsibility. He had for his most constant companion not a man or a woman, but an animal—his horse, on whom his work and his convenience and even at times his life depended. His duties took him endlessly riding over range country, where he sought for cattle to capture, calves or yearlings to brand, herds to drive to water, individual cows or bulls of a proper age or condition to cut out of a herd for segregation into another group. Such a group would then be driven to another location—a different pasture or a market.

In dealing with cows through the consent of his horse, the cow boy needed to know much of the nature of both animals. Through experience he learned to anticipate the behavior of cattle, and to judge the effect upon them of every stimulus. He saw that the laws that governed them were the laws of the crowd; and he developed extraordinary skill in handling great crowds of cattle at a time. His horse, broken to riding, and subject to his will, he had to know as an individual creature, and dominate relentlessly its nature by turns sensitive, stubborn, and gentle. Living with these two animal natures, the cow boy seemed to acquire in his own certain of their traits, almost as though to be effective at living and working with them, he must open his own animal nature to theirs and through sympathy resemble them. If he could be as simple as a cow, he could also be as stubborn; as fearless as a wild mustang, and as suspicious of the unfamiliar; as incurious as an individual bull, and as wild to run with a crowd when attracted. Even in his physical type, the cow boy might tend to resemble his animal companions—a certain flare of nostril and whiteness of eyelash could recall the thoughtless face of a calf; a leanness of leg and arm was a reminder of a horse's fine-boned supports and further suggested the physique best adapted to, and developed for, the horseman's job—the hard, sinewy body, light of weight but powerful, tall for high vision over the animal herd, long-legged for gripping the mount around its breathing barrel. His state of body and nerve had to be ready to fight, for his job sometimes included battle, when Indians or organized cattle and horse thieves came down upon his herd. Then like any soldier he had to shoot to kill, under the sanction of his duty. For his labors, he was paid in the 1870s from fifteen to twenty dollars a month in gold or silver. He saw himself at his task, and his self-image survived in his anonymous folk literature:

> All day long on the prairie I ride,
> Not even a dog to trot by my side:
> My fire I kindle with chips gathered round,
> My coffee I boil without being ground.

In any group of nineteenth-century cow boys, more were bearded than clean-shaven. Their costumes were much alike, though with individual variations. But all their garments were "coarse and substantial, few in number and often of the gaudy pattern." The cow boy wore a wide-brimmed hat with its crown dented into a pyramid or flattened. If the brim in front was sometimes turned up off his face, it could be turned down to protect him from the pressing light of the sky under which he spent all day. Around his neck he wore a bandana of tough silk. It served many purposes. Tied over his face it filtered dust before his breath. It served to blindfold a calf or tie its legs. It was a towel, a napkin, a bandage, a handkerchief, or simply an ornament. His shirt was of stout cotton flannel, in a bright color or loud design of checks or stripes or plaids. Over it he sometimes wore a cloth or leather vest but rarely a jacket. His trousers were either of heavy denim, dyed dark blue, sewn with coarse yellow thread, and reinforced at points of great wear with copper rivets; or were of odd colors and materials, mostly dark, that could stand tough use. They fitted tightly. The trouser legs were stuffed into boots that reached almost to the knee. At work, the cow boy often wore leggings of thick cowhide. They were made after the pattern of Indian leggings—two long tubes, with wide flaps at each side cut into fringes or studded with silver disks, that reached from ankle to groin, and were tied to a belt as though to the string of a breechclout. Their purpose was to shield him against thorns in the brush he rode through, and the violent rub of haired animal hides, and the burn of rope when he pulled it against his leg as he turned his horse to control a lasso'd creature. On his boots he wore large spurs, of silver or iron. He wore gloves to work in, and around his tight hips he wore a cartridge belt from which depended his pistol

—most often a Colt's single-action, 45-caliber revolver called the Peacemaker. He had no change of clothing. He went unwashed and unbathed unless he camped by a stream or a pond. "I wash," he said in his multiple anonymity,

I wash in a pool and wipe on a sack;
I carry my wardrobe all on my back. . . .

Like the object of his work and its chief instrument—the cow and the horse—his Texas saddle, in its essential form, came from Spain. Its high pommel and cantle, heavy stirrups, and great weight suggested the squarish, chairlike saddle of the jousting knight, though its design was modified by Mexican saddlers until all contours were rounded and smoothed, and the pommel, of silver or other metal, was developed to serve as a cleat about which to secure the lariat whose other end was noosed about a captive cow or horse. When not in use, the lariat was coiled and tied to the saddle. There was little other baggage on the saddle, except now and then a leather scabbard containing a short rifle. If two cow boys travelled together, they carried their camp equipment and bedrolls on a pack animal. Otherwise, when a large group worked daily out of a central camp, their equipment was carried in a camp wagon to which they returned during the day for meals and at night for fire, food, and companionship.

The wagon, pulled by four horses and driven by the camp cook, was a roving headquarters for the grazing party. Its form was invented in the 1850s by Charles Goodnight, who adapted an Army vehicle to the needs of the cow camp. Rolling in movement, it had a compact look, with its sheets over bows, that concealed the contents, which consisted of bedrolls for the workers and at its rear end a high, square chest standing upright. Parked, free of its horses, and with its tongue propped level to serve as a rack for harness, and with its sheets extended and supported by poles to make a generous pavilion of shade to one side, the wagon seemed to expand into several times its own size. It was amazing how much it carried, and how much immediate ground its unpacked equipment could cover. The chest at the rear was faced with a wooden lid which, when opened downward, became a work table supported by a central leg. Then were revealed in the chest many fitted drawers and hatches in which the cook kept every necessity for cooking and every oddment, including medicines. Behind it in the wagon bed, along with the bedrolls, he carried his heavy pots and skillets and tin dishes. Beneath the wagon frame hung buckets and to its sides were lashed water barrels.

The cooking fire, which at night served to give its only light to the camp gathering, was made a few feet from the wagon and its profuse scatter of equipment. There the cook prepared his meals, always the same. If brush or wood were scarce, he made his fire of dried animal droppings, like the Spanish soldiers who centuries before had found these the only useful product of fabled Quivira. If he had no matches, he could start his fire by pouring gunpowder into his pistol, wadding it loosely, and firing it with its muzzle close to a scrap of cloth or other dry kindling. He prepared a great pot of coffee boiled from whole beans. A cow boy drank a quart or more every day. Of such coffee it was said that "you would hesitate, if judging from appearance, whether to call it coffee or ink." It was drunk without cream or sugar. There was a kettle full of stew in which, using his pocketknife—his only table service—the cow boy probed for a lump of meat. With thick biscuit or cornbread he soaked up the gravy and like an Indian ate from his fingers. There were no green vegetables to be had. A pot of kidney beans finished the meal. The cow boys squatted near one another, or stood idling by the wagon, and ate in silence and with speed. A meal was not an occasion of social interest. It was an act of need, disposed of without grace or amenity. Inseparable from it were the taste and smell of dust and cowhair and horse sweat and leather—sensory attributes of everything in the cow boy's working life.

> For want of an oven I cook bread in a pot,
> And sleep on the ground for want of a cot.

But before the bedrolls were opened up from their heavy canvas covers, and the work party went to sleep, there was a little while for talk and other diversion. Such a miniature society created its own theatre. There was always someone who would be moved to perform, while the rest gazed at the intimate, never-failing marvel of how one whom they knew—a man just like them—became before their very eyes somebody else. The campfire put rosy light over the near faces of the gathered men and their cluttered possessions, and threw their shadows like spokes out on the flat ground until the immense darkness absorbed all. At the very center of light a fellow rose. He had a joke to tell. He acted it out. It may have been well known to all, but they listened in fixity. It was likely to be an obscene jape. The cow boy, observed a cattleman of the 'seventies, "rel-

ishes . . . a corrupt tale, wherein abounds much vulgarity and animal propensity." His delight was a practical joke on one of his
fellows. The joke was good if it made a fool of someone. It was better if it mocked the victim's personal peculiarity, and it was even
better if it played upon "animal propensity"—for the sake of symbolic relief of the enforced continence under which the work party
lived on the range.

There were other stories to hear—many dealt with experiences in
the Civil War, to which the early cow boys were still close in time.
There were wrestling and other trials of strength to perform. There
were songs to sing, some of whose texts were lewd parodies of senti-
mental ballads. All knew the songs of the cattle trail, and could sing
them together. If in one of his cubbyholes the cook carried a violin
for its owner, there would be fiddle music of an astonishing agility
that yet managed to seem tuneless, while a cow boy danced a clog
in firelighted dust, and the rest clapped hands. Often a mournful
piety stirred in someone, and when he began to sing a hymn, others
joined him, and like a sigh of innocence, their united voices rose
over their lonely fire where they camped, a little knot of men with
every potentiality, to one or another degree, for every human attribute. The bedrolls came out of the wagon and were spread. Nobody
had a book to read, and in any case, the firelight was dying and
would soon be down to coals.

> My ceiling's the sky, my floor is the grass,
> My music's the lowing of herds as they pass;
> My books are the brooks, my sermons the stones,
> My parson a wolf on his pulpit of bones. . . .

As his artless song implied, the cow boy belonged to the type of
man who was not, actually, domesticated. He chose freedom in the
wilds over responsibilities of hearth and home. He thought more
about work than he did of a family. He made love on almost a seasonal schedule, as though in rut. He visited a prostitute, or took a
sweetheart, only to leave her, with sighs about how he must go
roaming, as though all would understand his natural state. He departed for work or went off to fight wherever he would find other
men like himself. He preferred the society of men to that of
women; for only with men could he live a daily life that was made
up of danger, and hard exposure, and primitive manners. These did
not seem like disadvantages to him, for he liked them for them-

selves, and, further, they brought into his life excitement, freedom, and wilderness, all of which he sought.

If he saw himself as a simple creature, and if tradition so accepted him, both were wrong. His temperament and character were full of tempestuous contradictions and stresses. The life he chose resembled the Indian's more than any other, but it lacked the sustaining spiritual power of the Indian's nature-mythology, and so it could not really hold for him the unquestioned dignity of a system that tried to explain—in whatever error—the whole of human life. He was close to the frontiersman many of whose ways he repeated, but he was neither innovator, builder, nor explorer. His love of hardness and primitive conditions could be turned either to serve his comrades in unbreakable loyalty, or to lead him, as it did in individual cases, to a career as gunman or cattle thief. His longing for love was so great that he felt an exaggerated chivalry for womankind, but in his worship he made women unreal; and yet through his song literature he lamented, ". . . between me and love lies a gulf very wide." He sanctioned his state by romanticizing it in ballad and story; but he refuted it symbolically by his periodic violent outbreaks of gunplay, drunkenness, and venery. And with all his hardness, he gave in to a soft core of sentiment whose objects were the animals he worked with, and the comrades who worked with him.

"I and they were but creatures of circumstance," said a cow boy of his fellows in his domesticated old age, "—the circumstances of an unfenced world." From their unfencedness came their main characteristics. Solitude was put upon them by their chosen environment, which thus modified their character. "Adhesiveness," in the jargon of the nineteenth-century parlor science, was a human trait. The nearest living being to whom the cow boy could turn with affection was his horse. It was his daylong companion and helper. It obeyed his orders and made him master of distance and took him in and out of danger. Responding to his signals, it seemed to him to possess more than animal intelligence. His horse, a masterpiece of anthropomorphism, joined him in a partnership, and was paid every honor due to such a position. "My horse," continued the retired cow boy "my horse was something alive, something intelligent and friendly and true. He was sensitive, and for him I had a profound feeling. I sometimes think back on . . . remarkable horses I owned in much the same way that I think back on certain friends that have left me. . . . I went hungry sometimes, but if there was any possible way of getting food for my horse or if there was a place to stake him, even though I had to walk back a mile after putting him to graze"—and cow boys hated to walk—"I never let him go hungry. Many a time I have divided the water in a canteen with a horse." If it was expedient to take care of his horse in order to assure his own mobility and safety, and if it was ordinary human kindness to care for a dumb creature, there was yet more than such promptings in the cow boy's devotion to his mount, as many a song and story attested. The professional cow boy rarely had a cultivated mind; and in his incurious thought he was lowered and his horse was elevated until they drew together in common identity. It was a process typical of a juvenile stage of character, and it may have suggested why the cow boy and his legend should appeal forever after as a figure of play to little boys. In much the same sort of emotion the cow boy felt a mournful fondness for the animals he herded—the little "dogies" to whom he sang on the trail to keep them quiet, and to whom he attributed something of himself as they were objects of his vigilance and labor, day and night. In its innocence and pathos his system of projected sentimentality for animals suggested that only by making of them more than they were could he have survived his lonely and arduous duty with them. One of his songs said of the cow boy that "his education is but to endure. . . ."

Another song celebrated the life of cow boys together in their wandering yet coherent community. "The boys were like brothers," they sang of themselves, "their friendship was great. . . ." Alike in their extreme individualism, their self-reliance, their choice of a life wild, free, and rude, the companions of the cow camp gave to one another an extreme loyalty. It seemed like a tribute to the hard skills they had to master to do their jobs. A man who proved himself able at it deserved membership in a freemasonry unlike any other. Its physical tasks caused a high value to come upon the life of action, in which there was no place for the values of mind and spirit. These were relegated to the world of women; and in the towns and cities that later completed the settling of the last frontier West, for the better part of a century it would be the women's organizations that would try to rescue the fine arts, education, religion, and social amenity from being held as simply irrelevant to civilized life—an attitude even more withering to mankind's highest expressions than one of mere contempt. For its purpose in its time, the brotherhood of the cow camp was all that was needed to make an effective society. Diverse like all individuals, and sprung from various backgrounds and kinds of experience, the cow boys taken together seemed to merge into a type more readily than most workers in a common job. Their environment directly created the terms of their work, and their work in its uncomplicated terms created their attitudes and points of view. And if they were like one another in their principal traits, it was because so many of them chose their calling for the same general reason.

This—it was attested to again and again in the cow boy's anonymous ballad literature—this was flight from one kind of life to another. Many cow boys left home, "each," said a ballad,

> Each with a hidden secret well smothered in his breast,
> Which brought us out to Mexico, way out here in the West.

In this lay a suggestion of doom, a rude Byronism that was echoed in other songs by allusions to unhappiness, guilt, escape. Some were driven to the new society of the cow range by a faithless girl at home, or a dissolute life, or a criminal past; others by inability to become reconciled to their home societies following the Civil War, or by bitterness in family life, or even by a cruel stepmother. Romantic conventions of behavior in the nineteenth century could move the cow boy, who punished those who had betrayed him. "I'll go," he threatened,

> . . . to the Rio Grande,
> And get me a job with a cow boy band.

He did not mean a band of musicians, for not until the next century would the cow boy's public identity be chiefly that of an entertainer who in a commercial adaptation of the cow boy costume would spend more time with a microphone than with either horse or cow. No, with companions on the cattle range, the cow boy, deaf to dissuasion by loved ones who had proved faithless, promised to go

> . . . where the bullets fly,
> And follow the cow trail till I die.

Unable for whatever reason to accept the bindings of conventional society, within the one he sought and helped to make on the last frontier he was capable of sure dependability in any cause for the common good of his comrades, whom he did not judge, even if sometimes a propensity to go wrong should overtake them in the very land where they had thought to escape their doom. Who knew when a man might encounter the moral frailty of one of his friends of the brushlands?

> As I walked out in the streets of Laredo,
> As I walked out in Laredo one day,
> I spied a dear cow boy wrapped up in white linen,
> Wrapped up in white linen as cold as the clay.

It was a dirge for a young man who in his dying words revealed a longing for a gentler land than the dusty empire of his work, and confessed his errors. "Oh," he said,

> Oh, beat the drum slowly and play the fife lowly,
> Play the dead march as you carry me along;
> Take me to the green valley, there lay the sod o'er me,
> For I'm a young cow boy and I know I've done wrong.

Unashamed of their grief that sprang from their close living, his bearers saw themselves in him, and if he had sinned, they could not condemn him.

> We beat the drum slowly and played the fife lowly,
> And bitterly wept as we bore him along;
> For we all loved our comrade, so brave, young and handsome,
> We all loved our comrade although he'd done wrong.

For here was a clan feeling, a solidarity, with a realistic view of character and its capacity for error. Idealizing one another in the all-male society of their work and play, the cow boys remained loyal above, or even because of, the weaknesses they shared and assuaged with violence. In conclusion, the dirge moved from the individual to the group.

> Then beat your drum lowly and play your fife slowly,
> Beat the Dead March as you carry me along;
> We all love our cow boys so young and so handsome,
> We all love our cow boys although they've done wrong.

In another valedictory the cow boy spirit, after reciting the perils of "some bad company" which could only lead to being "doomed for hell," ended in the presence of the hangman with an admonition to morality.

> It's now I'm on the scaffold,
> My moments are not long;
> You may forget the singer
> But don't forget the song.

In the cow boy's lonely character there were extremes of feeling and behavior. If in his work there seemed to be a discipline of dedicated steadfastness, a purity of vocation, then when he went to town, he threw himself into indulgence. Perhaps the town was a reminder of the coherent social life he had fled at home, and perhaps it was now a guilty joy to outrage it by his behavior. Certainly the town was the very opposite of the desolate open range from which even the cow boy needed periodic change.

His best chance for it came when men of the range party were told off to drive a herd of cattle to the marketing and shipping towns. The main trails along which he drove went north from the Texas Rio Grande to Kansas, and another—the Goodnight-Loving Trail—led westward to New Mexico and California. It passed the Pecos River at Horsehead Crossing about a hundred miles above the Rio Grande, and presently divided into two forks. One pointed north to Colorado. The other crossed the Rio Grande at Las Cruces and followed the old road to San Diego.

The cattle made trails that showed many narrow grooves side by side—marks of the strict formation in which the animals in their thousands were driven for upwards of a thousand miles. A cow boy said that trail life was "wonderfully pleasant"—this in spite of continuing hazards. There still might be trouble with Indians. All the cattle were wild, and were easily stampeded by attacks, or by thunderstorms, or by hail. If the weather was wet, rivers rose, and to take thousands of cattle across swollen waters was at best a tedious job, and often a perilous one. Against the drovers on the move there pressed at one period a whole organized enterprise of thievery. Outlaws captured drovers, tortured them, sometimes killed them, and stole their herds. When one drover was captured, he tried to talk his way out of his trouble, but the bandits were immovable and a reporter of the incident said bitterly that "it was like preaching morality to an alligator."

But in swelling volume the animal trains passed through to their destinations, and the cow boys were happy on the trail. They played tricks on one another, and shot game on the prairies, and after supper sang, told stories, danced to a fiddle, lay back to look at the stars and speculate about them, and listen for the sounds of the herd settling down for the night. "I do not know anything more wholesome and satisfying," mused a cow boy long after his trail days, "than seeing cattle come in on their bed ground at night so full and contented that they grunt when they lie down." It was like a communion of creature comforts in which man and animal could meet. Three shifts of night guards were posted over the herds. A sleepy cow boy rubbed tobacco juice in his eyes to keep awake. Morning must come, and another day to be spent at the pace of cattle walking with odd delicacy in their narrow grooved trails, and after enough such days, the shipping town would take form like a few scattered gray boxes on the severe horizon, and the cow boy would feel his various hungers begin to stir.

It was in town that he got into most of his trouble. Every facility was there to help him do it. As a cattle shipper observed, in frontier towns "there are always to be found a number of bad characters, both male and female; of the very worst class in the universe, such as have fallen below the level of the lowest type of brute creation." These pandered to the cow boy's howling appetite for dissipation.

Sometimes he rode into town and without cleaning himself or changing his clothes but just as he had dismounted in hat, damp shirt, earth-caked trousers, and boots and spurs, he strode into a dance house, seized a "calico queen" or a "painted cat," as he called the dancing women, and with Indian yells and a wild eye went pounding about the dance floor under a grinding necessity to prove in public, most of all to himself, that he was at last having a good time. The music to which he danced was "wretched . . . ground out of dilapidated instruments, by beings fully as degraded as the most vile. Few more wild, reckless scenes of abandoned debauchery can be seen on the civilized earth," remarked the cattle shipper, "than a dance house in full blast in one of the many frontier towns. To say they dance wildly or in an abandoned manner is putting it mild. . . ."

And sometimes the cow boy, at large in town with his accumulated pay, went first to improve his looks. In a barbershop he had a bath, and then had his three to six months' growth of hair trimmed, and his full beard cut down, shaped, and dyed black. In a clothing store he bought completely new clothes, from hat to boots, and then, strapping on his pistol, he was ready to impose himself like shock upon the town. Gambling rooms, saloons, a theatre, a row of prostitutes' quarters like cattle stalls, dance houses—from one to the next the cow boy could make his explosive ways, to be catered to by "men who live a soulless, aimless life," and women who had "fallen low, alas! how low . . . miserable beings." Among the conventions of the cow boy's town manners was free use of his firearm, whether he might harm anyone or not. The pathos of folly long done and half forgotten would make his murderous antics seem unreal to later view. But they were real enough in the frontier towns of the 1870s. "It is idle," sighed the cattle shipper in that decade, "it is idle to deny the fact that the wild, reckless conduct of the cow boys while drunk . . . have brought the *personnel* of the Texan cattle trade into great disrepute, and filled many graves with victims, bad men and good men. . . . But by far the larger portion of those killed are of that class that can be spared without detriment to the good morals and respectability of humanity. . . ." And "after a few days of frolic and debauchery, the cow boy is ready, in company with his comrades, to start back to Texas, often not having one dollar left of his summer's wages." All he had was a memory that found its way into one of his songs, about "The way we drank and gambled and threw the girls around. . . ."

The cow boy triumphed at a lonely work in a beautiful and dangerous land. Those of his qualities that did the job were the good ones—courage, strength, devotion to duty. His worse traits, exercised for relief, were not judged in relation to his task. All aspects of his complex nature entered into his romance. He saw himself for his own achievement, and like the earliest individuals of the frontier, he consciously created his character and his tradition, and whether his emotion was honest or not, it was so energetic that by it he made his nation see him in his own terms. In him, the last American to live a life of wild freedom, his domesticated compatriots saw the end of their historical beginnings, and paid him nostalgic tribute in all their popular arts. Soon, like them, he would lose his nomadic, free and rough form of life before the westward sweep of machine technics by which Americans made their lives physically more easy —and socially less independent and self-reliant. In the very exercise of their genius for convenience in living, the American sacrificed to the social and commercial patterns of mass technics some part of the personal liberty in whose name the nation had been founded. The cow boy in his choice of solitude held on to his whole liberty as long as he could. But domestication of his West by machine technics began in the 1860s and, once started, went fast.

For in response to such technics, the cattle industry grew with suddenness, and then became stabilized. The first of these was the westward advance of the railroads with which the northbound cattle drives could make a junction. It was not easy to arrange for the earliest rail transport of Western cattle. A young Illinois cattle shipper, who was the first to establish a livestock market in Kansas, was astonished to have his new idea rejected by two railroad presidents and the leading businessmen of several Kansas towns to whom he went in turn. Finally the Hannibal & St. Joe Railroad gave the young shipper a contract "at very satisfactory rates of freight from the Missouri River to Quincy, thence to Chicago." He selected Abilene, Kansas, as the site for his stockyards, and in 1867, the first cattle were driven there from Texas. During the next four years 1,406,000 head of cattle were brought to Abilene. Other trails and shipping centers were soon established, and it was estimated that during a period of twenty-eight years nearly ten million cattle worth almost a hundred million dollars were moved from the Texas ranges to market. In the process of developing so great a business, the whole practice of cattle raising became formalized through changes that sought greater efficiency.

One of these used a technical machine product that soon conquered the open range where wild cattle once drifted according to weather. It was barbed wire, first used in 1875 to fence pastures in which with fewer and less skillful cow boys the herds could be restricted and more easily managed. When land was enclosed, ranch dwellings were needed. Permanent headquarters buildings followed. Cattle no longer were driven to rivers but found their water in earth tanks supplied by dug wells, with still another machine product to keep it flowing—the metal windmill. The main trunk lines of the railroads ran east to west across the continent; but soon feeder lines were built—sometimes following the flat terrain of the old trails—and machine transportation reached nearer and nearer to the great ranches of the border where the whole cattle industry had had its beginnings. The Missouri, Kansas and Texas Railroad was the great Texas cattle line. It tapped the Rio Grande brush country ranges. The Atchison, Topeka and Santa Fe main line crossed New Mexico and a branch line ran from Belen on the Rio Grande all the way down the valley to El Paso. The Texas and Pacific reached eastward from San Diego to El Paso in 1877, and bridges now came back to the Rio Grande to stay. The whole river empire was soon tied to the rest of the nation by rails. When packing houses were established at Kansas City, Fort Worth, and other Southwestern cities, the final pattern of the organized beef-cattle industry was realized. In it there was little room for the figure, the temperament, of the original cow boy, with his individual lordship over great unimpeded distances and his need of freedom as he defined it. His cow-camp literature recorded yet another stage—the last—of his history. "The cow boy has left the country," he could sing, "and the campfire has gone out. . . ."

On barbed-wire fences, like symbols of the new order of affairs over the controlled range lands, dead, skinned coyotes were impaled in a frieze—twenty or thirty of them at a time. They were stretched in midair with a lean, racing look of unearthly nimbleness, running nowhere; and their skulled teeth had the smile of their own ghosts, wits of the plains. In the dried varnish of their own amber serum they glistened under the sun. The day of unrestrained predators was over.

5 · A Larger Earth

It would take only a few generations for man's new resources of power and the technics of their application under the imperatives of modern society to bring across all the Southwest the style of material life common to the nation as a whole.

But true attributes of the past survive in the vast region, and where they are not exploited for commercial purposes, may still be encountered in their main characters—Indian, Latin, Anglo-American, with hints of the prehistoric time, the colonial epoch, and the nineteenth century frontier.

As in any historical projection, changes in the terms of social energy will continue to be the main theme of any observation of the Southwest. Meanwhile, those phases of change which occur only through aeons of geological time, affecting the landscape, with all its splendors of space, light, mountain, desert, river, canyon, high plains, sea coast, will always know a larger scale and a slower pace than man's.

The land of the heroic triad will continue to mean for later men what it meant to one of our time—the poet Witter Bynner, who wrote, in Santa Fe,

> . . . *a larger earth*
> *Absolved us*
> *Of ourselves.*

Acknowledgments

Apart from my great indebtedness to authors, whose works I list in the Bibliography, I owe thanks to many others who gave me active assistance in my labors related to the subject of this book. The acknowledgments for Great River, the parent volume of the present collection of essays in social history, are numerous, and it seems impossible to separate those which might be cited exclusively for this book, devoted as it is to particular aspects of southwestern life, from my inclusive listings of respectful gratitude in the original. Let me here, then, again thank all those whom I originally specified in Great River, and repeat only the names of those whose aid was so central to my whole purpose and my needs that without it I would have had no occasion to thank all the others in a finished work: Professor Allan Nevins, Mr. Ernst Bacon, the late Mr. J. Frank Dobie, Mr. Carl Carmer and Miss Virginia Rice; and Dr. Henry Allan Moe under whose sensitive and generous administration of the John Simon Guggenheim Memorial Foundation my work was greatly advanced through the aid conferred by two Guggenheim Fellowships. For excellent help in the preparation of the manuscript of the present book I am grateful to Mrs. Tania Senff and her staff secretaries of the Center for Advanced Studies at Wesleyan University.

—P. H.

Bibliography

The following listings, arranged according to the major divisions of this book, have been extracted from the general bibliography of *Great River: The Rio Grande in North American History.* They stand here with reference only to those chapters of *Great River* selected for this arrangement of my impressionistic presentations of the social history of the Southwest. Later studies must surely have offered further insights into the subject matter. I offer respectful thanks to those whose works, listed below, informed and sustained my own observations.

—P.H.

BOOK ONE. PROLOGUE / *Place*
PAGES FROM A RIO GRANDE NOTEBOOK
Reading from Source to Mouth

Croneis, Carey; Krumbein, Wm. C., and Lasley, C. *Down To Earth, An Introduction To Geology.* Chicago, University of Chicago Press, 1936.

Milham, Willis Ishister. *Meteorology.* New York, The Macmillan Co., 1929.

Talman, Charles Fitzhugh. *The realm of the air.* Indianapolis, the Bobbs-Merrill Co., 1931.

BOOK TWO. INDIAN / *Rio Grande Pueblos:*

The Ancients

Alexander, Hartley Burr. *North American (mythology).* V. 10 of
Mythology of all races, edited by Lewis Herbert Grey. Boston,
Marshall, Jones Co., 1916.

Bandelier, Adolph F. A. *The delight makers;* with an introduction by
Charles F. Lummis. New York, Dodd, Mead and Co., 1916.

―――― *Diaries.* Typescript from ms. 10 v. (unpublished, with the exception of v. 1, edited by Charles H. Lange and Caroll L. Riley.
Albuquerque, University of New Mexico Press, Santa Fe, School
of American Research, 1966).

―――― *Documentary history of the Rio Grande pueblos.* Part two,
Indians of the Rio Grande valley, by Adolph F. A. Bandelier and
Edgar L. Hewitt. Albuquerque, University of New Mexico Press,
1937.

―――― *Final report of investigations among Indians of the southwestern United States, carried on mainly in the years from 1880 to
1885.* Part II. Papers of the Archaeological Institute of America.
American series, IV. Cambridge, printed by John Wilson and Son,
University Press, 1892.

Benedict, Ruth. *Patterns of culture.* Boston, Houghton Mifflin Co., 1934.

Brand, Donald D. *Prehistoric trade in the southwest. New Mexico
Business Review,* v. 4, no. 4; October, 1935.

Bryan, Kirk. *Pre-Columbian agriculture in the southwest, as condi-
tioned by periods of alluviation. Annals of the Association of American Geographers,* v. 31, no. 4, December, 1941.

Castetter, Edward F. *The early utilization and the distribution of agave
in the American southwest,* by Edward F. Castetter, Willis H. Bell,
and Alvin R. Grove. Albuquerque, *University of New Mexico Bulletin,* Whole no. 335, December 1, 1939.

Coolidge, Mary Roberts. *The rain-makers, Indians of Arizona and New
Mexico.* Boston, Houghton Mifflin Co., 1929.

Crane, Leo. *Desert drums, the Pueblo Indians of New Mexico, 1540–
1928.* Boston, Little, Brown and Co., 1928.

Davenport, J. Walker. *Painted pebbles from the lower Pecos and Big
Bend regions of Texas,* by J. Walker Davenport and Carl Chelf.
San Antonio, Witte Memorial Museum, bulletin 5, ND.

Denver Art Museum. *Leaflet series,* 1936; 1939.

Dobie, J. Frank. *A vaquero of the brush country, partly from the
reminiscences of John Young.* New York, Grosset and Dunlap,
1929.

Douglas, Frederic H. *Indian art of the United States,* by Frederic H.

Douglas and René D'Harnoncourt. New York, The Museum of Modern Art, 1941.

Fergusson, Erna. *Our Southwest*. New York, Alfred A. Knopf, 1940.

Frazer, James George. *The golden bough, a study in magic and religion*. New York, The Macmillan Co., 1935.

Harrington, J. P. *Old Indian geographical names around Sante Fe, New Mexico*. American Anthropologist, v. 22.

Hewitt, Edgar L. *Ancient life in the American southwest*. Indianapolis, The Bobbs-Merrill Co., 1930.

—— *The Pueblo Indian world* . . . by Edgar L. Hewitt and Bertha P. Dutton . . . Albuquerque, University of New Mexico; Santa Fe, School of American Research, 1945.

Hrdlička, Ales. *Physiological and medical observations among the Indians of the southwestern United States and northern Mexico*. Smithsonian Institution, Bureau of American Ethnology, Bulletin 34. Washington, Government Printing Office, 1908.

Jeançon, Jean Allard. *Pueblo Indian clothing*, by Jean Allard Jeançon and Frederic H. Douglas. Denver Art Museum, Leaflet series 4.

—— *Pueblo Indian foods*, by Jean Allard Jeançon and Frederic H. Douglas, Leaflet series 8.

Kelley, J. Charles. *Association of archaeological materials with geological deposits in the Big Bend region of Texas*, by J. Charles Kelley, T. N. Campbell, and Donald J. Lehmer. Alpine, Texas, Sull Ross State Teachers College Bulletin, v. 21, no. 3.

Kidder, A. V. *An introduction to the study of southwestern archaeology with a preliminary account of the excavations at Pecos*. New Haven, Yale University Press, 1924.

Lummis, Charles F. *Mesa, canyon and pueblo*. New York, Century Co., 1925.

MacClary, John Stewart. *The first American farmers*. Art and Archaeology, v. 124, no. 3. September, 1927.

Martin, George C. *Archaeological exploration of the Shumla caves*. Southwest Texas Archaeological Society. San Antonio, Witte Memorial Museum, 1933.

Palmer, Rose A. *The North American Indians. The Smithsonian Scientific Series*, v. 4. New York, Smithsonian Institution Series, Inc. 1938.

Parsons, Elsie Clews. *Pueblo Indian religion*. 2 v. Chicago, University of Chicago Press, 1939.

Renaud, Étienne B. *Evolution of population and dwelling in the Indian southwest*. Social Forces, v. 7, 1928–1929.

Smith, Victor J. *A survey of Indian life in Texas*. Alpine, Texas. West Texas Historical and Scientific Society, Circular no. 5, 1941.

Thoburn, Joseph B. *Ancient irrigation ditches of the plains. Chronicles of Oklahoma*, Oklahoma Historical Society, v. 6, 1931.

Twitchell, Ralph Emerson. *The leading facts of New Mexican history,* v. 1 and 2. Cedar Rapids, The Torch Press, 1911.

United States Department of Agriculture. Field flood control co-ordinating committee. *Survey report. Run-off and water-flow retardation and soil-erosion prevention for flood-control purposes. Rio Puerco watershed, tributary of the upper Rio Grande.* Signed Hugh G. Calkins, Arthur Upson, Millard Peck. 1940.

United States Department of Agriculture. Soil Conservation Service, Region 8. *A report on the Rio Grande watershed with special reference to soil conservation problems.* Prepared by Rio Grande district staff in collaboration with the staff of the regional office. Signed E. R. Smith, District Manager, Rio Grande District. Albuquerque, November 22, 1936. *Tewa Basin study, v. 1, The Indian pueblos; v. 2, The Spanish-American villages; v. 3, Physical surveys and other studies.* Mimeographed. Albuquerque, April, 1935.

United States Department of the Interior. Bureau of Reclamation. *Reclamation Handbook.* Washington, Superintendent of Documents, 1942.

Watson, Don. *Cliff Palace, the story of an ancient city.* Ann Arbor, Michigan, 1947.

White, Leslie A. *The pueblo of Santo Domingo, New Mexico. Memoirs of the American Anthropological Association,* No. 43. Menasha, Wisconsin, 1935.

Wissler, Clark. *The American Indian.* New York, Oxford University Press, 1922.

BOOK THREE. LATIN / *Conquering Spaniards and Their Mexican Sons*

1. Collective Memory

Armstrong, Edward. *The Emperor Charles V.* London, Macmillan and Co., 1910.

Artiñano, Pedro M. de. *Spanish Art. The Burlington Magazine,* 1927.

Bell, Aubrey F. G. *Cervantes.* Norman, University of Oklahoma Press, 1947.

Buckle, Henry Thomas. *History of Civilization in England,* Vol. 2. New York, D. Appleton Co., 1879.

Cervantes Saavedra, Miguel de. *Don Quixote de la Mancha,* translated by Peter Motteux. New York, Illustrated Modern Library, 1946.

Crane, Leo. *As cited for Book II.*

Diaz del Castillo, Bernal. *True history of the conquest of Mexico, written in the year 1568.* Translated by Maurice Keating. 2 v. New York, Robert M. McBride, 1927.

Fitzmaurice-Kelly, James. *New history of Spanish literature*. London, Humphrey Milford, 1926.

Gautier, Théophile. *A romantic in Spain,* translated from the French by Catherine Alison Phillips. New York, Alfred A. Knopf, 1926.

Gibson, Charles E. *Story of the ship*. New York, Henry Schumann, 1948.

Goldscheider, Ludwig. *El Greco.* New York, Phaidon Press–Oxford University Press, 1938.

Hanke, Lewis. *The first social experiments in America, a study in the development of Spanish Indian policy in the 16th century.* Cambridge, Harvard University Press, 1935.

—— *The Spanish struggle for justice in the conquest of America.* Philadelphia. University of Pennsylvania Press, 1949.

Hewett, Edgar L. *As cited for Book II.*

Hume, Martin A. S. *Philip II of Spain*. London, The Macmillan Co., 1920.

Huntington, Ellsworth. *The red man's chronicle, a chronicle of aboriginal America. (Chronicles of America)*. New Haven, Yale University Press, 1921.

Leonard, Irving A. *Books of the brave, being an account of books and men in the Spanish conquest and settlement of the sixteenth-century new world.* Cambridge, Harvard University Press, 1949

Madariaga, Salvador de. *Fall of the Spanish American empire*. London, Hollis and Carter, 1948.

—— *Rise of the Spanish American empire.* London, Hollis and Carter, 1947.

Martialis, Marcus Valerius. *Epigrams,* with an English translation by Walter C. A. Kerr. New York, G. P. Putnam's Sons, 1930.

Maugham, W. Somerset. *Don Fernando, or variations on some Spanish themes*. Garden City, Doubleday, Doran and Co., 1935.

Meier-Graefe, Julius. *The Spanish journey*. Translated by J. Holroyd Reece. New York, Harcourt, Brace and Co., ND.

Prescott, William H. *History of the reign of Philip the second, king of Spain*. Boston, Phillips, Sampson and Co., 1855.

Priestley, Herbert Ingram. *The coming of the white man, 1492–1848*. New York, The Macmillan Co., 1929.

Trend, J. B. *The civilization of Spain*. London, Oxford University Press, 1944.

2. *The Desert Fathers*

Bandelier, Adolph F. A. *Historical documents relating to New Mexico, Nueva Vizcaya, and approaches thereto, to 1773*. Collected by Adolph F. A. Bandelier and Fanny R. Bandelier. Spanish texts and

English translations. 3 v. Edited . . . by Charles Wilson Hackett. Washington, Carnegie Institution, 1923.

Bell, Aubrey F. G. *As cited for Book III, Collective Memory.*

Benavides, Fray Alonso de. *Fray Alonso de Benavides' Revised Memorial of 1634* . . . edited by Frederick Webb Hodge, George P. Hammond, and Agapito Rey. (v. IV, Coronado Cuarto Centennial Publications, edited by George P. Hammond). Albuquerque, University of New Mexico Press, 1945.

Bourke, John G. *The folk-foods of the Rio Grande valley and of Northern Mexico.* (In *Southwestern Lore,* edited by J. Frank Dobie). Publications of the Texas Folk-Lore.

Crane, Leo. *As Cited for Book II.*

Dickey, Roland F. *New Mexico village arts.* Drawings by Lloyd Lozes Goff. Albuquerque, University of New Mexico Press, 1949.

Fergusson, Erna. *As cited for Book II.*

Gilpin, Laura. *The Pueblos, a camera chronicle.* New York, Hastings House, 1941.

Kubler, George. *The religious architecture of New Mexico in the colonial period and since the American occupation.* Colorado Springs, The Taylor Museum, 1940.

Leonard, Irving A. *As cited for Book III, Collective Memory.*

Madariaga, Salvador de. *As cited for Book III, Collective Memory.*

Maugham, W. Somerset. *As cited for Book III, Collective Memory.*

Sigüenza y Góngora, Carlos de. *The Mercurio volante of Don Carlos de Sigüenza y Góngora. An account of the first expedition of Don Diego de Vargas into New Mexico in 1692.* Translated, with an introduction and notes, by Irving Albert Leonard. Los Angeles, The Quivira Society, 1932.

Towne, Charles Wayland. *Shepherd's empire,* by Charles Wayland Towne and Edward Norris Wentworth. Norman, University of Oklahoma Press, 1945

United States Department of the Interior, Bureau of Reclamation. *As cited for Book II.*

3. *Hacienda & Village*

Bandelier, Adolph F. A. *Final report, as cited for Book II.*

—— *Historical documents, as cited for Book III, The Desert Fathers.*

Benavides, Fray Alonso de. *As cited for Book III, The Desert Fathers.*

Benedict, Ruth. *As cited for Book II.*

Beshoar, Barron B. *Western trails to Calvary.* Denver, The Westerners, Brand Book, 1949.

Bevan, Bernard. *Spanish art.* The Burlington Magazine, 1927.

Bolton, Herbert Eugene. *Coronado, knight of pueblos and plains.* New York, Whittlesey House, 1949.

—— *The Spanish borderlands. A chronicle of Florida and the southwest.* (Chronicles of America). New Haven, Yale University Press, 1921.

Boyd, E. *Saints and saint-makers of New Mexico.* Santa Fe, Laboratory of Anthropology, 1946.

Castañeda, Carlos E. *Our Catholic heritage in Texas, 1519–1936.* Prepared under the auspices of the Knights of Columbus of Texas, Paul J. Foik, editor. 7 v. Austin, Von Boeckmann-Jones Co., 1936.

Chavez, Fray Angélico. *Our Lady of the Conquest.* Santa Fe, Historical Society of New Mexico, 1948.

Dickey, Roland F. *As cited for Book III, The Desert Fathers.*

Dougherty, E. *The Rio Grande valley.* (In the *Magazine of History,* with notes and queries. Extra number, No. 138, 1867.) Tarrytown, New York, reprinted by William Abbatt, 1928.

Fergusson, Erna. *As cited for Book II, and Book III, The Desert Fathers.*

Fisher, Reginald. *Notes on the relation of the Franciscans to the Penitentes.* Sante Fe, *El Palacio,* v. 48, December, 1944.

Forrest, Earle R. *Missions and pueblos of the old southwest.* Cleveland, Arthur H. Clarke Co., 1929.

Hackett, Charles Wilson. In Bandelier, *Historical documents, as cited Book III, The Desert Fathers.*

Horgan, Paul. *Colonial life in Latin America, an exhibition of history and art.* Roswell, New Mexico, Roswell Museum, 1949.

James, George Wharton. *New Mexico, the land of the delight makers.* Boston, Page and Co., 1920.

Jaramillo, Cleofas M. *Shadows of the past (sombres del pasado).* Santa Fe, Seton Village Press, 1941.

Kincaid, Edgar B. *The Mexican pastor.* (In *Texas and southwestern lore,* edited by J. Frank Dobie.) Publications of the Texas Folk-Lore Society, no. 9. Dallas, the Southwest Press, 1931.

Kubler, George. *As cited for Book III, The Desert Fathers.*

Madariaga, Salvador de. *As cited for Book III, Collective Memory, and The Desert Fathers.*

May, Florence. *The Penitentes. Natural History,* v. 38, Dec. 1936.

Pérez de Villagrá, Gaspar. *History of New Mexico.* Translated by Gilberto Espinosa. Introduction and notes by Frederick W. Hodge. Los Angeles, The Quivira Society, 1933.

Priestley, Herbert Ingram. *The coming of the white man, 1492–1848.* New York, The Macmillan Co., 1929.

Salpointe, Jean Baptiste. *Soldiers of the Cross. Notes on the ecclesiastical history of New Mexico,* Arizona and Colorado. Banning, California, St. Boniface's Industrial School, 1898.

Twitchell, Ralph Emerson. *The Spanish archives of New Mexico.* 2 v. Cedar Rapids, The Torch Press, 1914.

Underhill, Ruth. *Work-a-day life of the Pueblos.* United States Indian Service, Indian life and customs, no. 4. U.S. Department of the Interior. Phoenix, Phoenix Indian School Printing Department, 1946.

United States Department of Agriculture. Field flood control coordinating committee. *As cited for Book II.*

United States Department of Agriculture. Soil Conservation Service. *As cited for Book II.*

Wilder, Mitchell A. *Santos, the religious folk art of New Mexico,* by Mitchell A. Wilder and Edgar Breitenbach. With a foreword by Rudolf A. Gerken, Archbishop of Santa Fe. Colorado Springs, The Taylor Museum, 1943.

BOOK FOUR. ANGLO-AMERICAN / *Sons of Democracy*

1. A Wild Strain: Mountain Men

Cleland, Robert Glass. *This reckless breed of men, the trappers and fur traders of the southwest.* New York, Alfred A. Knopf, 1950.

Ferris, W. A. *Life in the Rocky Mountains . . .* edited by Paul C. Phillips. Denver, Fred A. Rosenstock, Old West Publishing Co., 1940.

Irving, Washington. *The adventures of Captain Bonneville.* 2 v. New York, G. P. Putnam's Sons, 1895.

Pattie, James O. *Personal narrative of James O. Pattie of Kentucky . . .* edited by Reuben Gold Thwaites. (*Early Western Travels*). Cleveland, Arthur H. Clark Co., 1905.

Pino, Pedro Bautista, *et al. Three New Mexico chronicles; the Exposición of Don Pedro Bautista Pino, 1812; the Ojeada of Lic. Antonio Barreiro, 1832; and the additions of Don José Augustín de Escudero, 1849.* Translated with introduction and notes by H. Bailey Carroll and J. Villasana Haggard. Albuquerque, The Quivira Society, 1942.

Twitchell, Ralph Emerson. *Spanish archives, as cited for Book III, Hacienda and Village.*

2. The Mexico Trade

Barker, Eugene C. *The Austin papers.* Edited by Eugene C. Barker. (*Annual Report of the American Historical Association, 1919. 3 v.*) Washington, Government Printing Office, 1924.

Cleland, Robert Glass. *As cited for Book IV, A Wild Strain.*
Dickey, Roland F. *As cited for Book III, The Desert Fathers, and Hacienda and Village.*
Dunbar, Seymour. *A history of travel in America.* 4 v. in 1. New York, Tudor Publishing Co., 1937.
Gregg, Josiah. *Commerce of the prairies, the journal of a Santa Fe trader.* [Reprint from the edition of 1844.] Dallas, Southwest Press, 1933.
Pino, Pedro Bautista, et al. *As cited for Book IV, A Wild Strain.*
Rives, George Lockhart. *The United States and Mexico, 1821–1848.* 2 v. New York, Charles Scribner's Sons, 1913.
United States [government] Office of the Superintendent of Indian Affairs. *Passport issued to a party of prairie travelers;* signed by William Clark, Superintendent of Indian Affairs, July 22, 1820. Original document. (Excerpt quoted by permission of the Huntington Library.)

3. Collective Prophecy

Adams, Henry. *Selected letters of Henry Adams,* edited with an introduction by Newton Arvin. New York, Farrar, Straus and Young, Inc., 1951.
Adams, John, and John Quincy. *The selected writings . . .* edited and with an introduction by Adrienne Koch and William Peden. New York, Alfred A. Knopf, 1946.
Audubon, John James. *Audubon's America, the narratives and experiences of John James Audubon,* edited by Donald Culross Peattie . . . Boston, Houghton Mifflin Co., 1940.
Botkin, B. A. *A treasury of American folklore. Stories, ballads and traditions of the people,* edited by B. A. Botkin. New York, Crown Publishers, 1944.
Butterfield, Roger. *The American past, a history of the United States from Concord to Hiroshima, 1775–1945.* New York, Simon and Schuster, 1947.
Christensen, Erwin O. *Index of American design.* New York, Macmillan Co.; Washington, National Gallery of Art, Smithsonian Institution, 1950.
Crèvecoeur, Hector St. Jean de. *Letters from an American farmer* (Extracts in *This was America,* edited by Oscar Handlin). Cambridge, Harvard University Press, 1949.
Curti, Merle. *The growth of American thought.* New York, Harper and Brothers, 1943.
Dunbar, Seymour. *As cited for Book IV, The Mexico Trade.*
Grassi, Giovanni Antonio. *Notizie varie sullo stato presente della re-*

pubblica degli Stati Uniti dell' America . . . *(1819)* (translated excerpts in *This was America,* edited by Oscar Handlin.) Cambridge, Harvard University Press, 1949.

Gregg, Josiah. *As cited for Book IV, The Mexico Trade.*

Handlin, Oscar. *This was America,* edited by Oscar Handlin. Cambridge, Harvard University Press, 1949.

Kouwenhoven, John A. *Made in America, the arts in modern civilization.* Garden City, Doubleday and Co., 1948.

Lipman, Jean. *American folk art in wood, metal and stone.* New York, Pantheon, 1948.

McCoy, John C. *Paper read before Old Settlers Historical Society, Jackson County, Missouri, 1871.*

Mencken, H. L. *The American language, an inquiry into the development of English in the United States.* Fourth edition. New York, Alfred A. Knopf, 1936.

────── *Supplement I to the above.*

Miller, Alfred Jacob. *The west of Alfred Jacob Miller (1837),* from the notes and water colors in the Walters Art Gallery, with an account of the artist by Marvin C Ross. Norman, University of Oklahoma Press, 1951.

Montlezun, Baron de. *Voyage fait dans les années 1816 et 1817, de New-Yorck á la Nouvelle-Orléans et de L'Orénoque au Mississippi* . . . *(1818).* (Translated excerpts in *This Was America,* edited by Oscar Handlin). Cambridge, Harvard University Press, 1949.

Moreau de Saint-Méry, Méderic Louis Élie. *Voyage aux Étatus-Unis de l'Amérique, 1793–1798.* (Translated excerpts in *This was America,* edited by Oscar Handlin). Cambridge, Harvard University Press, 1949.

Moses, Montrose J. *The American dramatist.* Boston, Little, Brown and Co., 1925.

National Capital Sesquicentennial Commission. *American processional, 1492–1900.* Washington, The Corcoran Gallery of Art, 1950.

Parkman, Francis. *The journals of Francis Parkman,* edited by Mason Wade. 2 v. New York, Harper and Brothers, 1947.

Quinn, Arthur Hobson. *A history of the American drama from the beginning to the Civil War.* New York, Harper and Brothers, 1923.

Rice, Martin. *Old timers' poem,* read by the author Martin Rice at Old Settlers' meeting, Jackson County, Missouri, 1880.

Rosenfeld, Paul. *An hour with American music. The One Hour Series.* Philadelphia, J. B. Lippincott Co., 1929.

Rourke, Constance. *American humor, a study of the national character.* New York, Harcourt, Brace and Co., 1931.

────── *The roots of American culture, and other essays.* Edited with a preface by Van Wyck Brooks. New York, Harcourt, Brace and Co., 1942.

Smith, Henry Nash. *Virgin land, the American west as symbol and myth.* Cambridge, Harvard University Press, 1950.

Stone, John Augustus. *Matamora and other plays,* edited by Eugene R. Page. Princeton, Princeton University Press, 1941.

Tocqueville, Alexis de. *Democracy in America.* The Henry Reeve text . . . edited . . . by Phillips Bradley. 2. v. New York, Alfred A. Knopf, 1945.

Trollope, Frances. *Domestic manners of the Americans.* Edited by . . . Donald Smalley. New York, Alfred A. Knopf, 1949.

Whitman, Walt. *Leaves of grass.* New York, Heritage Press, ND.

—— *Prose works.* Philadelphia, David McKay, ND.

4. *The Last Frontiersman*

Abels, Robert. *Early American firearms* (*The American Arts Library*). Cleveland and New York, The World Publishing Co, 1950.

Botkin, B. A. *As cited for Book IV, Collective Prophecy.*

Brown, Dee. *Trail driving days.* Text by Dee Brown; picture research by Martin F. Schmitt. New York, Charles Scribner's Sons, 1952.

Dobie, J. Frank. *The longhorns.* Illustrated by Tom Lea. Boston, Little, Brown and Co., 1941.

—— *The mustangs.* Illustrated by Charles Banks Wilson. Boston, Little, Brown and Co., 1952.

—— *Vaquero, As cited for Book II.*

Kohlberg, Ernst. *Letters, 1875–1877.* Translated from the German. Original documents. El Paso Public Library. (Excerpts quoted by permission of El Paso Public Library.)

Lomax, John A. *Cowboy songs and other frontier ballads,* collected by John A Lomax. With an introduction by Barrett Wendell. New York, The Macmillan Co., 1927.

—— *Folk song, USA, the 111 best American ballads,* collected, adapted, and arranged by John A. Lomax and Alan Lomax; Alan Lomax, editor; Charles Seeger and Ruth Crawford Seeger, music editors. New York, Duell, Sloan and Pearce, 1947.

McCoy, Joseph G. *Historic sketches of the cattle trade of the west and southwest.* [Facsimile reprint of the edition of 1874.] Washington, The Rare Book Shop, 1932.

Richardson, Rupert Norval. *The greater southwest* . . . by Richard Norval Richardson and Carl Coke Rister. Glendale, The Arthur H. Clark Co., 1934.

Santleben, August A. *A Texas pioneer. Early staging and overland freighting days on the frontiers of Texas and Mexico.* New York and Washington, The Neale Publishing Co., c. 1910.

Siringo, Charles A. *Riata and spurs.* Boston, Houghton Mifflin Co., 1931.

—— *A Texas cowboy, or fifteen years on the hurricane deck of a Spanish pony, taken from real life, . . .* with bibliographical study and introduction by J. Frank Dobie and drawings by Tom Lea. New York, William Sloane Associates, 1950.

Smith, Erwin E. *Life on the Texas range.* Photographs by Erwin E. Smith; text by J. Evetts Haley. Austin, University of Texas Press, 1952.

United States Congress. 44th Congress. 1st session. House of Representatives. *Report no. 343. Texas frontier troubles.* February 29, 1876.

Wadleigh, A. B. *Ranching in New Mexico, 1886–1890. New Mexico Historical Review,* v. 27, no. 1.

5. *A Larger Earth*

Bynner, Witter, *Indian Earth,* New York, Alfred A. Knopf, 1929. (Excerpts used with permission of the publisher.)

Index

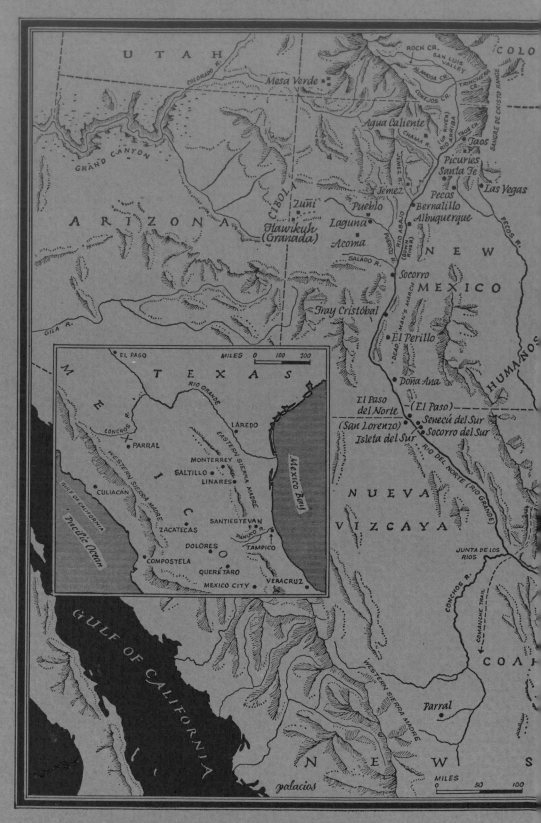